THE CLASSICS
OF **WESTERN
SPIRITUALITY**

THE CLASSICS OF WESTERN SPIRITUALITY
A Library of the Great Spiritual Masters

President and Publisher
Mark-David Janus, CSP

EDITORIAL BOARD

EDITH STEIN

Selected Writings

Edited by
Marian Maskulak, CPS

Foreword by
Sarah Borden Sharkey

Paulist Press
New York / Mahwah, NJ

Caseside photos used with permission of the Edith Stein-Archiv.; background image: Shutterstock / bluecrayola

For permissions to print previously published material, see Acknowledgments.

Caseside and book design by Sharyn Banks

Library of Congress Cataloging-in-Publication Data

Names: Stein, Edith, Saint, 1891-1942, author. | Maskulak, Marian, 1954– editor.
Title: Edith Stein : selected writings / edited by Marian Maskulak, CPS ; foreword by Sarah Borden Sharkey.
Description: New York : Paulist Press, 2016. | Series: The classics of Western spirituality | Includes bibliographical references and index.
Identifiers: LCCN 2016000390 (print) | LCCN 2016003079 (ebook) | ISBN 9780809106332 (hardcover : alk. paper) | ISBN 9781587686146 (Ebook)
Subjects: LCSH: Spiritual life—Catholic Church. | Christian life—Catholic authors.
Classification: LCC BX4705.S814 A25 2016 (print) | LCC BX4705.S814 (ebook) | DDC 230/.2--dc23
LC record available at http://lccn.loc.gov/2016000390

ISBN 978-0-8091-0633-2 (hardcover)
ISBN 978-1-58768-614-6 (e-book)

Published by Paulist Press
997 Macarthur Boulevard
Mahwah, New Jersey 07430

www.paulistpress.com

Printed and bound in the
United States of America

*In thanksgiving to God for the life of Edith Stein
and dedicated to all who, like her,
in a free and loving act of surrender,
place themselves into God's hands.*

CONTENTS

ABOUT THE CONTRIBUTORS

EDITOR OF THIS VOLUME

Marian Maskulak, CPS, is Associate Professor of Theology and Religious Studies at St. John's University, New York. She holds a PhD from the University of St. Michael's College, Toronto, Canada. She has also authored *Edith Stein and the Body-Soul-Spirit at the Center of Holistic Formation* (Peter Lang, 2007) and several articles on Edith Stein, as well as articles on various topics and figures related to the study of theology and Christian spirituality.

AUTHOR OF THE FOREWORD

Dr. Sarah Borden Sharkey, Professor of Philosophy, Wheaton College, earned her PhD from Fordham University. Her interests focus on the relevance of classical and medieval ideas for contemporary discussions. She has written extensively on Edith Stein, including *Edith Stein* in the Outstanding Christian Thinkers series (Continuum, 2003) and *Thine Own Self: Individuality in Edith Stein's Later Writings* (Catholic University of America Press, 2009), as well as a coedited volume on Stein's writings on Teresa of Avila (Institute of Carmelite Studies Publications, 2015).

FOREWORD

Edith Stein was born in a time of remarkable peace in Europe, but during her university years, she saw the devastation caused by World War I. She developed intellectually during the very difficult years following that war and leading to the Second World War. In the face of the tremendous societal upheaval, Stein's response was to call us to full humanity. She argued over and over—in her example and her writings—that we need to *become* fully human, to develop as the unique individual we are called to be, realizing the fullness of our humanity and refusing reductions of the person to physical needs, contextual setting, or mere political action. Her answer to the grave problems facing the nation at that time was holistic, full, distinctively human development.

As she developed her vision of such human development, Stein showed herself to be one of the great mystics. Mysticism is not, in her way of thinking, the experience of visions or other supernatural phenomena, but the desire for union with God. And like Augustine, she thought that all of us—whether we know it or not—were made for and long for that union with our Creator. To be with our Beloved, and to unfold fully in that intimate communion, is our distinct calling as unique human persons.

Although influenced by Thomas Aquinas, John Duns Scotus, Augustine, and other thinkers, it is clear that Teresa of Avila, and in particular Teresa's vision of God's presence in the innermost part of our soul, was dear to Stein's understanding of our fundamental nature. She even went so far as to claim that "it is impossible to give a proper picture of the soul (even a cursory and inadequate one) without speaking of that which concerns its innermost life."[1] Stein draws explicitly from the Carmelite mystical tradition, especially

Teresa of Avila and John of the Cross, in articulating that proper picture of the soul. For Stein, doing philosophical or theological anthropology well requires that one understand one's spiritual life—and giving such an anthropology is at the heart of what our world needs most, especially in times of profound societal and political crisis.

Marian Maskulak has provided a tremendous guide to these crucial themes in Stein, focusing on what is at the very heart of Stein's life and writings. This book covers major themes in Stein's account of human beings and our spiritual and religious life, including her notion of soul, vocation, the Mystical Body of Christ, the centrality of the cross, living at the hand of God, as well as the distinctively Carmelite dimensions of Stein's spirituality. Dr. Maskulak draws from much of Stein's corpus, pulling the relevant texts from her more theoretical works as well as from her letters and more personal papers. For those looking for a guide into Stein's writings about our spiritual lives—and thus what is most central to any life, regardless of the circumstances in which one finds oneself—this work is a true gem.

Sarah Borden Sharkey
Professor of Philosophy, Wheaton College

ACKNOWLEDGMENTS

I wish to express my special and most sincere thanks to Sr. Annette Buschgerd, CPS, for critically reviewing my translations and making many helpful suggestions. Sincere thanks also go to Nancy de Flon, Academic Editor, and Diane Flynn, Editorial Assistant, at Paulist Press, for all of their assistance. I would like to thank St. John's University for providing a semester of research leave that enabled me to bring this book to completion. I would also like to thank my graduate assistants, Taylor Bartlette and Andrew Outar, for typing some of the English selections of Stein's writings. Sincere thanks also go to Sr. Joanne Leccese, CPS, for her generous help with proofreading. I am very grateful for the prayerful support and loving encouragement of my religious community, the Missionary Sisters of the Precious Blood, my family, and my friends throughout this endeavor. Above all, I give thanks to the Triune God who dwells within each of us.

Grateful acknowledgment is made to copyright holders ICS Publications for copyright permissions, and Herder for translation rights, for use of selections (or texts) from the following works:

ICS Publications: The Collected Works of Edith Stein (CWES)

From *Edith Stein Letters to Roman Ingarden* translated by Hugh Candler Hunt © 2014 by Washington Province of Discalced Carmelites, Inc. ICS Publications 2131 Lincoln Road, N.E. Washington, DC 20002-1151 USA. www.icspublications.org

From *Finite and Eternal Being* translated by Kurt F. Reinhardt © 2002 by Washington Province of Discalced Carmelites, Inc. ICS Publications 2131 Lincoln Road, N.E. Washington, DC 20002-1151 USA. www.icspublications.org

EDITH STEIN

Herder: Edith Stein Gesamtausgabe (ESGA)

Edith Stein. *Der Aufbau der menschlichen Person: Vorlesungen zur philosophischen Anthropologie.* Edited by Beate Beckmann-Zöller. ESGA 14. Freiburg: Herder, 2004.

Edith Stein. *Bildung und Entfaltung der Individualität: Beiträge zum christlichen Erziehungsauftrag.* Edited by Beate Beckmann-Zöller and Maria Amata Neyer. ESGA 16. Freiburg: Herder, 2001.

Edith Stein. *Endliches und Ewiges Sein: Versuch eines Aufstiegs zum Sinn des Seins.* Edited by Andreas Uwe Müller. ESGA 11/12. Freiburg: Herder, 2006.

Edith Stein. *Die Frau: Fragestellungen und Reflexionen.* Edited by Maria Amata Neyer. ESGA 13. Freiburg: Herder, 2000.

Edith Stein. *Geistliche Texte II.* Edited by Sophie Binggeli. ESGA 20. Freiburg: Herder, 2007.

Original Translations

The works translated by me in their entirety for this volume are the following:

"Blessed Are the Poor in Spirit," from *Geistliche Texte II,* ESGA 20. Freiburg: Herder, 2007, 102-9.

"Eucharistic Education," from *Bildung und Entfaltung der Individualität,* ESGA 16. Freiburg: Herder, 2001, 63-66.

"The Holy Face," from *Geistliche Texte II,* ESGA 20. Freiburg: Herder, 2007, 49-51.

"The Participation of Religious Institutions of Education in the Religious Education of Youth," from *Bildung und Entfaltung der Individualität,* ESGA 16. Freiburg: Herder, 2001, 50-62.

"Sign of the Cross," from *Geistliche Texte II,* ESGA 20. Freiburg: Herder, 2007, 47-49.

"The Theoretical Foundations of Social Formation Work," from *Bildung und Entfaltung der Individualität,* ESGA 16. Freiburg: Herder, 2001, 15-34.

Following are the works from which I translated excerpts or pages:

Finite and Eternal Being excerpts, from *Endliches und Ewiges Sein,* ESGA 11/12. Freiburg: Herder, 2006.

EDITH STEIN

"The Foundations of Women's Formation" and supplement to "Foundations of Women's Formation," from *Die Frau*, ESGA 13. Freiburg: Herder, 2000), 30–45.

"I Will Remain with You," from *Geistliche Texte II*, ESGA 20. Freiburg: Herder, 2007, 179–82.

"The Life of Christian Women," from *Die Frau*, ESGA 13. Freiburg: Herder, 2000, 79–114.

"On the Idea of Formation," from *Bildung und Entfaltung der Individualität*, ESGA 16. Freiburg: Herder, 2001, 35–49.

"Recent Problems in the Education of Girls," from *Die Frau* ESGA 13. Freiburg: Herder, 2000, 127–208.

"Retreat in Preparation for Final Vows," from *Geistliche Texte II*, ESGA 20. Freiburg: Herder, 2007, 57–64.

"Truth and Clarity in Instruction and Teaching," from *Bildung und Entfaltung der Individualität*, ESGA 16. Freiburg: Herder, 2001, 1–8.

INTRODUCTION

In her 1936 essay "The Prayer of the Church," Edith Stein notes the importance of solitary dialogue with God as being an integral part of the church's prayer. She maintains that such solitary prayer prepares for events within the church that, in turn, help to transform the face of the earth. To illustrate her point, she names Bridget of Sweden and Catherine of Siena as examples of women who immersed themselves in the life and suffering of Christ and, consequently, contributed greatly to the church. She also mentions Teresa of Avila, who encouraged the renewal of the interior life as a means for addressing the widespread apostasy of her time. In like manner, Edith believes that anyone who surrenders unconditionally to God will be instrumental in building the kingdom of God.[1]

Those who become familiar with Edith's life and writings will recognize that what she wrote about these women applies to Edith herself—she immersed herself in the life and suffering of Christ, and saw her contemplative lifestyle as a means of helping others and countering the great afflictions caused by Nazism. God alone knows the fruit that her life of faith, prayer, sacrifices, and actions bore during her lifetime. Little did she know that only sixty-two years after penning the above thoughts, she herself would be counted among the Carmelite saints and then named copatroness of Europe along with Bridget of Sweden and Catherine of Siena. As part of his rationale for selecting St. Teresa Benedicta of the Cross (Edith's religious name) as copatroness, Pope John Paul II noted that she forged a sort of bridge between her Jewish roots and her Christian commitment, took part in the dialogue with contemporary philosophical thought, and by her death, shed light on the ways of God in contrast to the human horror of the Shoah. Thus, she has become "the symbol of a

1

human, cultural and religious pilgrimage which embodies the deepest tragedy and the deepest hopes of Europe."[2] The pope further elaborated:

> Today we look upon Teresa Benedicta of the Cross and, in her witness as an innocent victim, we recognize an imitation of the Sacrificial Lamb and a protest against every violation of the fundamental rights of the person. We also recognize in it the pledge of a renewed encounter between Jews and Christians which, following the desire expressed by the Second Vatican Council, is now entering upon a time of promise marked by openness on both sides. Today's proclamation of Edith Stein as a Co-Patroness of Europe is intended to raise on this Continent a banner of respect, tolerance and acceptance which invites all men and women to understand and appreciate each other, transcending their ethnic, cultural and religious differences in order to form a truly fraternal society.[3]

While directed toward Europe, the pope's words hold global significance, for surely Edith's relevance stretches far beyond Europe. Her relatability becomes evident when one considers the many ways in which she can be described: scholar; philosopher; seeker of truth; victim of gender discrimination; educator; author; translator; public speaker; loving daughter and sister; faithful and trustworthy friend; person appreciative of history, culture, and the arts; Catholic convert ever proud of her Jewish roots; woman who requested a papal pronouncement denouncing Nazism; Carmelite nun; victim of anti-Semitic policies and hatred; and above all, a lover of God. But at the core of her relatability stands her conviction that all human beings—past, present, future—are connected. Each human being is an unrepeatable member of the one great humanity to which each is called to contribute by developing and using one's own talents and potential. Everyone's contribution is necessary for the complete unfolding of humankind. Her unassuming manner as an adult reflects this perspective. Moreover, her freely chosen and loving surrender into God's hands made her open and ready to use her gifts wherever and however God directed her.

Edith's spiritual director, Archabbot Raphael Walzer, OSB, points to her unpretentious, very down-to-earth manner. In 1946, he wrote,

> As it was not hard for her to be simple with ordinary people, scholarly without all presumption with scholars, a seeker with seekers—I would almost like to add, a sinner with sinners—so she never felt the least difficulty sitting with the lay sisters at the same school desk of Carmel.[4]

Whether or not she would ever be declared a saint, Walzer was certain that "her picture, her praying and working, her silence and suffering, her last way towards the East will not disappear easily from the memory of coming generations, and [will] always radiate energy and awaken [the] desire of depth—depth in faith, in hope, and in charity."[5] Edith's canonization in 1998 has assured that her life will not be forgotten, even as it raised some questions and controversy concerning Jewish-Catholic relations. Now numbered among the saints, the earthly desire she expressed in 1930 can be fulfilled on a global scale—to lead to God anyone who comes to her.[6]

A number of areas stand out in terms of characterizing Edith's spirituality and its importance for contemporary Christians. Central to these are her holistic views regarding the human being and the individual's formation and development. From a philosophical and theological perspective, Edith perceives the human being as constituted of body-soul-spirit—not in any dualistic manner whatsoever, but rather as a unity that might be termed body-soul holism. She recognizes the need for human beings to develop on many different levels, all of which are interconnected—physical, intellectual, emotional, spiritual, interpersonal, cultural, and so forth—in order to become all that they were created to be and to attain the final goal of all human beings—union with God. Her views on the formation of the human person place her as a forerunner of contemporary notions of holistic spirituality.

While maintaining the unique and unrepeatable individuality of each person, Edith upholds the importance of community because being a member of community is part of the intrinsic makeup of each human being. As already mentioned, each person is part of the one humanity that also includes all humans who have come before the present generations and those still to come in future generations. She draws attention to the obligations that this carries. Likewise, Edith recognizes the interrelationships existing among all created being—inanimate, animate, human, and even angels. At the heart of her understanding of this interconnectedness lies the love of the Trinity, the archetype of community, who dwells within the human being and whose image is reflected in all of creation. Her holistic perspective promotes a balance between recognizing the importance of one's individual development without falling into individualism, and belonging and contributing to community without getting caught up in false ideologies or solely superficial relationships. Her thought is also applicable to today's ecological concerns.

Edith encourages a living faith—one that has a formative effect on one's life, influencing one's decisions and actions. Those who are grounded in and graced by the love of God are meant to reach out to others in love. Such a living faith needs to be nurtured through Scripture, prayer, and the Eucharist. As a laywoman, Edith made participation in daily Eucharist a priority and maintained a contemplative prayer life during years of a demanding schedule of teaching, lecturing, scholarly writing, and translating. She emphasizes the need for active participation in the liturgy as well as for times of intimate dialogue with God to nurture one's spiritual growth. In the contemporary world of fast-paced living and ever-evolving technology, such a contemplative attitude that includes times of quiet communion with the God who dwells within oneself seems to be precisely what is needed. With her insights and own example, Edith is a sure guide.

The paschal mystery—the life, suffering, death, and resurrection of Jesus—is the core of Christian spirituality. Here, too, Edith is an experienced mentor who reminds us that the goal of Christian formation is to be formed into the image of Jesus. Meditation on Scripture and active participation in the church's liturgical year facilitates this by bringing one into close contact with the life, teachings, and actions of Jesus. Such union with Christ inevitably entails encountering the sufferings of the cross within one's own life. Edith does not condone any type of injustice, suffering for the sake of suffering, or suffering that entails pathological pleasure.[7] Rather, she believes that uniting one's sufferings with Christ's redemptive suffering bears fruit through Christ and ultimately leads to resurrection. The kinds of suffering, violence, and terrors of war that marked Edith's era sadly continue into the present. At the same time, many people seek only a quick fix to a multitude of other types of suffering. The cross lies at the heart of the Christian message, and a correctly understood spirituality of the cross that condones neither injustice nor pathological suffering can help one to see unavoidable suffering through the lens of Christ's salvific act.

At the heart of Edith's spirituality lies her counsel to surrender oneself freely and lovingly into God's hands as in a trusting child-parent relationship. Ultimately, God is the primary formator who knows the deepest recesses of the soul that remain hidden even to the individual herself and who desires to lead us to full growth in union with God. Edith assures us that in God's hands, one will be well provided and cared for, and even in times of turbulence, one can rest there securely, confident in God's love and benevolence.

EDITH STEIN: A PORTRAYAL

Edith Stein has left behind an interesting and inspiring legacy conveyed through her life story and numerous writings. The first section of this biographical portrayal provides a brief overview of some significant events of her life. The remaining sections attempt to shed light on the unfolding of her life, beginning with the growth and development of some of her personal traits. While life in the first half of twentieth-century Europe differed markedly from today, readers will easily relate to some core facets of personal development that take place in the course of daily life and that extend beyond space and time. The third section highlights her faith journey, while the fourth focuses on the Benedictine influence that played a role in the life of this woman who felt called to be a Carmelite since the time of her baptism. The last section presents several instances of Edith's quite simple, yet no less real, spiritual experiences. No biographical narrative can do justice to another's life journey. This is all the more true when one considers Edith's conviction that the individual herself does not even know the depths of her own soul. Nevertheless, even glimpses into the life of another can have a formative effect on one's own life journey. The dynamics are perhaps similar to those studied by Edith for her dissertation on empathy—how a person experiences the experience of another—albeit here in narrative form rather than in real-time life.

Biographical Framework

The youngest of seven surviving children, Edith was born in Breslau, Germany (today Wroclaw, Poland), on October 12, 1891. Her mother, a devout Jew, placed great emphasis on the fact that her youngest happened to be born on the Jewish Day of Atonement.[8] When Edith's father died two years later, Mrs. Stein took over the family lumber business, leaving her older daughters to care for the two youngest girls. Edith and her mother kept a close bond throughout their lives despite her mother's strong opposition to her later conversion to Catholicism (1922) and subsequent entrance into Carmel (1933). Edith's sister Erna describes Edith's decision to be baptized as a strong blow to their mother. Her siblings tried to dissuade her, but reluctantly accepted her decision out of confidence in her inner convictions.[9]

Introspective, insightful, and sensitive by nature, Edith was quick to help others, sometimes acting as a liaison between family members in conflict situations.[10] Although she excelled as a student, she chose to stop her schooling just before turning fifteen, only to return to her studies about a year later. Edith attended the University of Breslau, where she showed an interest in psychology, for four semesters (1911–13). Drawn to Edmund Husserl's phenomenology, however, she transferred to Göttingen (1913–15) to study under "the Master" himself, whom she considered the preeminent philosopher of her time.[11]

World War I (1914–18) interrupted her university years. Wanting to contribute to the war efforts like friends who had joined the army, Edith worked in a Red Cross hospital for infectious disease for five months in 1915. The following year, she completed her PhD summa cum laude at the University of Freiburg since Husserl had taken a position there. She then worked as an assistant to Husserl at Freiburg for two years.

Denied a professorship at Göttingen due to the university's reluctance to hire a woman, Edith wrote a letter of complaint to the education minister. As a result, a circular was issued to all universities regarding the granting of professorships to women, but she correctly surmised that the circular would produce no concrete results for her.[12] When further efforts at obtaining a university position also failed, she gave private philosophy lectures in her family home to thirty participants.[13]

Following her conversion to Catholicism in 1922, Edith taught at St. Magdalena's in Speyer, a girls' high school and teachers' training institute run by Dominican nuns (1923–31). During these years, she also wrote, translated writings of Thomas Aquinas and John Henry Newman, and gave public lectures to women's and teachers' groups throughout Germany, as well as in Austria and Switzerland. As an example of how busy her schedule could be, between October 12 and 30, 1931, she presented fifteen lectures in fifteen different locations in the Rhineland-Westphalian area of Germany. That same year, she again unsuccessfully sought a professorship at Freiburg, and the following year, she obtained a position at the German Institute for Scientific Pedagogy in Münster.[14] In 1932, she also delivered radio addresses on a Bavarian Radio Network.[15]

Due to Nazi legislation forbidding Jews to hold public positions, her teaching position in Münster was terminated in 1933. Edith acknowledges that she felt "almost relieved" to be "caught up in the common fate."[16] When invited to present lectures during this time, she replied with piercing questions: "Do you know that I am a convert from Judaism? And do you dare to go against the prevailing trend by putting a Jewess into a position of influence on German youth?"[17]

No longer able to work in active ministry, Edith entered the Cologne Carmel (1933), where she took the religious name Sr. Teresa Benedicta of the Cross. It was a step she had long desired from the time of her baptism. After the devastating events of *Kristallnacht* on

November 9–10, 1938, Edith moved to the Carmel in Echt, Netherlands, so as not to endanger the Cologne community. There she was later joined by her sister, Rosa, also a convert to Catholicism. When the Nazis took over the Netherlands and declared non-Aryan Germans stateless, Edith and Rosa reported themselves as required by the Nazis, but filed a request to be removed from the list of emigrants so as to stay at the Carmel of Echt. Meanwhile, her superiors were trying to arrange for the two of them to go to a convent in Switzerland, although entry into Switzerland seemed impossible. In March 1942, Edith and Rosa had to appear before the SS in Amsterdam and were assured that they would not be able to emigrate before the war's end. They had given the United States as their destination. Despite their precarious circumstances, Edith reported that they "continue to lead [their] lives calmly and leave the future to him who alone knows anything about it."[18] On July 24, 1942, Edith received the news that the Carmel of Le Pâquier, Switzerland, was prepared to receive the Stein sisters, but they still needed permission to leave the country and to enter Switzerland. On July 26, 1942, the Dutch Catholic bishops protested the deportation of Jews by having a pastoral letter read in all churches. The Nazis retaliated at once by ordering the immediate deportation of all Catholics of Jewish descent. On August 2, Edith and Rosa were among three hundred arrested and transported to Auschwitz-Birkenau via the concentration camps at Amersfoort and Westerbork. They were gassed at Auschwitz-Birkenau on August 9, 1942.[19]

Edith was beatified in 1987, canonized in 1998, and in 1999, named copatroness of Europe, along with St. Bridget of Sweden and St. Catherine of Siena.

Personal Growth and Development

Edith understood the human person as a being who is in a continual process of unfolding or becoming in which all aspects of the individual's physical-spiritual being intersect and come into play in the process of formation—the physical, intellectual, psychological, emotional, religious, social, cultural, and so forth. This section provides several examples that highlight some instances of Edith's own personal growth process. They indicate that her capacity for self-reflection, her straightforward candidness, moral integrity, caring attitude, and dedication as a friend appear as core features of her character. Most of these examples are taken from her autobiography, *Life in a Jewish Family*, the bulk of which was written in 1933. While her autobiography ends with the account of the successful completion of her PhD in 1916, here and there she injects comments pertaining to events she is recounting and also mentions a few incidents that occurred after 1916. While some parts of her autobiography can come across as a bit self-congratulatory regarding her achievements, Edith also discloses some of her own faults and weaknesses. In both cases, it seems that her aim is to present a frank portrayal of events.

Edith describes herself as having been a lively and precocious child, stubborn and angry when she did not get her way. Her propensity for self-reflection showed itself early. As a young child, she pondered over whatever she saw or heard but rarely shared anything of her inner world with others. Edith considers her first transformation to have occurred around the age of seven and attributes it to reason having gained control in her. At that time, she concluded that her mother and older sister knew what was good for her and thereafter she obeyed them. Gone were her angry outbursts, and although it was not easy, she even sought forgiveness after having done something wrong. Edith ascribes this change to her distaste for angry outbursts by others that lessened their dignity.[20]

As is typical for young people when their experiences widen, Edith encountered views that contrasted with her own moral upbringing. She tells of being depressed for weeks as a university student in Breslau after reading the novel *Helmut Harringa*, which portrays the heavy drinking done in fraternities with its resulting moral lapses. She relates how hearing Luther's hymn "A Mighty Fortress" during a Bach concert cured her adverse disposition, and she found this to be "highly significant." As a young girl, she had enjoyed singing the hymn at her school's devotions. She writes that the following verse vanquished her pessimistic mood:

And though this world with devils filled,
should threaten to undo us,

we will not fear,…
truth will triumph through us.

Edith felt confident that she and her friends could conquer all "devils."[21] It is interesting that she omits the reference to "God's" truth found in the missing words of the given verse. During this time of her life, Edith neither practiced nor concerned herself with questions of faith and so it was obviously not the reference to "God's" truth that moved her, but simply "truth." But much later in life, she wrote what has become one of her frequently cited quotes: "God is truth. All who seek truth seek God, whether this is clear to them or not."[22] She wrote this in the context of conveying no concern whatsoever about Husserl's spiritual welfare near the end of his life. Her own search for truth had convinced her that God is truth.

Edith admits that during her university years, she paid attention to what others said to her and about her, and although hurt at times, she used such occasions for self-reflection. For example, when she was preparing to leave for studies in Göttingen, a respected friend wished her well in finding people there who would satisfy her taste since she seemed to have become too critical in Breslau. His words shocked her. Because she was accustomed to receiving only affection and admiration from her friends at that time, Edith became aware that she had naïvely begun to believe that she was perfect. She candidly admits to having made remarks about whatever she found to be negative and to having used ridicule or sarcasm to draw attention to others' weaknesses, mistakes, or faults. In looking back on this time, she observes that such is often the case with persons of no faith "who live an exalted ethical idealism. Because one is enthused about what is good, one believes oneself to be good."[23] Commenting on events after her student years, Edith notes a change in her attitude toward herself and others. She remarks that "being right" and winning over an opponent was no longer essential. Although she still quickly detected the human weaknesses of others, she now used this knowledge as a means to protect them rather than as a way to attack their vulnerabilities. This new outlook also influenced her tendency to correct others. Experience taught her that such corrections were useless unless individuals themselves wished to improve and were open to another's critique.[24]

Edith also indicates that there were times during and shortly after her university years when she went through periods of depression. Although she was a very gifted student, she writes that when struggling daily from early morning until midnight with her dissertation on the phenomenological question of empathy, she drove herself to near despair. At this time, she would wish to be run over by a vehicle when crossing a street or to fall off a cliff when out on an excursion. But since she was genuinely happy when with members of the philosophical circle, her distress went unnoticed by others. A positive assessment of her work by the phenomenologist Adolf Reinach finally gave her the boost she needed to complete her dissertation, and her desolation disappeared.[25] In a 1920 letter to her friend Fritz Kaufmann, whom she believed was in a depressed mood, Edith acknowledges the dangers of allowing things to fester in oneself:

> I would be very sad were this to be more than a passing mood on your part. In any case, I do want to tell you yet that I was very glad you told me everything right away. I know from personal experience—for I am much better acquainted with depressions than you perhaps surmise—what happens when one allows something like this to fester and tortures oneself with it in silence, whereby it takes on more and more monstrous dimensions.[26]

The placid student life that Edith and her friends enjoyed was, in her words, "blown to bits" with the onset of World War I in 1914. That year, when her male friends went off to the battlefield, Edith volunteered for five months in a Red Cross hospital for soldiers with contagious diseases in Mährisch-Weisskirchen, Austria. The details that Edith provides regarding some of the soldiers for whom she cared convey her attention to their individual needs and her tireless service and dedication. A few incidents there also showed her that some doctors and nurses adhered to a more liberal code of conduct in terms of partying and drinking, but Edith consistently maintained her own moral code. Upon leaving the hospital, she expressed her willingness to accept another Red Cross assignment but was not called upon.[27]

After completing her dissertation, Edith worked as Husserl's assistant. Despite her great respect for Husserl, she often became very frustrated and dismayed when he would not take time to address the questions she raised regarding his notes and writings that she was organizing to help him bring them into publishable form. Meanwhile, World War I dragged on. Regarding the political situation, Edith indicates in a letter to Roman Ingarden (April 1917) that she had crossed a sort of threshold that allowed her a new perspective even in the dark times:

> Certainly, I am not a blind optimist. Earlier, in fact, I even had the tendency to see only the dark side of things. Now, however, I am learning more and more to see something positive in everything. In doing so, I can rather clearly recognize all of the objectionable aspects of this life and suffer them accordingly, but they have lost their power and are no longer able to overwhelm me.[28]

Her positive perspective was greatly challenged in November 1917, however, with the news that her beloved professor, Adolf Reinach, had died on the battlefield. She was greatly saddened by this news. As will be seen in the next section, his wife's handling of his death had a profound effect on Edith's spiritual journey.

Edith's caring attitude also emerges in her dedicated commitment to her friends. Even in the midst of candid and sometimes feisty correspondence, her respect for her friends always comes through. Letters to Fritz Kaufmann and Roman Ingarden demonstrate her willingness to admit her own faults and to forgive quickly when misunderstandings or disagreements arose. In one such letter to Kaufmann, she writes,

> Thank you for your kind lines. Please don't plague yourself now with self-reproach. I can readily understand that my clumsy way of crossing your self-sacrificing efforts exasperated you thoroughly, and I have not been angry with

you for a moment. I think we will let this matter be buried now, and consider our old trusting relationship as the immovable foundation which underlies all words and dealings. Right?[29]

From Edith's standpoint, once a friend, always a friend.

In 1922, Kaufmann had estranged himself from her because of her baptism. Five years later, when he did reply to a letter from Edith, she responded, "The formation of an unshakeable bond with all whom life brings in my way, a bond in no way dependent on day-to-day contact, is a significant element in my life. And you can depend on that [tie] even when I do not always reply as promptly as this time."[30] Six years later, she wrote to Kaufmann about her growing number of friends and alludes to keeping a spiritual connection to them. "The circle of persons whom I consider as connected with me has increased so much in the course of the years that it is entirely impossible to keep in touch with the usual means. But I have other ways and means of keeping the bonds alive."[31] Kaufmann substantiates Edith's caring attitude in a letter he wrote to a colleague in 1945 after hearing about Edith's death:

> I am disconsolate at Edith Stein's death though I am still hoping—perhaps, against hope—that the news will not prove true. With Hans Lipps and her, my best Göttingen friends are gone, and life seems so much poorer. It is as if a door to a beloved room of the past has been definitely locked. You can hardly imagine what E. St. meant to me during the first World War when she did everything to keep me spiritually alive and abreast with the intellectual events within our movement and outside. She was the kind genius of our whole circle, taking care of everything and everybody with truly sisterly love (also of Husserl who was seriously ill in 1918). She was like a guardian angel to Lipps in the years of his distress. When I spoke to her last time in the Cologne Monastery—a lattice between her room and mine—the evening twilight made her fade to my eyes: I felt I was not to see her again.[32]

We also find Edith reassuring Ingarden of the value she placed on their friendship: "As to the other question: Of course, in no way do I want to deny that—overlooking everything—we have a genuine friendship and that I view it as something valuable."[33] Even after entering Carmel, she assures him: "I will always be interested in the concerns of my friends."[34]

Faith Journey

Like all human beings, Edith's faith journey was unique with its own twists and turns, joys and sorrows. In terms of her Jewish background, she relates that although her mother faithfully practiced the Jewish faith, she herself did not receive "a strictly-orthodox upbringing." However, the family did celebrate the Jewish High Holy Days. As a girl, Edith relished the fact that they did not attend school on these days, which gave her extra time to read a good book. Mrs. Stein placed great emphasis on the fact that Edith was born on the Day of Atonement, and while Edith enjoyed the other holy days with their feasting, the Day of Atonement held a particular attraction for her. She observed the full fast from the time she was thirteen, noting that she and her siblings always kept this fast even after they no longer shared their mother's faith.[35] Nevertheless, Edith reports losing her childhood faith at the age of fifteen, at which time she deliberately gave up praying. She found what she termed Talmudic sophistry distasteful and shares that when she later began to consider religious questions, she asked a Jewish friend "whether he believed in a personal God." His reply that nothing more could be said except that God is spirit left her very dissatisfied.[36]

While Edith had learned some Gospel verses that were used for devotions during her early schooling, her first fuller acquaintance with the Gospels came during her study of Old High German at the University of Breslau. She read Tatian's *Diatessaron* (Harmony of the Gospels) and Ulfilas's translation of the Bible. At the time, it held no religious meaning for her, and she noticed that it also did not seem to influence her Protestant friend with whom she studied. But it was in Göttingen (1913–14) that Edith became more fully acquainted with Christianity, and it was there that she became open to the idea of considering religious questions. Max Scheler gave lectures to the Philosophical Society of Göttingen and included numerous Catholic ideas in his talks. This was an unknown world for Edith, but Husserl had instructed his students to examine all things without prejudice. Observing that some of her associates whom she admired lived in the world of faith, Edith let down her "barriers of rationalistic prejudices."[37] But at this point, while she came to respect religious questions and those who had faith, she did not yet systematically investigate questions of faith. She even occasionally attended a Protestant church, but found that sermons that mixed politics and religion could not lead her to faith and actually annoyed her. She comments that she "had not yet found a way back to God."[38] Yet, a gradual transformation was taking place: "I was content to accept without resistance the stimuli coming from my surroundings, and so, almost without noticing it, became gradually transformed."[39]

Another simple incident made an impact on Edith when she visited points of interest in Heidelberg in 1916 with Pauline Reinach (Adolf Reinach's sister). They stopped into the Catholic cathedral to have a look around, and Edith was moved when she observed a woman carrying a market basket enter the church and kneel down to pray. Seeing someone stop into a church in the course of daily errands to pray as though in an intimate conversation was new to Edith and made an indelible impression on her. Until then, she had only seen people enter synagogues and Protestant churches to attend services.[40]

By February 1917, her interest in the question about God had grown stronger. She wrote to Ingarden,

> I find that many people will cut all corners (to totally avoid the religious experience) though it is impossible to conclude a teaching on person without going into the God question, and it is impossible to understand history. Of course, I am still not at all clear about this. However, as soon as I finish with *Ideen* [Husserl's unpublished papers], I would like to go into these things. It is the question that interests me. When you return perhaps we can read Augustine together. The only question is when.[41]

Ingarden never read Augustine with her, but in November of that year, she came face-to-face with the question of faith and the Christian belief in the afterlife when her beloved professor, Adolf Reinach, died while serving in World War I. She was deeply affected by this loss. When invited by his wife, Anna, to arrange his philosophical papers, her only hesitation was the fear of entering their home empty of Reinach's presence and expecting to find Anna as a grieving widow rather than the formerly happy wife. Edith was taken aback to find that Anna's deep sorrow had been transfigured by her strong faith in the power of Christ's cross. The Reinachs had become Christians only in 1916. Edith reportedly shared the following thoughts about this experience with a Jesuit priest: "This was my first encounter with the Cross and the divine strength that it inspires in those who bear it. For the first time I saw before my very eyes the Church, born of Christ's redemptive suffering, victorious over the sting of death."[42] In the next few years, Edith contemplated joining either the Catholic or the Evangelical Lutheran Church.[43]

In addition to her work for Husserl, which kept her from her own research and writing, Edith helped to put Adolf Reinach's philosophical papers in order. In apparent response to her family's remarks about her kindness to others, she wrote the following to her sister Erna on July 23, 1918:

It seems to me sometimes as though all of you have too high an opinion of me and that embarrasses me. For I am not at all a saint and have my hours of weakness, just as everyone else does. Besides, I believe that even a saint is not required to renounce all wishes and hopes, nor all the joys of the world. To the contrary: one is on earth in order to live. One should accept with gratitude all the beautiful things which exist. However, one should not despair if things go other than one had expected. When that happens, one ought to think of what one still has, and also, that one is only here on a visit as it were, that everything which depresses one so terribly now will not be all that important at the end; or it will have a totally different meaning than we now recognize.[44]

The fall of 1918 brought Edith a different kind of misery. She had been working as Husserl's assistant for two years, painstakingly organizing his many sheets of yet-unpublished work, but her "Master" whom she dearly respected still would not take time to address pressing questions and issues concerning the work she had completed for him. Edith conveyed her frustration in a letter to Ingarden, and one of her comments reflects just how fed up she was with her working situation. "The best way to come to terms with this wretched world would be to take one's leave of it. It is my conviction though, that one must not take such an easy way out."[45] Yet only four days later, she wrote to Ingarden about how her openness to the Christian faith gave her a more hopeful perspective:

> I do not know whether you have inferred from my earlier comments that I have overcome all the obstacles and increasingly have a thoroughly positive view of Christianity. That decision has freed me of all that had suppressed me and at the same time has given me the strength to see life anew and, thankfully, to start living again. Thus, I can speak of a "rebirth" in the deepest sense of the term. However, my new life is so closely connected with the experiences of last year that I will never dissociate myself from them in any way. They will always be vividly present for me and I no longer see misfortune in all the experiences. On the contrary, that part of my life is one of my most valuable possessions. Surely, it has to give you some satisfaction. For something that means so much to me, you must not think of it as just an episode. And you should not pretend (to me and to yourself) that it is a phantom "happiness" that has no reality and that is able more to frighten than to attract.[46]

It would seem that "the experiences of the last year" refer to the events connected with Reinach's death.

The Jesuit theologian Erich Przywara had a working relationship with Edith concerning her translation work on John Henry Newman and Thomas Aquinas during her years in Speyer. He relates that Edith told him that prior to her conversion to Christianity, she came across a booklet of *The Spiritual Exercises* of St. Ignatius in a bookstore and bought it. Her initial interest was more from a psychological perspective. She soon realized that the book, which is a manual for spiritual directors, was not meant for just reading, but for doing the exercises. Przywara states that Edith went through the thirty days of exercises by herself some time prior to her conversion.[47] While it is easy to imagine Edith doing the thirty days on her own, she herself makes no mention of this incident. What she does state is that in 1921, reading Teresa of Avila's autobiography had a definitive influence on her decision to be baptized in the Catholic Church.[48] Edith bought and studied a Catholic catechism and missal and then approached the pastor of St. Martin's Church, Bergzabern, about being baptized. She was baptized on January 1, 1922, and received her first Communion the next day. She was confirmed by the bishop of Speyer on February 2, 1922. Soon after, Monsignor Joseph Schwind, vicar general of the Diocese of Speyer, became her spiritual director. He suggested that she take a teaching position at St. Magdalena's School in Speyer, where she could board with the Dominican sisters and become more immersed in Catholic life.[49]

For her baptismal name, Edith chose Teresa Hedwig: Teresa after Teresa of Avila, and Hedwig after her friend and baptismal sponsor, Hedwig Conrad-Martius. Along with St. Teresa, Edith also names Augustine of Hippo and Francis of Assisi as Christian witnesses who made a strong impression on her.[50] Her familiarity with several of Augustine's writings is apparent in some of her writings, especially *Finite and Eternal Being*. Regarding Francis, it is interesting to note that the Stein family had a reproduction of Cimabue's St. Francis in their family home simply as a work of art. On her sister Erna's wedding day in 1913, Erna's seat was located below this painting, at the spot where Edith's desk usually stood. Edith recounts, "I looked at St. Francis above her head and found great consolation in his presence."[51] A possible later link with Francis may be Edith's practice of writing "*Pax!*" (Peace!) at the beginning of most of her letters dated since January 1930. She changed this to "*Pax Christi!*" (Peace of Christ!) in September 1933 and continued this practice until her last letter on July 29, 1942, prior to her deportation. Francis had instructed his friars to extend a greeting of peace to all they met. However, Edith does not state the reason for her own practice in this regard. In a play during her novitiate, Edith was cast in the role of Francis, and she once recommended the book *Little Flowers of St. Francis of Assisi* to a friend who had recently become Catholic. And at one time, like Francis, she even referred to her body as "Brother Ass."[52]

Following her conversion, Edith wished to become acquainted with the intellectual foundations of Catholic thought and so became acquainted with the writings of Thomas Aquinas. She also read Dun Scotus and Pseudo-Dionysius. Nevertheless, the two saints who had the greatest impact on her life were Teresa of Avila and John of the Cross. As already noted, reading Teresa's autobiography was a decisive factor in Edith's decision to be baptized in the Catholic Church and her desire to become a Carmelite. She wrote a booklet about Teresa that was published by the Cologne Carmel and also included an appendix on *The Interior Castle* in *Finite and Eternal Being*. For her private retreats prior to her clothing day (entrance into the novitiate), as well as before her first profession of vows, Edith reflected on the writings of John of the Cross—*The Ascent of Mount Carmel* before her clothing day and *The Dark Night*, as well as the Gospel of John, before her profession. In 1940, she states that after her clothing day, she delved a bit further into his writings but considered herself at the foot of the mount.[53] The following year, Edith began her manuscript on John's writings titled *The Science of the Cross* for the four hundredth anniversary of his birthday. At that time, Edith wrote that she was living nearly constantly immersed in the thoughts of John of the Cross.[54] Indeed, as reflected in her correspondence at that time, she was reading several studies that had been written about him.

Edith placed great importance on obedience to God, including obedience to a spiritual director. From the time of her conversion, she desired to live the Carmelite life, but for the sake of her mother and for the good that could be gained by the use of her intellectual gifts, both of her spiritual directors (first Monsignor Schwind and later Archabbot Walzer) advised her to continue to work in the active apostolate outside of the convent. When she could no longer teach because of Nazi law forbidding Jews to hold any sort of public position, she felt that this was now the time to apply to Carmel and her director consented.

Although her family found Edith's conversion to Catholicism on January 1, 1922, and her entrance into Carmel on October 14, 1933, incomprehensible, Edith always maintained loving ties with them and never disowned her Jewish identity. Quite the contrary, she was very proud of her Jewish roots. In fact, at that time, the church commemorated the Feast of Jesus' Circumcision on January 1. It was no coincidence that Edith chose that date to be baptized. Furthermore, she was confirmed on February 2, 1922, the Feast of the Presentation of Jesus in the Temple, known in Edith's day as the Feast of the Purification of Mary. Later in Carmel, Edith made other associations with Old Testament figures. As a devotional practice, the Carmelites drew the name of a Carmelite saint at the beginning of each month. Once when she drew the name Elijah, she wrote, "To my great joy, he is my patron this month and I have a lot of confidence in him, especially in this matter."[55] And even more strongly, she identified herself with Esther. When writing about her concern for her family and the question of their emigration during the escalating Nazi danger in 1938, she wrote,

> If only they knew where to go! But I trust that, from eternity, Mother [deceased Mrs. Stein] will take care of them. And [I also trust] in the Lord's having accepted my life for all of them. I keep having to think of Queen Esther who was taken from among her people precisely that she might represent them before the king. I am a very poor and powerless little Esther, but the King who chose me is infinitely great and merciful. That is such a great comfort.[56]

Benedictine Influence

Edith spent eight days at the Jesuit retreat house in Zobten near Breslau in August 1927,[57] but the private retreat she made the following year during Holy Week and Easter at the Benedictine Abbey in Beuron opened up a new stage in her spiritual journey. Beuron became a sort of monastic home for Edith. Not only did the liturgical atmosphere at the abbey appeal to her, but Archabbot Raphael Walzer, OSB, became her spiritual director and remained her trusted spiritual friend even after her entrance into Carmel, corresponding through letters.[58] She continued to make yearly private retreats at Beuron during Holy Week and Easter until 1933 and visited there at other times as well. Walzer writes that when Edith visited Beuron for the first time, she brought with her

> so many values that in this monastic atmosphere of the hidden Danube valley she discovered her real spiritual home immediately, without need…to experience any changes or to add new knowledge. It was a kind of harvest of fruit sown by others and grown up in her splendid soil…. But what did, in reality, the great attraction of Beuron and its services consist of for her? Certainly not their length…. Sportive piety was as far from her mind as love of comfort and eagerness for easy gain of graces and interior joys. She never tried to have extraordinary elevations or ecstasies. Neither her mind nor her heart would have anything to do with that. She liked simply to be there, to be with God, to hold before her in some way the high mysteries…. But as her physical, almost stiff posture, also her soul remained in the calm of happy vision and presence before God. As a grateful convert and deeply satisfied child of her mother the Church, seeing the choir of the monks whom she was very qualified to join, thanks to her liturgical and dogmatic knowledge, she recognized the great Praying Church. Adoring in Christ the Divine Head of the Mystical Body, in continuous prayer before his eternal Father, logically she considered the supernatural life most of all the official prayer of the Church by the realization of the apostolic order: "pray without cessation." She understood this command in its entire content, and so no divine service seemed too long for her, no effort too great or merely as a valuable sacrifice; it was natural for her faith, to join in and to disappear in the depth of the *laus perennis* [perpetual praise]. The strict observance of a high liturgical style, in its entire extension and discrete measure, certainly was her all and in a

sense, indispensable. Nevertheless, later when it was the question of the final decision of her entrance into the Carmel, she had no difficulty to renounce the Benedictine interpretation and possibility [of becoming] a member of the Praying Church. Nor did I make any effort to insinuate her entrance into one of the Benedictine abbeys that are under the jurisdiction of the Beuron Archabbot. Humanly speaking, she would have become a splendid daughter of St. Benedict. It was enough for her to choose the name of the holy Patriarch as a second religious name. Those souls who comprehend the spirit of totality, like her, may run the risk to continue at cultivating and ripening the same spirituality even in a more specialized form of religious life.

Also, the beauty alone of the strict liturgy was not decisive for her mind and heart. Surely, good form was a principal motive in her manner of speaking, seeing and producing... so she was delighted more than others with the official liturgical prayers and ceremonies. But no human element could here disturb her mind, neither some unhappy form of the Beuron abbey church nor other imperfections which did not escape her attention because of her typical universal knowledge.[59]

Several times Edith conveyed her experience of the spiritual nourishment she received at Beuron. Referring to a Dominican sister who had joined her on a retreat there, she wrote,

You will surely notice that Sr. Agnella still has the afterglow of Beuron about her. What one takes away from there is lasting. And in the space of twelve days there, one can gather a treasure that will keep for a very long time and will help to digest everything that comes from outside. That will answer the question about my condition.[60]

Three years later, she wrote the following to a former student about her visits to Beuron:

Also of course, I have often reflected whether my coming here so frequently is justifiable. But after all, one has to provide one's inner life with the nourishment it needs, especially when at other times we are required to give a great deal to others. Obviously, one cannot discuss this with persons who are oriented purely to material matters, and who have no sense for the values of spirit or soul.[61]

Edith also visited the Benedictine Abbey of Gerleve several times. When questioned about her patron saint for her religious name, she replied, "Of course it is holy Father Benedict. He adopted me and gave me the rights of home in his Order, even though I was not even an Oblate since I always had the Mount of Carmel before my eyes."[62] Even in 1940, Edith referred to Benedict as her "holy Father" in addition to John of the Cross.[63]

Spiritual Experiences

While Raphael Walzer describes Edith as "mystically gifted in the true sense of the word,"[64] he does not elaborate on what he means. Was he referring to the understanding held prior to the sixth century that *mystical* applied to realities concealed by surface appearance that were accessible to all Christians, such as the allegorical interpretation of Scripture, the hidden presence of Jesus in the Eucharist, the sacraments (*mysterion*), and the experience of God's presence in the world? Or was he thinking of the term later understood as referring to the knowledge of God attained by direct, immediate, and inexpressible contemplation?[65] He doesn't say. Edith's writings do not include any reports of personal mystical experience such as are found in Teresa of Avila's writings, but she does convey that earlier sense of mysticism as referring to the encounter with God in daily life that is possible for all persons. In 1927, Edith wrote to Ingarden about "real events" and not simply "feelings" that influenced her conversion. She found that living the interior life opens up a new and infinite world of passion and blessedness in which prior realities become transparent, motivating strengths become perceptible, and conflicts trivial.[66] Years after her death, Ingarden stated that he thought she had some sort of experience of God prior to her conversion to Catholicism.[67] Edmund Husserl also reportedly said of Edith,

> Every true Scholastic will be a mystic, and every true mystic a Scholastic.... It is remarkable—Edith stands on a summit, so to speak, and sees the furthest and broadest horizons with amazing clarity and detachment, and simultaneously, she looks in another direction within herself with equal penetration. Everything in her is utterly genuine, otherwise I would say: this is contrived and artificial.[68]

Describing her own meditation after her first year in Carmel, Edith notes, "Just so, my meditations are not great flights of the spirit, but mostly very humble and simple. The best of it is the gratitude that I have been given this place as a home on earth and a step toward the eternal home."[69] However, she does relate a few experiences that were significant for her and that convey a sense of a deep spiritual awareness or some sort of spiritual confirmation. She recounts two occurrences of experiencing real certainty during prayer in 1933 before entering Carmel. Events leading to the experience will put these happenings into context. Having heard unconfirmed reports about Nazi cruelties to the Jews, it occurred to Edith that the fate of her people would also be hers. After pondering what she might do to help the plight of the Jews, she planned to travel to Rome for a private audience with Pope Pius XI to request an encyclical denouncing Nazi policy. But she first wanted to discuss her plan with Archabbot Walzer during her Holy Week retreat in Beuron. Without giving details, she states that years before, she had taken private vows and was permitted to regard Walzer as "her abbot." On her way to Beuron, Edith stopped in Cologne to visit a catechumen whom she was instructing. She provides the following account of her prayer during a holy hour at the Cologne Carmel.

> I talked with the Savior and told Him that I knew that it was His cross that was now being placed upon the Jewish people; that most of them did not understand this, but that those who did, would have to take it up willingly in

the name of all. I would do that. He should only show me how. At the end of the service, I was certain that I had been heard. But what this carrying of the cross was to consist in, that I did not yet know.[70]

Ascertaining that only an audience with a small group would be possible, she resorted to writing a letter that was delivered to the pope unopened. It was upon returning to Münster after her retreat that Edith learned that she would not be able to continue teaching because of her Jewish background. She "felt almost relieved that [she] was now caught up in the same common fate."[71] Shortly after, it dawned on her that this might now be the time to enter Carmel. This had been her desire ever since she first read Teresa of Avila's autobiography in 1921, but as already mentioned, her spiritual directors counseled her to wait out of consideration for her mother and also because of the good she could accomplish through her professional and apostolic work. But now she could no longer work openly in Germany, and although she received an offer to teach in South America, Edith thought that her mother would prefer her to be in a German convent rather than in South America. On Good Shepherd Sunday (April 30, 1933), Edith went to a church holding a day of prayer. In a succinct manner, she notes, "I went there late in the afternoon and said to myself, 'I'm not leaving here until I have a clear-cut assurance whether I may now enter Carmel.' After the concluding blessing had been pronounced, I had the assurance of the Good Shepherd."[72]

A different sort of occurrence happened at the time of Mrs. Stein's death in Breslau. It was September 14, 1936, the Feast of the Exaltation of the Cross, a day when the Cologne Carmelites renewed their vows. Edith reported feeling a distinct sense of her mother's presence at her side when her turn came to renew her vows. A telegram later arrived reporting the news of her mother's death at the same hour as the renewal ceremony.[73] In similar fashion, when Husserl died six days after her final profession, Edith confided that she had expected that there would be a coincidence similar to the timing of her mother's death. She attributed this to God's prodigality in demonstrating God's love.[74]

BACKGROUND TO
THE SELECTED WRITINGS

Edith's literary legacy ranges from phenomenological studies to personal letters. At one end of the scale, her strictly phenomenological works provide very interesting but often difficult reading. At the other end, her letters, autobiography, and retreat reflections are very straightforward. In between are found other scholarly writings, academic lectures, essays, translations, and public lectures written after her baptism that deal with philosophical, pedagogical, and theological themes. In most of these, the influence of her training in the phenomenological method under Husserl surfaces to a greater or lesser degree, as seen by her use of descriptive analysis, attention to the meaning of terms, concern for understanding the essence and essential structures of the object of her research, openness toward all experience, and a holistic attitude that is alert to interconnections. Because of the technical language used in her phenomenological writings, only one brief selection is taken from this part of her corpus. The selections have been chosen to highlight various aspects of Edith's perception of God, the journey of faith, and spiritual growth. The writings reveal her keen intellectual abilities, her search for truth, her interest in the human person, her love for God, her concern for others, her encouragement to cultivate a living faith, and her very down-to-earth approach to life in general.

In some cases, only excerpts of an essay are included in the selections, but the endnotes for the following include the full pagination for the entire essay. Information about the writings is taken from the critical editions of the works.

"Blessed Are the Poor in Spirit"[75]—This essay is dated November 1, 1933, and was possibly published in the *Monatsbrief der Societas Religiosa* (Monthly letter of the Societas Religiosa), a secular institute of professional women.

"Eucharistic Education"[76]—Edith gave this lecture at the Eucharistic Congress for German-speaking countries in

Speyer on July 14, 1930, on the occasion of the nine-hundred-year anniversary of the laying of the foundation stone of Speyer's imperial cathedral. The lecture was part of a meeting of the Speyer Women's Section. It was published in the Speyer diocesan newspaper, *Der Pilger* (The pilgrim) 30 (July 27, 1930).

"Exaltation of the Cross—*Ave Crux, Spes Unica!*"[77]—Edith wrote this meditation for the prioress of the Echt Carmel to use for the Carmelites' renewal of vows on the Feast of the Exaltation of the Cross celebrated on September 14, 1939. She wrote five other meditations for the prioress to use on various occasions, including two others for the Feast of the Exaltation of the Cross.

Finite and Eternal Being: An Attempt at an Ascent to the Meaning of Being[78]—As a Carmelite, Edith was given permission in 1935 to pursue the scholarly work she had begun on the manuscript *Potency and Act*. But her focus changed direction, resulting in a new opus in which she applies Thomistic and phenomenological thought to fundamental ontological questions, particularly the question of the meaning of being. Completed in 1937, the book could not be published because of Nazi anti-Semitic policies. Edith refused the publisher's suggestion to have it published under another sister's name. It was published in 1950.

"The Foundations of Women's Formation" and Supplement to "Foundations of Women's Formation"[79]—Edith presented this lecture at a conference of the Federation of Catholic German Women at Bendorf on the Rhine on November 8, 1930. A participant at the conference asked Edith to elaborate further on some points of her lecture in an essay for the *Monatsbrief der Societas Religiosa*. Edith was only able to fulfill this request in January 1932, and the article appeared in the *Monthly Letter* under the title "Ways to Inner Stillness." However, this was not the title given by Edith.

"The Holy Face"[80]—A poem written for Mother Petra Brüning, OSU, in gratitude for sending Edith a picture of the face of Jesus from the shroud of Turin. The poem was written December 5, 1937.

"I Will Remain with You"[81]—An undated poem that includes two illustrations: (1) within a triangle, there is a heart entwined with a crown of thorns, above which is a flame encompassing a cross; (2) a monstrance. It was possibly written as a gift for the final profession of Sr. Maria of God, OCD, on June 20, 1938.

"Letter to Pope Pius XI"[82]—Written in 1933, Edith's letter to the pope was published when the complete Vatican archives of Pius XI (1922–38) were opened to historians in 2003.

Letters to Roman Ingarden[83]—Collection of 162 letters and postcards written to Edith's friend and fellow phenomenologist Roman Ingarden, dating from January 1917 until May 6, 1938. They met in Göttingen in 1913 and developed a friendship in Freiburg, where both Edith and Ingarden transferred to complete their doctoral degrees under Husserl. Ingarden attests that from the summer of 1916 until the beginning of January 1917, they met and conversed every day until he left for Poland. Upon his return to Freiburg in late September 1917, the two again met almost every day until the end of January 1918, when Ingarden moved back to Poland. After that, they only met twice for a few days.[84]

"The Life of Christian Women"[85]—Edith presented four lectures under this theme in Zurich in January 1932, at the invitation of the Organization of Catholic Women. She actually presented all four lectures twice, in two different locations. They were printed in the publication *Mädchenbildung auf christlicher Grundlage* (Education of girls on the basis of Christianity) in March and April 1932.

"On the Idea of Formation"[86]—Edith presented this lecture in Speyer for the Catholic teachers of the Palatinate on October 18, 1930. The text was published in the journal of the Association of the Catholic Teachers of Bavaria, *Zeit und Schule* (Time and school) 22 (November 16, 1930).

"The Participation of Religious Institutions of Education in the Religious Education of Youth"[87]—Edith Stein most likely gave this lecture at a conference of the Committee of Religious held in Würzburg at the end of August 1929. The text was published in the newspaper of the Bavarian Diocesan Priests' Association and its Economic Association, *Klerusblatt* 10 (Clergy newspaper) (1929).

"The Prayer of the Church"[88]—Written in 1936, this essay was published in the series *Ich lebe und ihr lebt. Vom Strom des Lebens in der Kirche* (I live and you live. From the current of life in the Church) (Paderborn, Germany: Bonifatiusdruckerei, 1937).

"Recent Problems in the Education of Girls"[89]—In 1932, Edith was appointed as lecturer at the German Institute for Scientific Pedagogy, Münster, and was assigned to teach fourteen lectures during the summer on the recent problems in the education of girls. The first three sections of the lectures were slightly revised and published under the title, "Problems of Women's Education" in Beuron's *Benediktinischen Monatschrift* (Benedictine monthly) 14, nos. 9–10 and 11–12; 15, nos. 1–2 and 3–4 (1932).

"Retreat in Preparation for Final Vows"[90]—These are Edith's personal reflections during a private retreat that she made in April 1938, from Palm Sunday until Easter Tuesday, prior to professing her final vows on April 21, 1938.

The Science of the Cross[91]—In 1941, Edith was asked by her prioress to write a study on John of the Cross for the four-hundredth anniversary of his birth in 1542. On August 2, 1942, the day Edith and her sister Rosa were arrested by the SS, the manuscript was found on her desk. It was published in 1950.

"Sentient Causality"[92]—This is one of Edith's phenomenological writings that presents an analysis of the person from a phenomenological perspective. Written in 1919, it was published with another one of her essays, "Individual and Community," in the 1922 *Jahrbuch für Philosophie und phänomenologische Forschung* (Yearbook for philosophy and phenomenological research).

Self-Portrait in Letters 1916-1942[93]—A collection of 342 letters and postcards written by Edith to over 60 different recipients between 1916 and 1942.

"Sign of the Cross"[94]—A poem written November 16, 1937, possibly for Sr. Renata Posselt, OCD.

"The Theoretical Foundations of Social Formation Work"[95]—Edith gave this lecture at the convention of the Association of Catholic Teachers of Bavaria in Nuremberg on April 24, 1930. The text was published in the Association's journal, *Zeit und Schule* (Time and school) (June 1 and June 16, 1930).

"Truth and Clarity in Instruction and Teaching"[96]—This is the first known public lecture given by Edith at a teachers' conference held in Speyer on September 11 and in Kaiserslautern on September 12, 1926. It was published in the journal *Volksschularbeit: Monatsschrift für aufbauende Erziehung und Bildung* (School work: Monthly publication for constructive teaching and formation) 7, 11 (1926).

1

THE TRIUNE GOD

INTRODUCTION

A seeker of truth and a phenomenologist at heart, Edith had a great love for philosophy, but her search for truth led her to see the limits of philosophy. She discovered that the truths of faith enabled her to go beyond those limits. Subsequently, the Trinity—the divine, tripersonal, infinite being—takes center stage in her study of being, so that her ontology can be considered a trinitarian ontology.

God—the Blessed Trinity—dwells within each individual. Edith articulates this belief a number of times, such as in the first two selections. The first, a stanza from the poem "I Will Remain with You," identifies the innermost being of the human soul as the Trinity's favorite abode. The second is an excerpt from a letter to a Dominican sister whose community was forced to live in private dwellings after the Nazis had closed schools run by religious orders.[1] Edith reminds her of this truth now that the sisters did not have the physical presence of the Blessed Sacrament with them as they had had in their convent. Her reference to priests and religious in prisons without the Eucharist would apply to Edith herself four years later.

The selections taken from *Finite and Eternal Being* provide the reader with a glimpse into Edith's philosophical approach to God as informed by her faith. In the first of these selections, Edith contrasts the fleeting being of the human with God's enduring being. Within the continual flow of the current of time, the momentary experience of actual being, as it occurs between the already past and the not yet future, gives a hint of eternal being. The human being is not sustained and supported by himself, but by God's enduring being. The way of faith supports this understanding by revealing God as the

God "who is," the Creator, the one who stands more faithfully with us than a parent, and the one who is love. While philosophy tries to demonstrate the existence of God through discursive reasoning and comes up with some important concepts, Edith asserts that the concepts alone do not bring one closer to God. She points out that even St. Augustine, who stressed in various ways that our own being points beyond itself to true being, equally emphasized that humans are not capable of comprehending the incomprehensible God. Those who think otherwise do not understand the nature of God or the nature of the human being. The way of faith reveals the God of personal nearness, the loving, merciful God, and it bestows a certitude not found through natural knowledge. While the way of faith is dark, God communicates Godself in a manner proportionate to human understanding.

In the second selection from *Finite and Eternal Being*, we find Edith approaching the ultimate questions of being (ontology) by starting with God's personal name, YHWH, "I AM" (Exod 3:14). Following Augustine's lead, she accepts that God is "being in person," where "person," like all assertions about God, must be understood analogically. For instance, Edith also applies the term *person* to both human beings and angels to indicate the conscious, free, and self-determining "I." In this case, all persons call themselves "I" and each "I" possesses something incommunicable—something that is not shared with any other existent. However, this aspect of incommunicability does not apply to the persons of the Trinity, who share the one divine nature.[2]

Without beginning and end, God's "I AM" is eternally living presence, the plenitude of being without any voids, darkness, or changing contents. The "I AM" signifies that God is the I live, I know, I will, I love in the perfect unity of the eternally one divine act. In contrast, the life of the "I" in the human being has a beginning. It is present in every fleeting moment even though what it experiences in each moment (its experiential contents) is only momentarily present. Yet, without these various experiences that fill it, the "I" is empty. However, Edith maintains that if one removes everything that is non-being from the human "I," it analogically bears a resemblance to divine being.

The third selection from *Finite and Eternal Being* compares the "we" of the Trinity to the "we" of human beings that occurs when one finite "I" encounters another. The community of human persons does not nullify the multiplicity and diversity of persons or essences, but leaves room for the personal individuality that the "I" shares with no one else. The Trinity is a perfect unity of "we" in which there is no diversity of essence, only the diversity of the Divine Persons that makes possible the "we." In its fullest meaning, the divine unity of "I" and "you" is a unity of love. Since love, in its perfection, is a "being-one" founded on mutual self-giving, Edith holds that God who is love must be the "being-one" of a plurality of persons. She equates the divine name "I AM" with the meaning "I give myself wholly to a 'you,'" "I am one with a 'you,'" and "We are." This mutual eternal love of the Trinity is the highest form of love that surpasses any love between God and creatures.

Edith dedicates an entire chapter of *Finite and Eternal Being* to discussing the image of the Trinity in the created world. The final selections are taken from this chapter. Although dense reading at times, they shed light on Edith's perception that all created being—both animate and inanimate—bears some sort of image of the Trinity, even if only a distant image-like resemblance. Here she differs with Aquinas, who recognized a vestige or trace of the Trinity in the entire created world, whereby the causality of the cause can be inferred from its effect—such as when fire can be inferred by the presence of smoke. Aquinas saw an image of the Trinity only in rational beings possessing reason and free will—humans and angels. Edith is convinced, however, that a certain image character is found in the entire created world and distinguishes between a proximate and more remote image character.[3] She demonstrates her point by methodically (and at times laboriously) moving through the realms of inanimate corporeal things, nonpersonal animate beings, and human beings. Although Edith does not make explicit reference to the need for humans to respect creation, it is surely implicit in her view that all creation carries a certain image character of the Trinity. She herself enjoyed being in the outdoors, whether taking a walk, mountain hiking, or picking apples in the apple orchard of her friends Hans Theodor Conrad and Hedwig Conrad-Martius.

A few points can help facilitate the reader's understanding of these last selections, which are among the most challenging of all the selections in this volume. First of all, two German words translated as "body" carry two specific meanings. *Leib* indicates a living or ensouled body, whereas *Körper* indicates the merely physical or corporeal body. Second, Edith understands the soul as the form of the body (*Leib*), whether plant, animal, or human. She views the human being as being constituted of body-soul-spirit in a totally holistic way—"the entire human being is *one* substance"—such that body and soul thoroughly permeate each other. She does not endorse any sort of dualistic approach, and in fact, she clearly refutes dualism.[4]

THE TEXTS

Poetry

"I Will Remain with You"[5]

The innermost chamber of the human soul
Is the Trinity's favorite abode
Its heavenly throne on earth.

Letter

To Sr. Agnella Stadtmüller, OP, October 20, 1938[6]

Pax Christi!
Dear Sister Agnella,

...Yesterday, greetings from you were passed on to me in a letter from the Lichtenbergers. I hope you have settled in somewhat in the meantime. Certainly it is difficult to live outside the convent and without [having] the Blessed Sacrament [reserved in the house]. But God is within us after all, the entire Blessed Trinity, if we can but understand how to build within ourselves a well-locked cell and withdraw there as often as possible, then we will lack nothing anywhere in the world. That, after all, is how the priests and religious in prison must help themselves. For those who grasp this it becomes a time of great grace. We have already heard this of some people [in such a situation]....

In Jesus' love, your
Sister Teresa Benedicta, OCD

Finite and Eternal Being

CHAPTER II. §7 THE BEING OF THE "I" AND ETERNAL BEING[7]

...Anxiety, to be sure, is under ordinary circumstances not the dominant mood of human life. It overshadows everything else only under pathological conditions, while normally we go through life almost as securely as if we had a really firm grip on our existence. This may in part be explained by the fact that we feel tempted to pause at any superficial view of life which simulates an appearance of "lasting" existence within a "static temporal continuum" and which under the veil of our multiple "cares" hides from us the sight of life's nullity. Generally speaking, however, this feeling of security in human existence cannot be called a mere result of such an illusion and self-deception. Any circumspect reflective analysis of the being of people shows clearly how little reason for such a feeling of security there is just in actual human existence, and to what extent the being of people is indeed exposed to nothingness.

Does this mean then that the feeling of existential security has been proven objectively groundless and "irrational" and that therefore "a passionate...consciously resolute and anxiety-stricken *freedom toward death*"[8] represents the rational human attitude? By no means. The undeniable fact that my being is limited in its transience from moment to moment and thus exposed to the possibility of nothingness is counterbalanced by the equally undeniable fact that despite the transience, I *am*, that from moment to moment I am *sustained in my being*, and that in my fleeting being I share in enduring being. In the knowledge that being holds me, I rest securely. This security, however, is not the self-assurance of one who under her own power stands on firm ground, but rather the sweet and blissful security of a child that is lifted up and carried by a strong arm. And, objectively speaking, this kind of security is not less rational. For if a child were living in the constant fear that its mother might let it fall, we should hardly call this a "rational" attitude.

In my own being, then, I encounter another kind of being that is not mine but that is the support and ground of my own unsupported and groundless being. And there are two ways in which I may come to recognize *eternal being* as the ground of my own being. One is the *way of faith* when God reveals himself as *he who is*, as the *Creator* and *Sustainer*, and when our Redeemer says, "He who believes in the Son possesses eternal life" (John 3:36). Then I have in these pronouncements clear answers to the riddle of my own being. And when he tells me through the mouth of the prophet that he stands more faithfully at my side than my father and my mother, yea that he is love itself, then I begin to understand how "rational" is my trust in the arm that carries me and how foolish is all my fear of falling prey to nothingness—unless I tear myself loose from this sheltering hold.

The way of faith, however, is not the way of philosophic knowledge. It is rather the answer of another world to a question which philosophy poses. But philosophy has also its own specific way: it is the way of discursive reasoning, the way or ways in which *the existence of God is rationally demonstrated.*

The ground and support of my being—as of all finite being—can ultimately be only one being which is not some received being (as is all human being). It must be a *necessary being*, i.e., it must differ from everything that has a beginning in that it alone cannot not be.[9] Because the being of this existent is not received being, there cannot be any separation between *what* it is (and what could or could not be) and its actual existence: it must be its very act of existing.[10]

This necessary being *a se* [by itself], which is without a beginning and itself the cause of all beginning, must be *one*; for if there were several such beings, a distinction would have to be made between those characteristics in which they differ and which make one of them that *particular being*, and those qualities which the one shares with the others. But the first existent does not admit of such a distinction.[11]

It may be that my fleeting being has a "hold" on something finite and yet, being finite, this something could not possibly be the ultimate hold and ground. Everything temporal is *as such* fleeting and therefore needs an eternal hold or support.[12] If my own being is tied to some other finite being, we are *together* sustained in being. The security which I experience in my fleeting existence indicates that I am immediately anchored in an *ultimate* hold and ground (notwithstanding the fact that there may also be some mediate supports of my being). But this experience is a rather dim and indefinite feeling that can hardly be called *knowledge*.

St. Augustine, who groped his way to God preeminently from the experience of his inner being and who emphasized in ever new verbal expressions the fact that our being points beyond itself to true being, is always equally emphatic in affirming our incapability of comprehending him who is incomprehensible. "Those who...believe," he writes, "that it could occur to someone, while in this mortal life, to attain to the radiant brightness of the light of immutable truth and to adhere to it steadily and unswervingly with the mind totally detached from the habits of this life—these people have not understood the nature of what they seek nor the nature of those who seek...."[13] And again, "When you begin to step nearer, conscious of some similitude with him, and when you then try to probe the being of God—in a measure proportionate to your growing love (for your love is also of God)—then you experience something you expressed in words and something you did not and could not express in words.... For prior to your search you thought you had enunciated something pertaining to God, but once your search has begun, you feel how impossible it is to make articulate the object of your search."[14]

This groping search in darkness reveals to us the incomprehensible one as inescapably near, as the one in whom "we live, move, and are" (Acts 17:28), but who remains incomprehensible, nevertheless. Our discursive reasoning is certainly capable of coining clear concepts, but far from grasping the incomprehensible one, these concepts rather move him still farther away into that peculiar distance in which all conceptual knowledge is shrouded.

The way of faith gives us more than the way of philosophic knowledge. Faith reveals to us the God of personal nearness, the loving and merciful God, and therewith we are given a certitude which no natural knowledge can impart. But the way of faith, too, is a dark way. God himself attunes his language to the measure of human understanding, so as to make the incomprehensible intelligible to some extent.

When he commissioned his servant Moses and told him, "I am who am" and "Tell the sons of Israel: He who is has sent me to you"—for this true being is hard to grasp by the human mind, and Moses was sent as a human being to human beings (though not by a human being)—he immediately added, "Tell the sons of Israel that the God of Abraham, the God of Isaac, and the God of Jacob has sent me to you. This is my name for all eternity.... What I told you—I am who am—is true, but you cannot comprehend it. But when I said that I am the God of Abraham and the God of Isaac and the God of Jacob—this is true and comprehensible as well.... For this, *I am who am*—that pertains to me. But this, *the God of Abraham and the God of Jacob*, pertains to your understanding."[15]

CHAPTER VI. §4.3 THE NAME OF GOD: "I AM"[16]

I shall now attempt to approach the ultimate ontological questions from an entirely different point of view, namely by taking as my frame of reference that name by which God has designated himself: "I am who I am" [Exod 3:14].[17] It seems to me highly significant that in the scriptural text we do not read, "I am *being*" [*das Sein*], or "I am *he who exists*" [*der Seiende*], but "I am who I *am*." One hardly dares interpret these words by using other ones. However, if the Augustinian interpretation is correct, we may conclude that he whose name is "I am" is *being in person*.

That the so-called first existent must be a person appears evident from much that we have previously stated. Only a person can *create*, i.e., call into being by virtue of his will. And the efficacy of the first cause can be conceived only as a free act, because any efficacious activity that is not a *free act* has a cause and is therefore not the *first efficacious activity.* Furthermore, the rational order and the purposiveness of the universe point to a person as their author. Only a rational being can posit and sustain a *rational order*; and only a knowing and willing being can posit ends and ordain certain means to these ends. Reason and freedom, however, are the essential marks of the person.

The name by which every person designates himself or herself *qua* person is the name "I." Only an existent who in its being is conscious of its being and simultaneously conscious of its differentiation from every other existent can call itself an "I." And of every "I" there is only one. It possesses something which it shares with no other existent, i.e., something that is *incommunicable* (the Thomistic understanding of individuality). This does not mean, however, that every "I" is *unique* in the sense that it does not share its quid (what it is) with any other existent. For, after all, the name "I" has a universal meaning which is fulfilled wherever and whenever it is duly applied. The question of whether there pertains to every person in addition a *particularity* which this person shares with no other person need not be considered here. At any rate, such a meaning is not implied in the name "I."

The incommunicability which pertains to every "I" as such is a *peculiar characteristic of being.* From every "I" emanates its own being, which we call life. It streams forth from moment to moment forming a *self-enclosed* existent, and every "I" *subsists for itself* and subsists in no like manner for any other existent, nor does any other existent subsist for the "I" in any like manner.[18]

Every human being is "an I." Every human being sooner or later refers to itself as an "I." This means that, for every human being, "being I" has a beginning. It may happen that a human being pronounces the *word* "I" before it is able to realize its meaning. It is also possible that the human being understands the meaning of the word (simply as a form of "conscious life," without its being as yet able to form the *concept* "I"), before the being begins to make use of it verbally.

There are minor discrepancies between the intellectual life and its natural verbal expression, caused by the peculiarities of language as a physically conditioned means of expression as well as by the fact that speech has to be acquired by a process of learning.

Such discrepancies do not, however, void the significance of language as an essential means of expression, so that the use of the word "I" in the sense described is a sign of the awakened life of the ego. The life of the "I" is the ego's being, but this being does not coincide with the being of the human being, and the beginning of the awakened ego life is not equivalent to the beginning of human existence.

The peculiar being of the ego was discussed previously.[19] We pointed out that the ego enjoys a twofold ontological prerogative with respect to those contents which fill its life: 1) The ego life is actual or actually present at every moment, whereas each of its contents has only one moment in which the height of actuality is made present; and 2) the ego life is the *carrier* of experiential contents, and the latter receive their being alive from the life of the ego and are unified by it and in it.

But despite these prerogatives, the being of the "I" is deficient and by itself null and void. It is empty unless it is filled with content, and it receives this content from those realms—the "external" and the "internal" world—which lie "beyond" its own sphere. Its life comes out of one darkness and moves into another darkness. There are lacunae in it which cannot be filled, and it is sustained only from moment to moment. And thus we see that while the being of the "I" is separated from divine being by an infinite distance, it nevertheless—owing to the fact that it is an "I," i.e., a person—bears a closer resemblance to divine being than anything else that lies within the reach of our experience. If we remove from this being of the "I" everything that is non-being, this will make it possible for us to conceive—albeit only analogically—of divine being.

In God there is not—as there is in the human being—a contrast between ego life and being. God's "I am" is an eternally living presence, without beginning and without end, without any voids and without any darkness. This divine ego life has all its plenitude in itself and from itself. It receives nothing from anywhere else, for it is that from which everything else receives everything. It is that unconditioned reality which conditions everything else. In this divine "I" there are no changing contents, there is nothing that emerges and dies away. There is no passing from potentiality to actuality or from a lower to a higher actuality. This consummate plenitude is eternally present because it is all that which is.

The "I am" means: I live, I know, I will, I love—and all this not in the manner of a successive or coordinated series of temporal *acts*, but in the perfect unity of the eternally *one* divine *act* in which all the diverse significations of *act*—actual being, living presence, perfect being, intellectual striving, free activity—absolutely coincide. The divine "I" is no empty ego, but an "I" which harbors, encompasses, and in sovereign self-possession, masters all plenitude.

This perfect unity may be expressed even more clearly in a language which encloses the meaning of the "I am" in one single word, as in the Latin *sum*. In the case of that "I" whose very being is life, we can best understand that *I* and *life* or *being* are not two different things but inseparably one. They are the *personally formed plenitude of being*.

CHAPTER VI. §4.5 A COMPARISON BETWEEN THE RELATIONSHIP OF THE CREATOR TO HIS CREATION AND THE INNER RELATIONSHIP WHICH EXISTS AMONG THE DIVINE PERSONS[20]

...Divine being-a-person is the archetype of all finite being-persons. The finite "I," however, finds itself confronted with a "you," i.e., "another I" like unto itself, an existent to whom the person may turn, demanding understanding and response, an existent of whose life the "I" partakes in the unity of a "we" by virtue of an experienced common or communal ground of the being "I."

This "we" is the form in which we experience the oneness (i.e., the being one) of a plurality of persons. And this oneness does not annul the multiplicity and diversity of persons. The diversity is not even a diversity of *being* in the sense in which we have learned to know being as pertaining to the essence of the "I." The being-incorporated into a higher unity does not annul the *monadic*, closed structure of the ego-life. But there is also a diversity of *essence*. The community of species, which is the basis of the being-we, leaves room for a *personal individuality* which the "I" shares with no one and nothing else.

Now such a diversity of essence is not found in the Divine Persons. God's "personal individuality" is all-encompassing being which, *as* all-encompassing, is unique and distinct from everything finite. Nor is there found any contrast of *universal* and *particular*, and of essential and actual being.

The Three Persons have their entire essence in common, so that there remains only the diversity of the Persons as such. There is thus a perfect unity of the we, such as can never be attained by any community of finite persons. And there is yet within that unity a separateness of the I and the Thou [*Du*] without which no we is ever possible.

In addition to the revelation of the divine name "I am," there occurs in the Old Testament that saying of Genesis, "Let us make man according to our own image" (Gen 1:26), a phrase which our theologians traditionally interpret as a first intimation of the mystery of the Trinity. And there are furthermore the clear words of our Savior, "I and the Father are one" (Jn 10:30). The we, then, as a unity of I and thou, is a higher unity than that of the I. In its most authentic meaning, it is a unity of love.

Now love as a simple yea in view of some good is possible also in the self-love of an I. But love is more than such a yea, more than a mere affirmation of value. It is giving of the self to a thou, and in its perfection it is a being-one that is founded on mutual self-giving. And because God is love, divine being must be the being-one of a plurality of persons, and the divine name "I am" is thus equivalent to an "I give myself wholly to a Thou," an "I am one with a Thou," and therefore also with a "We are."

The love between God and creatures is different from that love which is the life-principle of the Divine Persons, which as such has no equal, because the love between God and creatures can never be love in its highest perfection (not even in that state of perfection which can be attained by the rational creature in the light of glory). The highest love is a mutual eternal love. While it is true that God loves his creatures from eternity, he is not loved by them from eternity. Thus, if divine love were dependent on creatures, it would be subject to change, it would lack perfect fulfillment, and God himself would be made to depend on his creatures. Thus the love between

God and creatures always remains imperfect, because, even though in the total self-giving of the life of glory, God is capable of receiving into himself the creature, no creature—nor all creatures together—can ever comprehend or encompass God.

God's inner life is the perfectly free, immutable, and eternal mutual love among the Divine Persons, independent of all created things and beings. And what the Divine Persons give to each other is one, eternal, and infinite nature and being, wholly encompassing each of them separately and all of them together. This nature and being the Father gives from eternity to the Son by generating him, and from this gift proceeds, as the fruit of mutual love, the Holy Spirit. The being of the Second and Third Persons is thus a received being and yet—unlike created being—no newly originated being. Rather, it is the *one* divine being, simultaneously given and received, since the giving and receiving pertain to divine being as such.

Another access to the mystery of triune being may be sought in the following way. God's being is *life*, i.e., a movement from the inside out, and ultimately a generating being. The divine being is not—as is the case with finite, created things and beings—a movement into existence. Nor is it a movement transcending the individual self, as is the case in any finite generation, but it is an eternal movement within the self, an eternal self-drawing or self-creating out of the depth of God's own infinite being, an infinitely generous giving of the eternal I to an eternal Thou, and a correspondingly eternal and ever-renewed self-receiving and self-giving. And because the oneness which eternally springs from this giving and receiving brings forth once more in a *communal manner* that which has been given and received, the circle of the intradivine life completes and closes itself in the Third Person who is gift, love, and life.

Chapter VII. §6 Meaning and Fullness, Form and Matter, the Contrast between the Creator and His Creation and the Image Relationship[21]

...In their unity of meaning and life, all created structures are images of the divine essence from which they are distinguished by their materiality. And we shall now make an attempt to describe finite being in terms of its image relationship to divine being. However, we can only do this by turning our eyes first on divine being.

We have ascended to divine being by starting out from creaturely being and by proceeding from the finite and conditioned to the infinite and unconditioned author and archetype of everything finite and conditioned. We have also already crossed that borderline which is indicative of what can be learned about the Creator from creatures and of what God has himself revealed concerning his own nature. Without crossing this borderline, it would be impossible to learn anything about creaturely being as viewed from the perspective of divine being. We thus look in the Triune Deity for the archetype of what in the realm of creaturely being we have designated as meaning and fullness of life.

As far as *meaning* is concerned, we may refer to our earlier discussions.[22] We regarded the *Eternal Word* (the Logos) as that *unity of meaning* which, as the archetype of all finite units of meaning, encompasses the total plenitude of meaning. The church designates in her creed the Holy Spirit as the author of life, as the "vivifier" or "life-giver." Ultimately, however, only the one who does not receive life but is "life in person" can vivify or give life. In the *Holy Spirit* we thus see the divine fullness of life.

It need hardly be emphasized that this statement does not imply a partition or division of the divine essence. The one essence owned in common by all the Divine Persons is life and love, wisdom and power. Aside from the relations of the Three Persons to one another, nothing can be predicated of one of them that does not pertain to all of them. And if, within the indivisible unity of God, we distinguish certain *attributes* and ascribe some of them to this person and others to that person, we are thereby merely attempting to make the incomprehensible intelligible. And yet what the creaturely image reveals to us of the divine archetype serves to make us see creaturely being in a new light.

But to make us understand (as far as one can speak of "understanding" these matters) the Holy Spirit as the dispenser of life and as the archetype or paradigm of all creaturely life, something must first be said concerning the position of the Third Person in the Deity.

As was emphasized in our earlier discussion, the only distinctions among the Divine Persons concern their relations to one another, relations which are explained by the different manner of their procession. Thus, the Father is called *Father* because everything proceeds from him, while he proceeds from no one and nothing else. The Son is called *Son* because he proceeds from the Father. And "he is called the *Word of the Father* because he proceeds from the Father as an effect or act of the intellect, as a conception of the spirit, and this latter name is also applied to the word that is inwardly produced by the intellect in us."[23] The Third Person is called the *Holy Spirit* "because this person proceeds from the Father through the Son in a single spiration in the manner or mode of love, and it is this first and highest love which moves and guides hearts to a sanctity which is essentially love for God."[24]

We have been trying to understand the plurality of the Divine Persons from the fact that God is *love* and that love is a free self-giving of an I to a Thou, and a union of both in a We.[25] Because God is spirit, he is fully transparent to himself and generates from eternity the "image" that pertains to his own being, an image in which he sees himself as he is in himself—his co-essential Son, Eternal Wisdom, or the Word. And because God is love, the "image" which he generates of himself is love also, and the mutual relationship of Father and Son is a loving self-giving and a union of love. But because love is the highest kind of freedom,[26] a giving of self as the act of one who fully possesses himself (i.e., a *person*)—in the case of God, however, the act of a person who is and loves not in the human manner, but who is love or whose very being is love—the divine love must itself be a Person: the Person of *Love*.

However, love is *life* in its highest perfection. Love is being which eternally gives itself without suffering any diminution, and it is thus infinite fecundity. The Holy Spirit is therefore the *gift* as such: not merely the mutual self-giving of the Divine Persons to one another, but the self-giving of the deity *ad extra*. The Holy Spirit thus comprises in itself all the gifts of God to his creatures.[27] Because God's wisdom foresaw from eternity all created things and being, the Logos as Wisdom in Person is the universal archetype of the determinateness of all creaturely essences, the eternal paradigm of everything they are to be. And because God's creative will, his existence-creating and life-imparting love have from eternity apportioned to creatures their "power of being" or the "power" of unfolding their essence, the Holy Spirit—as the person of life and love—is the archetype of all creaturely life and efficacious acting as well as of that spiritual radiance of their essence which is a property even of material structures. And if, finally, in the standing-upon-itself of every independent actuality (*prote ousia*) we may see an image of the Father as the primary unconditioned principle, then the entire structure of created existents ("that which is") turns into an image of the Triune Deity. But because all that which is, is *one* and because there is never an *empty form* without fullness, and the fullness of the essence is simultaneously a meaningfulness and powerfulness which form themselves into existence, all that which is analogically mirrors the unity of the divine essence.[28]

Chapter VII. §7. The Image of the Trinity in Inanimate Corporeal Things[29]

...We thus encounter in the realm of material being a twofold triunity: first, in the structure of existents, inasmuch as they stand upon themselves as thingly carriers of their essence and inasmuch as, by virtue of their essence, they are meaningful and unfold their being with the aid of that potent force which pertains to the essential form. And, second, this unfolding of being proceeds again in a triune manner—it is a self-forming into a structure that pertains to a particular essence. It implies possession of a thoroughly formed essence. And it is a self-transcending in efficacious action *ad extra*, in active involvement in the causal texture of corporeal nature and in a radiation of the individual essence that extends into the spiritual world. Lastly, the triple unfolding of being in the material realm has an analogue in the three basic modes of space-filling—the liquid, solid, and gaseous formation of matter.

Chapter VII. §8. The Image of the Trinity in Nonpersonal Animate Beings[30]

That which is efficaciously operative in the formation of animate beings and exercises its efficacy as the "center" of a structural unity we have designated as supra-material form, living form, or soul. This form or soul, though delimiting and enclosing itself from within, receives into itself, embodies in its structure, and transforms extraneously existing material elements, and it produces or generates new independent structures of the same species. We are dealing here with a kind of formation in which *life* is *auto*-motive—a self-enclosed cyclic movement that yet procreatively reaches out beyond itself. This kind of life is an image of divine self-sufficiency and self-sustenance as well as of divine self-giving and creative productivity.

That which is alive or animate is more self-sustaining than the material-corporeal thing because it has a genuine primordial source in its own self, and it is therefore a more strongly marked image of the Father. As a self-enclosed and self-delimited structure, the animate being is a complete unity of meaning and as such a more strongly marked image of the Logos. It bears within itself the power of unfolding its own essence and of generating new structures, and in this vitality and fecundity it is more strongly a marked image of the Holy Spirit.

The *power of being* or the *life force* of the animate creature is, on the other hand, proportioned to the structural unity into which it is to unfold as well as to the new "births" which it is to produce. And just as its essence is not already completely actualized from the outset but is evolving and becoming more and more actual in a temporal process, so it also does not bear within itself from the outset the measure of power that is proportionate to its essence, but must progressively gain possession of it. To attain this goal as well as to complete itself in its structural unity, the animate creature has to rely on the material elements of the corporeal world. Just as it is capable of receiving into itself and of formally appropriating foreign material elements, so it is also capable of making use of these elements' internal forces and of transforming these forces into vital energy. For this reason, the more or less perfect unfolding of the animate creature's essence depends on its *environment*.

In plants, formation is no more than a mere forming of matter. Plants have not yet attained to the state of "being their own selves" and thus of forming themselves from within. The *animal soul* has reached that stage. It continues, like the lower forms, in the spatial forming of matter, but beyond this its *life is an internal movement* and the *forming of a soul structure*. The intake of food is "felt." The taste of the received material elements is experienced as a sensory impression "from without," and satiation is felt as resulting from bodily functions and as a physical state. Both the taste of food and satiation with food are intimately associated with an "internal impress," with satisfaction or repugnance, and with the more durable inner states of contentment or discontentment. And even the actual measure of power as well as its increase and decrease are felt in specific *vital emotional states*.

All of this has its *raison d'être* in the essence of the soul, which on this level has a tendency to unfold in a threefold manner: in the direction of material corporeality, in the direction of its own self, and in the direction of self-transcendence. For every external sense impression is an encounter with the surrounding world, and the contrast between the *self* and the external world is *felt*, so that the life of the soul compels a constant reckoning and coming to terms with the external world. And body and soul are being formed in these encounters.

This forming of the individual being, however, is preceded by that original formation which results from the specific determinateness of the essence. The *life force* is here a *body-soul* power. And this means not only the power of forming matter into a living body, but the capability of moving and activating in space the already formed body in diverse ways—always, however, in accordance with the specific essence. And in this process, the body receives its complete "actual formation." Moreover, it means that the animal soul is capable of moving itself and of being active in diverse ways, and in these movements and activities, the original "design" of the soul structure expresses itself in a concrete manner.

What the animal "encounters" in its surrounding world sets it in motion internally and causes it to assume specific attitudes with respect to the things and beings encountered. Reactions of fear, rage, etc., are responses to received impressions. Although they originate internally, they tend to manifest themselves externally, and they produce several effects. These "responses" impress a definite stamp upon the body—a bodily *expression* of the soul, which may be a temporary formation or a set of "features" of enduring character. And these responses cause certain externally manifest bodily activities, such as movements of flight or grasp, and they leave definite "traces" in the soul, such as an inclination and readiness for the resumption of identical positions and attitudes as well as enduring inner modes of behavior (what Scholasticism calls *habitus*).

In these attitudes and responses, the *single* power of the soul is being articulated and formally developed into a manifold of "powers" (faculties, skills, inclinations) without yet losing its unity. And the "life" in which this power of the soul unfolds itself is being formed into vital movements of varying content.

All these manifestations of the animal soul reveal a supramaterial quality which far surpasses that of the plant soul. The animal soul possesses an inner individual life that is detached, as it were, from space-filling matter, that is mirrored in the already formed material structure (the body) by constantly occurring transformations (in the phenomenon of expression), and that turns the body into an instrument of the individual's activities in the external world. This is made possible by the dual nature of the body [*Leib*], which is a body [*Körper*] in the corporeal world and simultaneously an animate structure formed by the soul, and by the dual nature of the soul, whose life is an internal movement and simultaneously an external formation of matter. The result is the transformation of soul movement into body [*leiblicher*] movement and of body [*leiblicher*] movement into purely material corporeal [*körperlicher*] movement.

On the other hand, however, the life of the animal soul remains tied to and conditioned by the body. Everything that befalls the animal soul is occasioned by the body [*Leib*], and it affects the body [*Leib*] in one way or another. And the power of the soul which exerts and consumes itself in its inner life (as well as in its external forming of matter) is nourished by the influx it receives from the corporeal world through the medium of the body [*Leib*]. But this same power is also diminished and consumed by the resistance it meets in its encounters with the external world.

With the awakening of an inner life, an entirely new kind of image relationship to the Deity appears—a relationship which is an analogical counterpart of the duality of inner personal life and a self-transcending forming of an external world. And this inner life bears within itself the seal of the Trinity. As a life that *stands upon itself* it is an image of the Father. As a *meaningful* life—full of meaning by virtue of its contents, even though these contents are not yet rationally understood by an ego—it is an image of the Son. And as *life*, as manifestation of *power*, as radiation of the essence, it is an image of the Holy Spirit. But the entire inner life, the forming of the body, and the active operation upon the external world are at this stage still things that merely "happen." They happen without being either understood or freely willed and are therefore not personal acts of the free spirit.

Chapter VII. §10 The Threefold Formative Power of the Soul. Body, Soul, and Spirit[31]

At this time we must again remind ourselves that the being of the human soul is not exhausted in its spiritual life. If we go back to the root of human being, we find a threefold direction in its unfolding: the forming of the body, the forming of the soul, and the unfolding of spiritual life. All this is done by the formative power of the soul, although this power (in its threefold formative efficiency) is *one*. It effects the forming of the body in the manner [of a plant soul and yet is thoroughly a human soul]. What is formed by this power is a human body, a means and field of expression for a free spirit—not a plant structure. This formative power is alive in the body and forms itself in the manner in which an animal soul is formed, and yet quite differently, since the life of the senses in its entirety is united with and formed by the spirit. And this formative power of the soul rises to a spiritual life of equal rank with the life of pure spirits [angels], but this spiritual life, nevertheless, has its own particular form, because it is rooted in bodily sensory life. In this manner the separate realms of the created world are joined in human beings in the unity of an essence, while outside of human beings they are linked only by a causal nexus and an interconnection of meaning.

The threefold formative power of the soul must be regarded as a tri-unity, and the same is true of the end product of its forming activity: body-soul-spirit. If we attempt to relate this tri-unity to the divine trinity, we shall discover in the soul—the wellspring that draws from its own sources and molds itself in body and spirit—the image of the Father; in the body—the firmly circumscribed expression of the essence—the image of the eternal Word; and in the spiritual life, the image of the divine Spirit. If we further keep in mind that *body* [*Leib*] is not to be understood as merely an animate physical entity [*Körper*] but as the "outborn" structure of the essence; that, correspondingly, *soul* signifies not merely the essential form of a corporeal animate being, but every kind of primal life source; and that, lastly, *spirit* denotes free self-transcending, we shall be able to discern this tri-unity even in the soul as such. The soul draws from its own source. It forms itself into a firmly circumscribed structure. And it steps forth from itself (transcends itself) in its spiritual life. Its self-forming into foreign matter in the process of the formation of the body may then be compared to the becoming incarnate of the Word, and its stepping forth from itself into an external world—upon which the soul impresses its own stamp—may be compared to the sending of the divine Spirit into the created world.

The soul in its threefold formative power and the threefold deployment of its being—even on its natural level—can be regarded as an image of the Triune Deity. And when it then opens itself in its innermost being to the influx of divine life, the soul (and through it, the body) is formed into an image of the Son of God. The "streams of living water" emanate from it—streams which effect a renewal of the face of the earth out of the Spirit. The human spirit, when it is permeated and guided by the Divine Spirit, recognizes in the divine light—underneath all the disfiguring veils—the original form of the created world and becomes capable of cooperating in the task of its restoration.

2

SECURE IN
GOD'S HANDS

INTRODUCTION

The theme of resting securely in God's hands or placing one's life in God's hands recurs in Edith's thought. It conveys an attitude of confident trust in divine providence as well as a sense of security in being led by God. Edith was well aware of the focus on human angst in the face of nothingness propounded by her contemporary Martin Heidegger. She acknowledges that existential anxiety is experienced through human fears and that it is ultimately the fear of nonbeing. However, as seen in the selection from chapter 2 of *Finite and Eternal Being* included in the last chapter, Edith maintains that, apart from pathological conditions, anxiety is not the dominant mood of human life. Rather, humans go through life quite securely even though there is little reason found in human existence itself to feel secure. She attributes this feeling of security to a sense of being sustained in our fleeting being by enduring being. Edith compares this to the security of a child being carried by a strong arm and states that it would be irrational for a child to live in constant fear that its mother would let it fall. For Edith, Eternal Being is the ground and support of all being.[1]

But surrendering oneself into God's hands does not in any way preclude fully and proactively using one's gifts and talents in life's situations. For example, at the time when the publication of *Finite and Eternal Being* first came to a halt because of the publisher's financial situation, Edith writes, "My consolation is that the Lord will take care of the book, if it can be of use to him. Otherwise, it may as well remain unprinted."[2] However, she actively sought another publisher, but after procuring one, the book's publication was again prevented because of Nazi restrictions. She declined the publisher's suggestion to have another sister named as the author, and then attempted to find a publisher outside of Germany, including the United States, but without success. Of this she writes, "All efforts have failed. I do not know what more to do, other than to leave the whole thing up to the Lord."[3] She could not have guessed that not only *Finite and Eternal Being*, but every piece of her extant writing would eventually be published and translated into several languages.

The first excerpt, taken from one of Edith's phenomenological essays, "Sentient Causality," was written in 1919, three years before her conversion to Catholicism. Marianne Sawicki suggests that the reference here to resting in God may not indicate a religious stance because Edith's mention of fate and the deity indicates that she is referring to a stoicism such as that espoused by Epictetus, who understood fate as divine and impersonal.[4] By 1917, however, Edith was interested in questions of faith and surely would not have missed the more personal, religious interpretation of resting in God.

The remaining selections include excerpts from letters and lectures. In the letters, references to being secure in God's hands appear both as advice to others and as a description of her own personal stance. Edith also drew on this theme when giving various lectures to women's and teachers' groups. In the letter to Sister Adelgundis found below, Edith actually refers to this theme as her *Ceterum censeo*—one might say, her signature theme.

THE TEXTS

"Sentient Causality"[5]

Beyond these influxes of impulse power, which presuppose a certain amount of lifepower already—namely, that required for the experiencing of power-giving contents—there is obviously still another that isn't tied to that presumption. There is a state of resting in God, of complete relaxation of all mental activity, in which you make no plans at all, reach no decision, much less take action, but rather leave everything that's future to the divine will, "consigning yourself entirely to fate." This state might have befallen me after an experience that exceeded my power, and that has completely consumed my mental lifepower and deprived me of all activeness. Compared to the cessation of activeness from the lack of lifepower, resting in God is something completely new and unique. The former was dead silence. Now its place is taken by the feeling of being safe, of being exempted from all anxiety and responsibility and duty to act. And as I surrender myself to this feeling, new life begins to fill me up, little by little, and impels me—without any voluntary exertion—toward new activation. This reviving infusion appears as an emanation of a functionality and a power which is not my emanation and which becomes operative within me without my asking for it. The sole prerequisite for such a mental rebirth seems to be a certain receptivity, like the receptivity supporting the structure of the person, a structure exempted from the sensate mechanism.

Letters

To Fritz Kaufmann, January 6, 1927[6]

Dear Herr Kaufmann,

...And advice? I have given you my advice: become like a child and lay your life *with* all the searching and ruminating into the Father's hand. If that cannot yet be achieved, then plead; plead with the unknown and doubted God for help in reaching it. Now you look at me in amazement that I do not hesitate to come to you with wisdom as simple as that of a child. It *is* wisdom *because* it is simple, and all mysteries are concealed in it. And it is a way that most certainly leads to the goal....

Best regards and most cordial wishes, your
Edith Stein

To Sr. Adelgundis Jaegerschmid, OSB, April 28, 1931[7]

Dear Sister Adelgundis,

...Your criticism is not quite clear. It is, of course, true that the third part is not detailed enough. (The entire religious formation should have been included, as I once treated the matter in Munich.) But then, it appears that you did not want the supernatural to be brought up at all. But, if I could not speak about that, I would probably not mount a lecturer's platform at all. Basically, it is always a small, simple truth that I have to express: *how to go about living at the Lord's hand.* Then when people demand something else from me and propose very clever themes which are foreign to me, I can take them only as an introduction in order to arrive eventually at my *Ceterum censeo.*[8] Perhaps that is a very reprehensible method. But my entire activity as lecturer has hit me like an avalanche, so that I have been unable as yet to reflect on it in principle. Most likely, I will have to do that some time....

With most cordial wishes for you and your work I am your

Edith

To Ruth Kantorowicz, October 4, 1934[9]

Pax Christi!
Dear Fräulein Dr. Kantorowicz,

...Now to your questions. Before all else I would like to tell you to lay all care for the future, confidently, in God's hands, and allow yourself to be led by him entirely, as a child would. Then you can be sure not to lose your way. Just as the Lord brought you into his church, so he will lead you to the place in it that he wants you to have. Despite your 33 years, I would advise you to set aside, for the time being, the question of a religious vocation. God's will is not halted by any boundary of age. After all, I was accepted at 42 years of age, and many others even later. Naturally everything is easier when one enters while still young....

With sincere best wishes for your further path, in the love of Christ, your sister

Teresa Benedicta a Cruce, OCD

༄༅

To Mother Petra Brüning, OSU, April 16, 1939[10]

Pax Christi!
Dear Reverend Mother,

...My basic attitude since I've been here is one of gratitude—grateful that I may be here and that the house is as it is. At the same time I always have a lively awareness that we do not have a lasting city here. I have no other desire than that God's will be done in me and through me. It is up to him how long he leaves me here and what is to come then. *In manibus tuis sortes meae* [My days are in your hands (Ps 31:15)]. There everything is well cared for. I need not worry about anything. But much prayer is necessary in order to remain faithful in all situations. Especially [must we pray] for those who have heavier burdens to carry than I have, and who are not so rooted in the Eternal. Therefore I am sincerely grateful to all who help....

With all sincere wishes in the love of the Risen One, your grateful

Sister Teresa Benedicta a Cruce, OCD

Lectures

"Truth and Clarity in Instruction and Teaching"[11]

...We said earlier that we have brought the child to the *right* way if we have brought him so far that he wants to live in the *imitation of Christ*, i.e., that he renounces his own will and places the direction of his life into God's hands.

...Whoever places his life in God's hands can be certain, and *only that one* can be certain, that he will become wholly himself; i.e., that he will become that which God has quite personally assigned for him.

"ON THE IDEA OF FORMATION"[12]

...God created the human being according to his image [Gen 1:27]. But on the other hand, as it is, only God alone sees this image in perfection. We see it in many images which portray it, each imperfectly, each from another angle—in creatures. We see it most perfectly in the most perfect of all creatures, in God's Son and in the Word of revelation which God announces to us. We are to take into ourselves as much of this image as we possibly can, so that it becomes an inner form and forms us from within. Also, as far as our strength allows, we are to strive to know ourselves and that for which we are made, and likewise to know others whose formation is entrusted to us. But we will never attain possession of a perfect knowledge, neither for ourselves nor for others, and therefore, will never be in a position to be able to set about our formation work for ourselves and for others with unfailing certainty. We will only be certain if we unconditionally entrust ourselves to the hand of the One who alone knows what is to become of us and who alone has the power to lead us to this goal—provided that we are of good will.

LOGOS

INTRODUCTION

If one were to ask Edith Stein whether there is meaning in life, she would respond with a resounding yes! She maintains that there is meaning in all created being. The subtitle of her major work, *Finite and Eternal Being*, is very telling in this regard—*An Attempt at an Ascent to the Meaning of Being*.

Edith recognizes that there is a coherence among all beings in both existence and meaning that is rooted in the divine Logos. The first selection below from *Finite and Eternal Being* highlights her conviction that the divine Logos is not only the Lord of all being, but also the Lord of all meaning. To elucidate her point, she draws on a few Scripture passages, including John 1:1, for which she renders three translations from the Greek: "In the beginning was the Word," "In the beginning was meaning," and "In the first being was the Logos." She is quick to note that her descriptions are figures of speech taken from human language that must be understood analogically when considering the divine Logos and the human logos. Edith understands the coherence by which everything exists in the Logos as a totality of meaning, or the unity of a meaning-totality. To illustrate what she means, she uses an example of the coherence of one's own life. While we can understand events that we plan as comprising a meaningful coherence, there are also unplanned or "chance" events that occur that we would not view as having meaningful coherence. Yet, later reflection may show that some of these unplanned events have had a greater impact on one's life than things planned. From Edith's perspective, one's life in all its details is a perfect coherence of meaning in God's eyes that the person will only fully understand in the life of glory. Within her discussion is found one of her frequently cited quotes, "What did not lie in *my* plan lay in God's plan." However, this must not be interpreted as some sort of determinism or stance of predestination, both of which are foreign to Edith's thought. Such coherence applies to all being so that the coherence in the Logos— the totality of meaning—is like a perfect work of art where every feature fits into the harmony of the entire structure. In relation to this meaning-totality, our understanding of the meaning of things can be compared to lonely tones from a distant symphony.

Another significant point from the first selection that can be easily overlooked needs to be highlighted. Edith describes creatures as being "called" into existence. This stands in stark contrast to Martin Heidegger's notion of human beings being "thrown" into the world. Nevertheless, Edith herself does use the phrase "thrown into existence" at times, such as when contrasting Jesus' humanity with that of all others.[1]

The second selection, also from *Finite and Eternal Being*, underscores Edith's view that creation is meant to reflect the divine splendor. Since everything created finds its archetype in the divine Logos, she perceives finite being as an image of the divine essence that is intended to reflect a ray of the divine splendor. Despite the condition of fallen nature, everything created is still a mirror of divine perfection, although a broken mirror. The creative works of human beings are also meant to continually carve out the God-likeness of nature. Such creative works should not only be useful for humans, but should also be beautiful in the sense that they reflect the eternal.

THE TEXTS

Finite and Eternal Being

Chapter III. §12 Essential and Eternal Being[2]

...That which gives me being and together with it fills this being with meaning must not only be the Lord of being, but also the Lord of meaning. All plenitude of meaning is contained in eternal being, and from nowhere else than from itself can eternal being "create" the meaning with which every creature is filled as it is being called into existence. Thus, we are not to think of the being of essentialities and whatnesses [quiddity] as an independent being alongside eternal being. It is the eternal being itself which forms in itself the eternal forms—not in a temporal occurrence—according to which it creates the world in time and with time. That sounds puzzling and yet known and familiar:

"*En archē ēn ho logos*"—thus answers Eternal Wisdom to the puzzling question of the philosopher. The theologian translates: "In the beginning was the *Word*" [John 1:1] and by that understands the *Eternal Word*, the second Person of the Triune Divinity.

But we do no violence to the words of St. John if we, in connection with the reflection which has led us here, attempt to say with Faust, "In the beginning was *meaning*."[3] One is indeed accustomed to comparing the Eternal Word to the "inner word" of human speech and only the incarnate Word to the "external," spoken word.[4] We will add to that what Eternal Wisdom says through the mouth of the Apostle Paul: "*autos estin pro pantōn kai ta panta en autō synestēken*"— "He is before all things and in him all things have their firm existence and coherence" (Col 1:17).

Evidently, both of these Scripture verses carry us far beyond what our searching mind has deduced. But perhaps the philosophical meaning of the Logos to which we have advanced can help us to understand the theological meaning of the Logos and, on the other hand, revealed truth can further help with the philosophical difficulties.[5]

We will first try to make clear the meaning of both Scripture passages. By *meaning*, the Gospel of John refers to a *Divine Person*, therefore, not something *un*real but, on the contrary, to what is *most real*. He also immediately adds, "*panta di' autou egeneto*—through him all things came into being"[6] [John 1:3]. And the verse cited from Paul which ascribes "existence and coherence"[7] to the things "in the Logos" follows this analogously. Thus, by divine *Logos* we have to understand a real essence; according to the doctrine of the Trinity, the *divine* essence. That the divine essence is called *meaning* is to be understood by the fact that it is the divine essence as something *understood*, i.e., as *content of the divine knowledge*, as its "intellectual meaning."

The divine essence can also be called *word* because it is the content of that which God speaks, the content of revelation, thus *linguistic meaning*; yet more fundamentally, because the Father expresses himself therein and brings it forth through his speaking. But this meaning is real and it is not possible to separate its essential being from its real being because the eternal being is essentially real and as the *first* being, author of all being.

That the first being's essential being cannot have had a beginning already lies in the essential being and in the meaning as such. But it can also be understood from the perspective of the divine *intellect*. The real (= current) being of the intellect is *life* and *living understanding*. God as "pure act" is changeless aliveness. But intellectual life—understanding—is not possible without content, without "intellectual" meaning. And this meaning must be as eternal and changeless as the divine intellect itself.

Is it possible at all, even only *intellectually*, to separate the essential being of the Logos from its real being, as it is possible in the case of a finite essence? The Trinity itself seems to imply a separation of this kind. The Son is designated as *co-eternal* with the Father,[8] but as "*generated* by the Father." And that means he *receives* his eternal being from the Father. Now the *divine essence* is *one* and therefore cannot be designated as generated. What is *generated* is the *Second Person*, and the being which the Second Person receives cannot be the essential being of the divine essence, but only its real being in a Second Person. Because the person of the Son and its real being is something "new" with respect to the person of the Father, for that reason one can also say that the person of the Son receives the essence. But the essence does not receive its essential being. Even the *En archē ēn ho logos* allows such an interpretation if we think about the meaning which *archē* has in Greek philosophy. It is indeed not "beginning" as in "the beginning of time," but rather the "first being," the primordial being. Thus, the mysterious phrase acquires the meaning: in the first being was the Logos (the "meaning" or "the divine essence")—the Son in the Father—the meaning encompassed by the primordial reality.[9] The "generating" means the positing of the essence in the new person-reality of the Son, which, nevertheless, is not any positing outside of the primordial reality of the Father.[10]

...These figures of speech now also lead us to the relationship of the divine Logos to the *meaning* of finite essences. We found that the name "Logos" for the Second Divine Person is substantiated by the fact that this name expresses the divine essence as known, as that encompassed by the divine intellect. These are figures of speech which are derived from human knowledge and the naming of finite things. We attribute to the Logos the place in the divinity which corresponds to the "meaning," as to the objective content of things, and at the same time, as to the content of our knowledge and speech in the realm of the comprehensible. This is the *analogia* [analogy], i.e., the similitude-dissimilitude between *Logos* and *logos*, between the eternal Word and the human word.

However, not only is a relationship of similitude maintained in the Scripture passages which we have drawn upon which makes it possible for us "to behold with understanding the invisible nature of God...through what is created" (Rom 1:20), but rather, it is expressed that the creatures are created *by the Logos* and *in him* have *coherence* and *existence*. What is meant is explained as well by a version of John 1:3–4 which was customary in the Middle Ages. Today we read "without him (the Logos) nothing was made that was made." At that time, one added, "what was made was life in him." That seems to express that created things have their being in the divine Logos—and indeed, their real being. In the passage thus interpreted is evidently found the "Augustinian" understanding of the ideas as "creative essentialities in the divine intellect."

How we are *not* to understand the being of things in the Logos is expressed in a doctrinal decision of the church:[11] created things are not in God as the parts are in the whole, and the real being of things is not the divine being, but rather their own being distinct from the divine being. Then what can their "existence and coherence" in the Logos mean?

Let's first try to understand the *con*-stare, the [standing] "together" of things in the Logos. It evidently means the unity of all being. Our experience shows us things as unities that are self-contained and separated from each other, but nevertheless, in reciprocal relations of dependence which leads us to the idea of a universal causal coherence of all real things. But the causal coherence appears as something external. If we try to investigate the structure of the material world, we indeed come upon the fact that the causal coherence in which they can occur is established in the essence of things. On the other hand, it is the causal coherences which disclose to us something of the essence.[12] But both show that the essence is something lying deeper than the causal coherences. Therefore, the universal *causal coherence* does not yet mean *any* universal coherence of meaning of all things. Moreover, the totality of all real things still does not altogether encompass all finite being. Many "unreal" things also belong to the totality of all being: numbers, geometric figures, concepts, and more. They are all encompassed by the unity of the Logos. The coherence in which "everything" exists in the Logos is to be thought of as the unity of a *meaning-totality* [totality of meaning].

The coherence of our own life is perhaps best suited to illustrate what is meant. In the ordinary manner of speaking, one distinguishes between "that which is planned" (and at the same time is considered as "meaningful" and "intelligible") and "that which is accidental," which in itself appears meaningless and unintelligible. I plan on certain studies and for that reason, choose a university which promises me special support in my field. That is a meaningful and intelligible coherence. That I meet a person in that city who "accidentally" also studies there and one day I "accidentally" get talking about questions of worldview with him—that initially does not at all appear to me as an intelligible coherence. But when I reflect on my life years later, then it becomes clear to me that that conversation had a decisive influence upon me, perhaps "more essential" than all my studies, and the thought comes to me that perhaps I "had to go" to that city "specifically for that reason." What did not lie in *my* plan lay in God's plan. And the more often I come across that sort of thing, the more lively becomes the faith conviction in me that—as seen by God— there is no "accident," that my entire life in all its details is sketched out in the plan of divine providence and before God's all-seeing eyes is a perfect coherence of meaning. Then I begin to look forward to the light of glory in which this coherence of meaning shall be unveiled even to me.

However, this applies not only to the individual human life, but also to the life of the entire humanity and beyond that to the entirety of all being. Their "coherence" in the Logos is the one meaning-totality [totality of meaning], a perfect work of art in which every single feature fits in *its* place in the harmony of the entire structure in accordance with the purest and strictest lawfulness. What we grasp of the "meaning of things," what "enters into our understanding," that relates to that meaning-totality [totality of meaning] like single, forlorn tones which the wind carries to me from a symphony sounding in the far distance.

In the language of theologians, the coherence of meaning of all being in the Logos is called the "divine plan of creation" (*ars divina*).[13] Its realization is the process of the world from the very beginning. But behind this "plan," behind the "artistic sketch" of creation stands (without being separated from it ontologically) the eternal plenitude of divine being and life.

Chapter IV. §4.7. Pure Form and Essential Form of Material Structures. Their Symbolic Character. Essence as "Mystery"[14]

...We said earlier that everything created has its archetype in the divine Logos.[15] We have to look at all finite being as an image of the divine essence which is meant to reflect a ray of the divine splendor. Originating in God and placed in itself, it is gifted with its own essence and independent existence (*ousia = substance*). Its essence is definitely determined by the divine essence, but must lag behind the divine essence in multiple ways. In its finitude, it cannot encompass the infinite plenitude of the divine essence and it cannot attain the divine perfection either in scope or degree. Its share of being (essence and existence) is allotted to it, while there is no measure for the divine being (not even by qualifying divine being as the archetype of a finite being). Moreover, real things lag behind the highest measure attainable to them. And *this* lagging behind is only understandable by the "*status naturae lapsae*" [state of fallen nature], by the degeneration of all things in the condition of fallen nature. Thus, even the luster of "gold" has been "dimmed" (Lam 4:1). In this way, a rupture has come into the determination of the essence of things. They are still a mirror of divine perfection, but a broken mirror. A conflict exists in them between what they actually ought to be and what they actually are; and likewise, a conflict between what they in themselves could become and what actually becomes of them. The latter no longer concerns merely individual matter in its determination of kind, but the context of natural occurrences and matter in its capacity as "material" for human achievements. We have indeed seen that they carry potentialities within them which can only be realized by external influences—their external condition is determined by what happens to them. We may assume that in the original order, all natural occurrences were to have helped things toward a full unfolding of their essence and thereby to a pure rendering of their divine archetype; that the powers placed in them were proportionate and subservient to the perfect formation of each individual and the entire "cosmos," and could not work meaninglessly or destructively as "raw powers." And thus the "creative work" of the human being was also to serve the purpose of carving out more and more the God-likeness of nature. Every "work" should not only be "useful" (i.e., subject to the goals of the human being), but also "beautiful" (i.e., a mirror of the eternal). Through the curse on creation, the elements are now not merely "degenerated," but also in rebellion against each other so that the natural occurrences can lead to a reciprocal hindrance of the unfolding of their essence and act destructively. And if the human being must "eat his bread by the sweat of his brow," then that is not only due to the earth which bears thistles and thorns for him and brings forth good fruit only after hard toil, but also due to the resistance of all matter to which he puts his laboring hand.

4

THE SOUL

INTRODUCTION

In her dissertation *On the Problem of Empathy*, which treats the phenomenological question of how one person experiences the experience of another, Edith includes a discussion about the constitution of the human person. She tells us that this topic of the constitutive makeup or structure of the human person was close to her heart and continually occupied her in her later works.[1] Likewise, in her preface to *The Science of the Cross*, she writes that she has made "a lifelong effort to grasp the laws of spiritual being and life."[2] She explains that her attempt to interpret the writings from John of the Cross and other secondary sources that she includes in that text are based on this lifelong effort. This is especially true regarding her explanations about spirit, faith, and contemplation found throughout the book and particularly in the selection from *The Science of the Cross* provided below. Edith specifically notes that what she writes about the "I," freedom, and person derives from her, not from John; while some points of departure for these topics are found in his texts, constructing a philosophy of the person was not his goal.

The "I" is the subject of conscious experience or current being that is alive in every "now." Its life comprises the sum of all past experiences in which it was alive and all of its future experiences in which it will be alive. It is neither the soul nor the body, but "dwells" in both and so applies to the whole human being. In the human being, the awake, conscious life of the "I" is the entryway to the soul just as the life of the senses is the entryway to the body. As noted in chapter 1, Edith designates the conscious, free, self-determining "I" as the "person."[3]

Edith maintains a holistic view of the tripartite constitution of the human being as body-soul-spirit. Today, the terms *mind*, *soul*, and *spirit* are often used interchangeably with little or no effort to make any distinctions. In contrast, Edith is typically very precise in her use of language. As *Finite and Eternal Being* and *The Structure of the Human Person* show, however, this does not at all imply simple definitions. Rather, she incorporates the phenomenological method of descriptive analysis in her search for fundamental principles, taking into consideration various perspectives of the soul.[4]

As sentient soul, the soul abides in all parts of the body, receiving impulses and influences from it and working upon it formatively. As spiritual soul, the soul rises above itself and gains insight into, communicates with, and is influenced by the world of things, persons, and events that lie beyond its own self. As soul in the strictest sense, the soul abides in its own self and constitutes the home of the personal "I." It is within this interior that everything which enters the soul is weighed and judged. Here, too, occurs the appropriation of all that becomes a constituent part of the self. Edith considers the innermost being of the soul to be its most spiritual part, and when the "I" lives out of this interiority, it lives fully and attains the fullness of its being. She also recognizes the innermost being of the soul as the "abode of God," whereby the soul is capable of opening itself and surrendering itself freely to God to bring about a union of love that is only possible between spiritual persons.[5]

Indeed, some scholars today purposely avoid the term *soul* because they automatically equate it with dualism. Edith was dismayed that in the modern era, research concerning the human being's inner world had abandoned all theological considerations of the soul, resulting in a nineteenth-century "psychology without a soul." She writes,

Both the nature and faculties of the soul were designated as mythological concepts and therefore eliminated until, in the end, the impulses and activities of the soul were explained as composites of simple sensations. Even all the powers of the intellect, of sentiment, and of life itself were drained out of the soul.[6]

Edith thought that the tide was turning with the research being done in her time, especially in the humanities and social sciences, but did not anticipate the strong influence of reductive materialism or the situation in which the mention of the soul is often immediately dismissed because of an assumed identification with dualism.

The tripartite makeup of the human being does not mean that the spirit is somehow juxtaposed alongside the soul. The "soul is 'spirit' (*spiritus*) in its innermost essence" and the "one spiritual soul unfolds its being in several ways."[7] Edith's perception of the human being needs to be understood as a unified whole: a body-soul holism. As she states in the selection below and elsewhere, the soul is one with the body "in the unity of one being." Also, although spatial images of height and depth or interior and exterior are used, there is nothing "spatial" about the soul. For example, saying that the soul is drawn to the "outside" simply indicates that the soul is farther from its inmost region and is occupied with the outer world.

It is also important to understand that for Edith, the term *spiritual* does not carry a solely religious connotation. Spirit refers to nonmaterial reality. She regards "'matter' and 'spirit' as different genera of reality which do not trace back to each other."[8] That which is spiritual is "non-spatial, invisible, and intangible."[9] The kinds of being that belong to the realm of the spirit include God, who is pure spirit; angels; human souls; and "meaning." For personal being, the essence of spirit includes freedom and a going-out-of-oneself.[10] In another excerpt from *The Science of the Cross* included in chapter 8, Edith explains that "the spirit may be spoken of in different ways, in different instances.... For insofar as spiritual being is life and change, it cannot be captured in static definitions, but must rather be a continual movement seeking fluid expression."[11]

For the human being, spiritual life concerns the intellect and will. In the aforementioned excerpt in chapter 8, she notes that Augustine and John of the Cross also include the memory.[12] However, from Edith's perspective, nonpersonal objects also carry a certain type of spiritual life in the sense of "meaning" that they convey to the observer. She refers to this as "objective spirit." All of nature, from the simple elements of colors, sounds, and shapes to an entire landscape, possesses a meaning—"something spiritual also speaks out of them." "Their spiritual meaning is that which is of value in them; that which can enter into us, which can delight us, lift us up, inspire us."[13] Edith writes,

> Spiritual life is kindled not only in living with spiritual persons, but also in the encounter with non-personal objects in which a peculiar spiritual life hides. We call them "objective spirit" and, as far as they are creations of the human spirit, we call them "culture." The human spirit is aimed at creating, understanding, and enjoying culture. It cannot fully unfold if it does not come into contact with the variety of cultural fields, and the individual human being cannot attain to that for which he is called if he does not learn to know the field to which his natural aptitude points him.[14]

From Edith's perspective, "the realm of the spirit embraces the entire created world."[15]

One of the most interesting sections of the selection below is Edith's discussion of the "thoughts of the heart," where "heart" indicates the innermost region of the soul and "thoughts" refer to first movements rising from the depth of the soul. The innermost region of the soul is where the soul is really at home, but paradoxically, the soul is typically "not at home." Edith states that there are very few souls who live in and from their deepest interior, and even fewer who constantly do so. Drawing on Teresa of Avila's image of the soul as the interior castle, she explains that most people, due to fallen nature, remain in the outer rooms of the castle where things from the outside draw them outside. God's insistent call is needed to move them to enter into themselves. The goal is for human beings to live in and from their inmost region. They are free to use this inmost region in complete freedom, but have the duty to guard it as a precious gift, for

God has chosen it as his dwelling. Also, God so respects human freedom that God does not take possession of a soul by means of mystical union without the soul wanting it herself. God does everything at the stage of mystical union because the soul has totally surrendered herself to God. This total surrender of the soul to God is the highest act of her freedom.

In the last part of the selection, Edith considers whether the majority of humans who do not arrive at mystical union can enter their inmost region and make decisions from there. To do so, she uses the practical example of a person desirous of sensory delights who is faced with the decision to help someone. This section demonstrates her style of occasionally inserting an example from daily life when considering the many facets of a question.

THE TEXTS

The Science of the Cross

13. CREATED SPIRITS[16]

2) The Soul in the Realm of the Spirit and of Created Spirits

a. Construction of the Soul; God's Spirit and Created Spirits

The soul as a spirit is positioned in a realm of the spirit and of spirits. She, however, possesses her own structure. She is more than a simple form that animates the body, more than the *interior* of an *exterior*. Rather, within her there lies an opposition between internal and external.[17] The soul can be said to be at home at her most interior point, at her essence or the deepest ground of the soul. She goes out through the activity of her senses to a domain inferior to her realm. It influences the soul in what she does and does not do and limits her freedom in a certain sense. It is unable to penetrate to the soul's innermost center, but it can distance the soul from that center within.

In her ascent to God, the soul raises herself above herself or is raised above herself. But at the same time, by this more than by anything else she actually attains her innermost center. That sounds contradictory, but corresponds with the facts and is grounded in the realm of the spirit's relationship to God.

God is pure spirit and the archetype of all spiritual being.[18] So, really, it is only by beginning with God that it is possible to understand what spirit is; however, that means it is a mystery that constantly attracts us because it is the mystery of our own being. We can approach it, in a certain way, since our own being is spiritual. We can also approach it by way of all being to the extent that all being, which has meaning and which can be comprehended intellectually, has something of spiritual being about it. But it reveals itself to a greater depth in proportion to our knowledge of God, though it is never totally unveiled, that is, it never ceases to be a mystery.

God's spirit is totally transparent to himself; is totally free to dispose of itself (in that unrestrictedness that is intrinsic to being-through-itself). It freely goes out of itself, yet always remains within itself. The Spirit sets up all other being out of itself, envelops it, penetrates, and rules it. Created spirit is a limited image of God (in all the forenamed features): as an image [*Abbild*] it is similar to God; as *limited* it is God's opposite. It is more or less extensively capable of receiving God, in the highest degree; it has the possibility of being united to God in mutual, free, personal surrender.

We speak of a *realm* of the spirit and of spirits, inasmuch as all spiritual beings have at least a possible connection among themselves and form part of a whole. We call it the realm *of the spirit* because *spirit* includes more than all spirits, namely all that is spiritual and that, in a certain sense, is everything that has being. But we say further: realm *of the spirits* because in this realm *spirits*, that is personal-spiritual beings, play a prominent role.

God is at the peak of this realm, infinitely surpassing all that is spiritual and all spirits. A created spirit can only ascend to him by transcending itself. However, since he bestows being on all that has being, and preserves it in being, God is the sustaining ground of everything. Whatever ascends to him descends at the same time, by that very act, into its own center or resting place.

b. The Soul's Dealings with God and with Created Spirits

Using a spatial image borrowed from the natural science of his time, the saint calls God the soul's *resting point* her *deepest center*.[19] According to that scientific view, bodies are pulled most forcefully toward the center of the earth since that is the point with the strongest power of attraction. A stone within the earth would already be at a certain point of rest, but not yet at the deepest center because it would have the capability, power, and inclination to fall farther, as long as it is not at the center point. Thus the soul has found its final and deepest resting point in God, "when, with all her might, she knows, loves, and enjoys God." That is never completely the case in this life. When, therefore, through the grace of God she is at her resting place, it is not yet the deepest center because she can always penetrate more deeply into God. For the power that draws her to God is love, and here love can always reach a higher degree. The higher the degree, the deeper love's anchor plumbs the soul, the more profoundly is she seized by God. On the rungs of the ladder the soul rises to God, i.e., to union with him. The higher she ascends to God, the deeper she descends within herself: the union is consummated in the innermost soul, in the deepest ground of the soul. If all of this seems contradictory, it is to be remembered that these are only different spatial images that—by reciprocally complementing themselves—wish to indicate something that is totally alien to space and for which natural experience cannot supply any adequate delineation.

God is in the inmost depth of the soul and nothing that is in her is hidden from him. But no created spirit is capable by itself of entering this enclosed garden or of getting even a glimpse of it. The created spirits comprise both good and bad spirits (which are also called *pure spirits* because they have no body) and human souls. Little is to be found in John about the mutual interaction of human souls. Actually, there is only *one* human relationship that he frequently refers to: that of the spiritual soul to her director. But he is not interested in the manner in which they come to understand one another. He remarks a single time that persons to whom the grace of discernment of spirits is given can recognize the inner state of another by slight external signs.[20] This points out the normal way of acquiring knowledge about the life of a stranger's soul: it is by way of sensory expressions of the spiritual life and leads as far within as that interior reveals itself.

For all external going-out-of-oneself perceptible in physical expressions, in sentient utterances, and words, in deeds and works, has, as a prerequisite, an internal going-out-of-oneself—whether this be voluntary or involuntary, conscious or unconscious. If it comes from the interior, then something of the interior will illumine it. But this will not have sharp outlines; not be something securely and distinctly grasped, as long as one is dependent on a purely natural way and is not led through extraordinary divine illumination. Rather, it will remain something mysterious. And when the interior is closed, no human glance, by its own power, will penetrate it.

The soul has connections not only to others of her own kind, but also to created *pure spirits*, good and evil. Along with the *Areopagite* [Pseudo-Dionysius], John assumes that human beings receive divine illumination through the mediation of angels; to be sure, he does not hold that grace's being handed down along the descending steps of the *heavenly hierarchy* is the only possible way for it to be received. He knows about a direct union of God with the soul and this is what actually matters to him. He considers the snares of the devil to be more powerful than the influence of the good angel. He sees the devil continually sneaking around souls in order to divert them on their way to God.

What possible connections exist between human souls and pure—that is, incorporeal—spirits? One feasible way of knowing leads here also via bodily expression and other sensory manifestations. This is possible for human beings since, in order to make themselves understood, pure spirits have the power to appear in visible form or to be heard through audible words. But this is a highly dangerous way, for one is exposed on it to manifold deceptions and errors: one can regard as spiritual visions what are only sensory deceptions or illusions of the imagination. The devil can appear in the luminous guise of a good angel in order to lead souls astray more easily. The soul can, for fear of such deceptions, reject genuine heavenly apparitions as deceit of the senses or of the devil.

On the other hand, can one take into consideration that the pure spirits find access to the soul's interior via the sense-oriented exterior? One can hardly interpret the stories in the Books of *Job* and *Tobit* in any way other than that the devil and angels keenly observe and supervise the external behavior of human beings. That the angels have knowledge of the world as it is accessible to the senses, and so also of the human exterior, is a concept consonant with the doctrines of faith, since it is a requisite for the service angels give to human beings.[21] If this can be done without requiring bodily senses, it indicates that there are still other possibilities of perceiving corporeal nature: "a knowledge of the sensory, without senses."[22]

It is not our task to examine these possibilities now. In any case, for pure spirits what is external is not the only entrance into the interior life; they can also perceive the interior, spiritual words and expressions. The guardian angel "hears" the prayer that, without sound, rises to him from the heart. The evil enemy observes certain of the soul's movements, which can give him a handhold for his whispered suggestions.

And the spirits, for their part, have the possibility of making themselves heard in spiritual ways: through soundless words that, without any mediation of the external senses, are spoken in the interior and perceived there interiorly; or through effects that one feels in oneself, but which are occasioned from outside, for example, mood changes or impulses of the will that are incomprehensible in connection with one's own experience. What has not entered the outer senses is not, on that account alone, generally free from all sensuality and therefore is not *purely* spiritual in the sense in which John of the Cross speaks of pure spirituality. True, he does call memory, intellect, and will spiritual faculties, but their natural activity is still conditioned by the senses and shares therefore in *sensory life*. Only that is purely spiritual that takes place in the inmost heart, the life of the soul from and in God.[23] Here, created spirits have no entry. The *thoughts of the heart* are concealed from them in natural ways—we say in natural ways because God can reveal these thoughts to them.

c. The Interior of the Soul and the Thoughts of the Heart

The thoughts of the heart are the original life of the soul at the ground of her being, at a depth that precedes all splitting into different faculties and their activity. There the soul lives precisely as she is in herself, beyond all that will be called forth in her through created beings. Although this most interior region is the dwelling of God and the place where the soul is united to God, her own life flows out of here before the life of union begins; and this is so, even in cases where such a union never occurs. For every soul has an inmost region and its being is life.

But this primary life is not only hidden from other spirits but from the soul herself. This is so for various reasons. Primary life is formless. The *thoughts of the heart* are absolutely not *thoughts* in the usual sense of the word; they are not clearly outlined, arranged, and comprehensible constructions of the thinking intellect. They must pass through various formulations before they become such constructions. First, they must rise out of the ground of the heart. Then they arrive at a first threshold, where they become noticeable. This *noticing* is a far more original manner of being conscious than is perception by the intellect. It too lies before the splitting into faculties and activities. It lacks the clarity of purely sensible perception; on the other hand, it is richer than a bare grasping by the intellect. That which arises is perceived as bearing a stamp of value on the basis of which a decision is made: whether to allow what is rising to come up or not. It must be mentioned here that, already, what rises in purely natural ways and becomes noticed is no longer the purely interior life of the soul, but is rather already an answer to something that she has brought into motion. But this leads in a direction in which we cannot follow further here.

At the threshold where the rising movements are perceived, types of recognizable spiritual faculties begin to split off and conceivable structures are formed: to these belong thoughts elaborated by the intellect with their reasonable arrangement (these are *interior words* for which, then, *exterior words* can be found), movements of the mind and impulses of the will that, as active energies, enter all that is connected with the spiritual life.

Spiritual life is now no longer the primal life in the depth, rather it is something that can be grasped by *interior perception*. And interior perception is a totally different art of comprehending than is that first noticing of what arises out of the depth. So, too, this emergence out of the depth is different from the surfacing of an already formed image that was stored in the memory and now has become alive again.

By no means is all that rises and becomes perceptible actually perceived. Much rises up, becomes interior and exterior word, turns into wish and will and deed "before one is aware of it." Only those who live completely recollected in their inmost region keep faithful watch over these *first movements*.

With this we arrive at the second reason why people keep their inmost region hidden. It has been said that the soul is really at home here. But—as odd as this may sound—she is as a rule *not* at home. There are very few souls who live *in* their inmost self and *out of* their inmost region; and still fewer who constantly live *from* and *out of* their deepest interior. According to their nature—that is, their *fallen* nature—persons keep themselves in the *outer rooms* of the *castle* which is their soul. What approaches them from outside draws them to the outside. It is necessary that God call and draw them insistently so as to move them to "enter into themselves."[24]

d. The Soul, the "I," and Freedom

It is important to clarify as much as possible, spiritually and without imagery, what these spatial images express. These images are indispensable. But they are ambiguous and easily misunderstood. What approaches the soul from without belongs to the *outer world* and by this is meant whatever does not belong to the soul herself; as a rule, it also includes whatever does not belong to her body. For even though the body is called her exterior, it is *her* exterior, at one with her in the unity of one being and not as external as that which confronts her as totally strange and separate.[25] Among these strange and separate ones, there is the difference between things which have a clearly *exterior* being, i.e., are spatially extended, and such as have an *interior* like the soul herself.

On the other hand we had to speak, in the soul herself, of an exterior and an interior. For when she is drawn outside, she does not leave herself, she is only farther away from her inmost region and with that, at the same time, devotes herself to the outer world. What approaches from outside has a certain right to claim her attention, and, depending on its *weight*, the value, and meaning it has in itself and for the soul, it deserves to be admitted to an appropriate depth of the soul. So it is objectively reasonable that she accepts it from there. But to do so, she is not required to sacrifice her position at a deeper level; because she is a spirit and her *castle* is a spiritual realm, there are totally different rules valid here than in the external sphere.

When she is in the deepest and inmost region of this, her inner realm, then she rules over it completely and has the freedom to go to whatever *place* in it she pleases, without having to leave *her place*, the place of her rest. The possibility to move within oneself is based on the soul's being formed as an "I." The "I" is that in the soul by which she possesses herself and that which moves within her as in its own *space*. The deepest point is at the same time the place of her freedom: the place at which she can collect her entire being and make decisions about it. Free decisions of lesser importance can, in a certain sense, also be made at a point located farther toward the outside. However, these are superficial decisions: it is a *coincidence* when such a decision proves to be appropriate, for only at the deepest point can one possibly measure everything against one's ultimate standards. Nor is it an *irrefutably* free decision, for anyone who does not have herself completely in hand cannot decide in true freedom but rather, allows herself to be determined by outside factors.

Human beings are called upon to live in their inmost region and to have themselves as much in hand as is possible only from that center point; only from there can they rightly come to terms with the world. Only from there can they find the place in the world that has been intended for them. In all of this, they can never *see through* this inmost region completely. It is God's mystery, which God alone can reveal to the degree that pleases him. This inmost region, however, has been laid in the hand of human beings; they can make use of it in complete freedom but they also have the duty to guard it as a precious good entrusted to them. In the realm of spirits, it must be given great value. The angels have the task of protecting it. Evil spirits seek to gain control of it. God himself has chosen it as his dwelling. The good and evil spirits do not have free entrance into the inmost region. The good spirits are no more able, in natural ways, to read the "thoughts of the heart" than are the evil spirits, but they receive illumination from God about all they must know of the heart's secrets.

Furthermore, there are spiritual ways in which the soul can make contact with the other created spirits. She can address herself to another spirit with whatever has become an *interior word* in her. This is how St. Thomas imagines the *language* of the angels with which they mutually communicate: as a purely spiritual self-offering with the intention of sharing with another what one has in oneself.[26] In this [way], also, is the soundless cry to the guardian angel to be imagined, or an interior summoning of evil spirits.

But even without our intention to share, the created spirits have a certain access to what occurs within us: not to that which is concealed in our inmost region, but probably about whatever has entered the interior regions of the soul in a perceptible form. From that point, they are also able to draw conclusions about that which may be concealed from their sight. We must assume that the angels protect the locked sanctuary with reverent awe. They desire only to bring the soul there in order for her to surrender it to God. But Satan strives to wrest into his possession that which is God's kingdom. He cannot do this by his own power, but the soul can surrender herself to him. She will not do this if she herself has entered her inmost region and come to know it as happens in divine union. For then she is so immersed in God and so secure that no temptation can approach her anymore. But how is it possible that she can hand herself over to the devil when she has not yet fully taken herself into possession as can happen only upon entrance to the inmost region? One can only think she does it by blindly grabbing hold, as it were, while she is still outside. She gives herself away without knowing what she surrenders by that. And neither can the devil break the seal on that which, still closed, has been handed to him. He can only destroy what remains forever hidden from him.

The soul has the right to make decisions that concern herself. It is the great mystery of personal freedom, before which God himself comes to a halt. He wants his sovereign authority over created spirits only as a free gift of their love. He knows the thoughts of the heart. He sees through the deepest foundations and abysses of the soul, where her own glance cannot penetrate unless God specifically grants her light to do so. But he does not want to take possession of her without her wanting it herself. Yet he does everything to achieve the free surrender of her will to his as a gift of her love in order, then, to be able to lead her to the bliss of union. That is the gospel John of the Cross has to announce and for which all his writings serve. What was said last about the structure of the soul's being, especially about the relation of freedom to her inmost region, does not come from the expositions of our holy Father St. John. It is therefore necessary to prove whether it is in harmony with his teaching, and may, in fact, even serve to clarify his doctrine. (Only if this proves to be the case can this interjection be justified in this context.) At first glance, some of what has been said may well appear incompatible with certain of the saint's expositions.

Every human being is free and is confronted with decisions on a daily and hourly basis. But the inmost region of the soul is the place where God lives "all alone" as long as the soul has not reached the perfect union of love.[27] Holy Mother Teresa calls it the seventh dwelling place that opens for the soul only when the mystical marriage takes place.[28] So then, is it only the soul that has arrived at the highest degree of perfection that decides in perfect freedom? Here it must be considered that the autonomous action of the soul apparently diminishes the more she nears her inmost self. And when she arrives there, God does everything in her, she no longer has anything more to do than to receive.[29] However, it is precisely this act of receiving that expresses her free participation. But beyond that, freedom comes into play at a far more decisive moment. God does everything here only because the soul has totally surrendered herself to him. And this surrender is the highest act of her freedom. John himself depicts the mystical marriage as voluntary surrender of God and the soul to each other and ascribes so great a power to the soul that has arrived at this step of perfection that she has not only herself but even God at her service.[30] For this highest stage of the personal life there is perfect agreement between the mystical doctrine of our holy parents and the view that the inmost region of the soul is the place of the most perfect freedom.

But how do matters stand with the large mass of humans who do not arrive at mystical marriage? Can they enter the inmost region and make decisions from there, or are they only capable of more or less superficial decisions? The answer is not a simple yes or no.

The structure of the soul's being—her greater and lesser depths as well as the inmost region—are hers by nature. The movement of the "I" within this space similarly exists as a possibility resulting from the soul's essence. This "I" sets itself up now here, now there, according to the *motivations* that appeal to it. But it undertakes its movements from a position it prefers to occupy. This position, now, is not the same in everyone; rather, it is distinguished according to the various types of persons. The one who desires sensory delights is mostly engrossed in a sensual satisfaction or preoccupied about gaining such satisfaction; his position is located very far from his inmost region. One who seeks truth lives principally at the heart of an actively searching intellect. If he is really concerned about *the* truth (not merely collecting single bits of knowledge), then he is perhaps nearer to the God who is Truth, and therefore to his own inmost region than he himself knows.

To these two examples we wish to add only a third which seems to have particular meaning: the "I–human being," that is, the one for whom his own "I" stands as the central point. Considered superficially, one might think such a human being to be particularly close to his inmost region. Yet, perhaps for no other type is the way there as obstructed as for this one. (Every human being has something of this in himself as long as he has not suffered through to the end of the *Dark Night*.) We must examine for all these types the possibilities for the mobility of the "I," the possibilities of free decision making, and the possibility of reaching the inmost region.

When the sensual human being, who is engrossed in some satisfaction, is presented with the possibility of procuring something even more satisfying, he will perhaps, without further consideration or choice, move from satisfaction into action. When the *drives* lie on the same level, a movement takes place but not an actually free decision; nor a breakthrough to a greater depth. But it is possible for the sensual human being to be approached by something that belongs to a completely different area of values. No type is exclusively restricted to one area. At a given time one area simply has the ascendancy over the others. He may, for example, be asked to deny himself some pleasure in order to help another human being. Here, the solution will hardly be reached without a free decision. At all events, the sensual person will not make a sacrifice as a matter of course; rather he will have to pull himself together to do so. If he declines—whether after some evaluation or with an immediate "that's out of the question"— that, too, is a decision of the will. In an extreme case one can even think of him continuing in his enjoyment without dismissing the perspective of sacrifice. In this case, the spirit is so suffocated in sensuality that the challenge cannot even reach him. The words are heard, and perhaps their immediate meaning may be understood, but the area where the real sense of the call would be received is buried in rubble. In this extreme, not only does a single free decision fail to materialize but freedom itself was already abandoned previously. Where one declines, the meaning is probably grasped, even though, apparently, it is not evaluated at full range.

In such a refusal to take the full range into consideration lies both the superficiality of the decision and a bridled freedom. One does not allow certain motives to appeal with their full import and takes good care not to return to that depth where these motives could instigate involvement. In this case, one surrenders oneself to a single area of decision making. One never takes oneself, that is, all the deeper levels of one's own being, into one's hands and so deprives oneself of the possibility of taking a stand after evaluating the true circumstances, that is, what is truly reasonable and truly free. Besides this superficial rejection, one can think of course of something that would be more appropriate: having allowed the call for help to be weighed fully by the soul, with full consideration of all the aspects, one could feel obliged to refuse when evaluation of all the pros and cons establishes it as unjustified. Such a refusal is on the same level as compliance after objectively weighing the pros and cons. Both are possible only when the sensual human being has abandoned his attitude *as* a sensual person and has gone over to an *ethical* attitude, that is, the attitude of one who wants to recognize and do what is morally right. To do this he must take up a position deep within himself: so deep that the crossover resembles a formal transformation of the human being. And this may not even be possible in a natural way, but only on the basis of an extraordinary *awakening*. Yes, we may well say: an *ultimately* appropriate decision can be made only at the extreme depth of the soul. For no human being is by nature in a position to scan *all* the pros and cons that have a say about a decision. The decision can only be made according to one's own best knowledge and conscience, within the circumference of one's own vision. However, a person with faith knows that there is one whose view is not circumscribed but truly comprises and perceives everything. The conscience of the one who lives in this certainty of faith can no longer quiet itself by following its own best knowledge. It must strive to recognize what is right in God's eyes. (For this reason only a religious position is the truly ethical one. There is in all likelihood a natural seeking and longing for the right and good, as well as finding this in some cases, but only in seeking for the divine will can human beings truly reach their goal.)

The question is answered once and for all by the one who is drawn by God himself into the soul's own inmost region and has surrendered there in the union of love. Nothing further is necessary than to allow God's Spirit to direct and lead, for the Spirit will distinctly urge him on, and he will always and everywhere be certain he is doing the right thing. In that one great decision made with the utmost freedom, all future ones are included and can then, almost as a matter of course, be made accordingly. But, instead of simply searching for the right decision in a particular case, to arrive at this height there is a long way to go—if indeed there is a way to it. A person who, only here and now, seeks what is right and accordingly decides by what he believes he knows is on the way to God and on the way to himself even when he does not know this. But he does not yet have such a hold on himself as that which is given in the ultimate depth; therefore he cannot fully make disposition of himself nor can he make perfectly free decisions about *things*.

Whoever *fundamentally* seeks to do what is right, that is, whoever is determined to do it always and everywhere, has made a decision about himself and has set his will within the divine will, even when it is not yet clear to him that the good action corresponds to what God wills. But if this is not clear to him, the sure way of discerning what is right is still wanting; and he has made disposition of himself as though he had himself completely in hand, although the ultimate depth of his inmost region has not yet opened to him. The final decision only becomes possible eye to eye with God. But when a person has arrived so far in the life of faith that he has committed himself to God completely and no longer wants anything but what God wills, has he not then arrived at his inmost region, and is his state still different from that of the highest union in love? It is very difficult to draw a boundary line here, and difficult, also, to know how our holy Father St. John draws it. Still I believe—objectively and as he teaches—it is necessary to acknowledge a boundary and to bring it into relief. Whoever truly wants, in blind faith, nothing more but what God wills, has, with God's grace, reached the highest state a human being can reach. His will is totally purified and free of all constraint through earthly desires; he is united to the divine will through free surrender. And still, for the highest union of love, the mystical marriage, something decisive is lacking.

5

LOVE

INTRODUCTION

The selections included in chapter 1 on the Triune God demonstrate that Edith understands the love shared among the Trinity to be the highest form of love. She elaborates on this theme in the first three selections below taken from *Finite and Eternal Being*. The first speaks of the command to love one's enemies. As the saints have shown, this is possible with God's grace, even if at first there is a reluctance to do so. In the second selection, Edith points out that the mutual eternal love of the Trinity cannot be attained by finite beings who, unlike God, cannot love from eternity or encompass God. She holds that the closest approximation to this trinitarian love is found in the surrender of a finite person to God. This surrender is simultaneously the surrender to oneself as loved by God as well as the surrender to all creation. In the third selection, we read that such a surrender to God is only possible when a person comes to know God as the Loving One, and only God can reveal Godself to us in this way.

The remaining selections taken from her correspondence capture more of Edith's thoughts pertaining to love, especially in relation to the Carmelite vocation. Her reply to a friend's viewpoint regarding the life of Thérèse of Lisieux provides a glimpse into Edith's own desires. Convinced that Thérèse's life was formed by the love of God, Edith adds that she would desire to have as much of that love as possible in her own life and in the lives of those dear to her.

During July–August 1933, prior to her formal entrance into Carmel, Edith spent a few weeks at the convent as a guest of the Carmelites. She was most impressed by the spirit of love that characterizes Carmel and that she witnessed to be very much alive. Even before her entrance, Edith was certain that, despite the enclosure of Carmel, she would be permitted to write letters to friends and others as a labor of love since love supersedes all other rules. Edith's focus on her own call to love is seen on a remembrance card from her final profession in 1938. A line from John of the Cross's poem *The Spiritual Canticle* is found at the top of the card: "From now on my only calling is to love more."[1]

In the last excerpt, Edith demonstrates her familiarity with the writings of John of the Cross and displays her strong conviction that we should certainly strive for perfect love since that is the purpose for which we were created. But her conviction and enthusiasm is grounded in the reality that God's grace provides what is most essential while we faithfully carry out our part. She likewise advises against judging one's own progress. Only God knows that, and only God knows and can purify the depth from which our faults arise.

THE TEXTS

Finite and Eternal Being

Chapter VII §9.5 Capability, Obligation, and the Inner Life[2]

...[God] *makes* possible what would be naturally impossible.[3] Saints who, trusting in God's power, resolved to practice heroic love of enemies experienced that they had the freedom to love. Perhaps a natural aversion will still assert itself for a time, but it is powerless and is not able to influence the behavior that is led by supernatural love. In most cases, it will soon yield to the superior strength of divine life which fills the soul more and more. After all, in its ultimate meaning, love is the surrender of one's own being and becoming one with the beloved. Whoever does God's will comes to know the divine Spirit, the divine life, and divine love—and all of that means nothing other than God himself. For by doing what God demands of him with the innermost surrender, the divine life becomes *his* life: he finds God in himself when he enters into himself.

CHAPTER VII. §9.7 THE IMAGE OF GOD IN THE NATURAL SPIRITUAL LIFE OF THE HUMAN BEING[4]

...In the realm of creatures, the closest approximation to this pure love which is God is the surrender of the finite person to God. Indeed, no finite spirit is capable of wholly encompassing the divine spirit. But God—and God alone—wholly encompasses every created spirit. Whoever surrenders himself to God attains to the highest perfection of being in loving union with God—attains to that love which is at the same time knowledge, surrender of the heart, and free act. The love is wholly turned toward God, but in union with divine love, the created spirit—recognizing, blessed, and freely assenting—also encompasses itself. The surrender to God is at the same time the surrender to one's own self that is beloved by God and to the entire creation, particularly to all spiritual beings united with God.

CHAPTER VII. §9.8. THE SUPERNATURAL IMAGE OF GOD THROUGH THE INDWELLING OF GOD IN THE SOUL[5]

However, of himself alone, the human being by his own nature is not capable of such a surrender of love. Already, if he can attain to the knowledge and really fulfilled love of other people only if they open themselves up lovingly to him—everything else which we call human knowledge and human love are only paths and preliminary steps to this—how then is he to attain to the love of God whom he doesn't see without first being loved by God? After all, all natural knowledge of God rising from creatures does not open up God's hidden essence. Despite all analogy which must unite the creature and Creator, natural knowledge can still always comprehend God only as the totally Other. In uncorrupted nature, this could already suffice to recognize that a greater love is due to the Creator than to any creature. But in order to lovingly surrender to God, we must come to know God as the Loving One. And so, only God can reveal himself to us. In a certain way, the word of revelation does this. And loving devotion already pertains analogously to the believing acceptance of divine revelation. However, loving devotion perfects itself only when

God imparts his divine life to the surrendered soul itself in the life of grace and glory and draws the soul into his divine life.

Letters

To Sr. Adelgundis Jaegerschmid, OSB, March 17, 1933[6]

Pax!
Dear Sr. Adelgundis,

...What you wrote about the little Thérèse [of Lisieux] amazed me. For the first time, I saw how one *can* look at it from that point of view. My impression was simply that there the life of a human being has been formed entirely, from first to last, only and exclusively, by the love of God. I know of nothing more sublime, and I would wish to have as much of that as possible in my own life and in the lives of all who are near to me.

Most cordially, your
Edith

To Mother Petra Brüning, OSU, July 26, 1933[7]

Pax!
Dear Reverend Mother,

...You see, I am already permitted participation in all of the spiritual exercises in the daily schedule, with my prie-dieu in the sanctuary set right next to the grille [in the choir]. Of course, it will be even nicer once I may stand on the other side of the grate, in the choir. But even now, it is a superabundant grace. The first Mass I attended here was for the Vigil of the Feast of Carmel. The Introit begins: "I led you into the land of Carmel, that you might eat of its fruits and produce" [Jer 2:7]. And every day supplies me with a generous portion. But the best part is that the spirit of Carmel is love, and that this spirit is very much alive in this house....

In sincere gratitude and reverent love, your
Edith Stein

‹∼›

To Sr. Agnella Stadtmüller, OP, August 27, 1933[8]

Pax!
Dear Sister Agnella,

...Of course, you may also write to me later, but whether I may reply will depend on my superiors. I am convinced the permission will always be given when a labor of love for a [needy] soul is involved. After all, for us, *"maior horum caritas"* ["and the greatest is love" (1 Cor 13:13)] supersedes all other rules....

In caritate Christi, your
Edith Stein

‹∼›

To Sr. Agnella Stadtmüller, OP, March 30, 1940[9]

Pax Christi!
Dear Sr. Agnella,

..."Pure love" for our holy Father John of the Cross means loving God for [God's] own sake, with a heart that is free from all attachment to anything created: to itself and to other creatures, but also to all consolations and the like which God can grant the soul, to all particular forms of devotion, etc.; with a heart that wants nothing more than that God's will be done, that allows itself to be led by God without resistance.

...Should we strive for perfect love, you ask? Absolutely. For this we were created. [Perfect love] will be our eternal life, and here we have to seek to come as close to it as possible. Jesus became incarnate in order to be our way. What can we do? Try with all our might to be empty: the senses mortified; the memory as free as possible from all images of this world and, through hope, directed toward heaven; the understanding stripped of natural seeking and ruminating, directed to God in the straightforward gaze of faith; the will (as I have already said) surrendered to God in love.

This can be said very simply, but the work of an entire life would not attain the goal were God not to do the most essential. In the meantime we may be confident that he will not fail to give grace if we faithfully do the little we can do. The little—taken absolutely, is for us a great deal. And while we are about it, we have to be careful not to wish to judge for ourselves how far we have come. Only God knows that. That brings me to Psalm 18[10] (so simple, as I understand the phrase). What we recognize of ourselves, and of our faults and behavior, is only the illuminated surface. The depth they come out of is to a large extent hidden from ourselves. God knows that depth and can purify it. The *ab alienis* [from unknown (faults)] can probably be understood in different ways. I think of it principally as what burdens us through unknown faults. But one could also think of that in which we are implicated by others. *Delictum maximum* [greatest fault] probably is not to be understood as anything definite. To me it seems to point far more to divine mercy's immensity and salvation's almighty power, for to them nothing is too great....

In Corde Jesu, your least
Sister Teresa Benedicta a Cruce, OCD

6

VOCATION

INTRODUCTION

Edith speaks about vocation in various contexts—personal vocation; the traditional vocations of the married, single, and religious life; occupational vocations; and the Christian vocation. In one of her most sweeping comments concerning vocation, she states, "To be united with God in a continual communion of life—that is the highest form of life to which one can be called. It is the vocation of every individual human soul, it is the vocation of the church."[1]

The first selection from *Finite and Eternal Being* elaborates on this idea of union with God. Edith asserts that the vocation to union with God is a vocation to eternal life and each soul with its own unique individuality is meant to reflect God's image in an entirely personal manner. She incorporates into her discussion the passage from Revelation 2:17 that speaks about giving a white stone to the victor on which will be written a new name that only the recipient knows. Edith equates this name with the person's innermost essence. Because of her training in phenomenology, the concept of essence holds particular significance as a technical term for her. Husserl's phenomenological method placed much emphasis on essences. The essence of an "object," whether material or not (for example, "object" can designate a physical entity, a feeling of joy, the soul, a number, and so forth) refers to those qualities that are necessary to make an object what it is. In other words, it refers to qualities that an "object" cannot do without in order for it to be what it is. Furthermore, "essence is a unified whole and always more than the sum total of all individual characteristics which we may be able to discover, and in its unity and wholeness it can ultimately only be designated by some name."[2] Edith believes that what human beings sense of their innermost being remains veiled during this life and they will only know themselves as God knows them in the next life.

Once again, Edith highlights the theme of love in this selection. The soul that opens itself to God is in a loving union with God, which is only possible between spiritual persons. Moreover, this love bears the stamp of personal individuality.

In the first of two excerpts taken from her letters, Edith highlights the diversity of vocations as reflecting the great diversity of people, gifts, and purposes. She also advises prayer and guidance when seeking one's individual vocation. In the second excerpt, she discusses union with God and union with God's will in response to a friend's question concerning mystical graces. Here again, Edith demonstrates the very practical side of her spirituality by stating her belief that one simply ought to do all that is possible to become an empty vessel for divine grace.

The final selection is taken from a lecture concerning the education and formation of girls. In it, Edith stresses that each individual has a "special" vocation, even if history only preserves the names of a few. Each human soul created by God bears its own unique "stamp" from God and each has a corresponding vocation to a work that is sketched out in her personal individuality. Thus, in the process of one's formation, it is important to develop this personal individuality. Even more important than various educational opportunities, one needs to believe in oneself, have the courage to be oneself, believe in one's individual vocation to a certain work, listen to the call, and be ready to follow it.

THE TEXTS

Finite and Eternal Being

Chapter VIII. §3.1. The Vocation of the Soul to Eternal Life[3]

We have come to know the innermost being of the soul as the "dwelling of God." By its pure spirituality, it is capable of receiving the

Spirit of God into itself. By its free personhood it is thus able to surrender itself as is necessary for this reception.

The vocation to union with God is a vocation to eternal life. As a purely spiritual form, the human soul is already *naturally* immortal.[4] Moreover, as spiritual-personal, the soul is capable of a supernatural enhancement of life, and faith teaches us that God *wills* to give it eternal life, that is, an eternal share in God's life.

So, the individual soul with its "unique" individuality is not something transitory that is only destined to reveal in itself its type of particularity for a fleeting length of time and during this length of time, to pass it on to "descendants" so that it may remain preserved beyond its individual life. The soul is destined for eternal being, and that makes it seem understandable that it is to reflect God's image in an "altogether personal way."

Sacred Scripture offers quite a few clues for such an interpretation. Thus, we may understand from the psalm verse, "He has formed the heart of each one individually" (Ps 33:15), that each individual human soul has come forth from the hand of God and bears a special seal; and when it is said in John's Book of Revelation, "To the victor I will give...a white stone, and on the stone will be written a new name which no one knows except the one who receives it" (Rev 2:17). Shouldn't that name be a *proper* name in the full sense of the word, which expresses the innermost essence of the recipient and opens up to him the mystery of his being that is hidden in God? It is a "new" name not for God, but for the person. On earth that person carried a different name. Indeed, human language doesn't have any genuine proper names; language names things and even persons after some characteristics that are generally comprehensible. Human beings "characterize" while they bring together as many of such characteristics as possible. Their innermost and most distinct being most often remains hidden to them. It is concealed by the characteristic features that the human nature in them takes on during the course of their life under the influence of their environment and especially through interaction in "society." What they sense of it in themselves and in others remains dark and mysterious, and is "something inexpressible" for them. But when earthly life ends and everything transitory falls away, then every soul will know itself "as it is known" (1 Cor 13:12), that is, as it is before God—as what and for what purpose God has quite personally created it, and what it has become in the order of nature and grace—and to this essentially belongs: by virtue of its free decisions.

We also have to think about what it means to receive God into the innermost being of the soul. The omnipresent God is, of course, always and everywhere present: in inanimate and irrational creation, which cannot receive God in the same way as the soul, in the "outer dwellings" of the soul where the soul itself notices nothing of God's presence, and in its innermost being, even when the soul itself doesn't stay there. Therefore, it is out of the question that God comes to a place where God was not before; rather, saying that the soul receives God means that it freely opens itself to God and surrenders to that union which is only possible between spiritual persons. This is a *loving* union: God is love and the share in divine being granted by the union must be a loving together with God.

God is the plenitude of love. But created spirits are not capable of receiving into themselves and realizing the entire plenitude of divine love. Their share is proportionate to the measure of their being and this means not only a "so much," but also a "certain manner"—love bears the stamp of personal individuality. And again, this makes it understandable that God may have created a "unique" dwelling in each human soul so that by the diversity of different kinds of souls, the plenitude of divine love would find further scope for its communication.

Letters

To Rose Magold, August 30, 1931[5]

Pax!
Dear Rose,

...There is no general solution to the question of how to choose between entering a religious order, or [joining] a pious union, or leading, on the other hand, a solitary life in the service of God. The decision has to be made for each individual case. The multiplicity of religious orders, congregations, and associations is not an accident, nor a mistake; rather, it reflects the multiplicity of purposes and people. No individual is suitable for everything; nor is there any form of union or other organization that can accomplish everything. *One* body—but many members. *One* Spirit—but many gifts. Where the individual belongs is a vocational question, and so it is *your* most important question now that examinations are over. The question of vocation cannot be solved merely through self-examination plus a scrutiny of available possibilities. One must pray for the answer—you know that—and, in many cases, it must be sought by way of obedience. I have given this same advice several times, and those involved have arrived at peace and clarity following it.

I think the very best thing for you would be to get yourself some firm guidance. I do not know whether you have a confessor at this time to whom you could entrust yourself completely. If not, I know of two confessors near you in whose ability to help you I have complete confidence....

Most cordially,

Edith Stein

∽∾∾

To Sr. Callista Kopf, OP, October 20, 1938[6]

Dear Sister Callista,

...[You ask] whether the life of mystical graces is reserved for a few? Your brother [Dominican], Garrigou-Lagrange, has attempted to show with great emphasis (and many have concurred in his opinion) that it is but the unfolding of the three theological virtues and that all Christians are called to what is the *essential* [element] of it, namely, to union with God. This [union] is not extraordinary, but only the ecstasies, visions and the like that accompany it in some cases. The obstacles people put up account for the fact that only a few actually attain to that [union]. Our holy parents in the order are not completely of that opinion. In any case, for the consolation of those not mystically graced, both emphasize that what is decisive is union with God in the will, that is, conformity to the divine will. But our Holy Mother saw a vocation to Carmel as synonymous with a vocation to contemplation. That surely holds for every "contemplative" order. Anyway, I think there is more security in doing all one can to become an empty vessel for divine grace. "Tear your heart away from all things. Seek God, and you will find him." (Maxim of our Holy Mother)....

In the love of Jesus and Mary, your

Sister Teresa Benedicta a Cruce, OCD

Lecture:
"Recent Problems in the Education of Girls"[7]

III.A.3. IDEA OF INDIVIDUALITY

Consideration of the redemptive order has already shown us that there is not *one* fully undifferentiated goal for all women. Mary herself is the clearest example of this because with her choice of virginity, she departed from what, according to the whole tradition of her people, was women's role. If her role is unique in the history of humankind, nevertheless, again and again we see women in the course of time who clearly have a special vocation: already in the Old Testament the women who are seen as prototypes of Mary, Judith and Esther; later in the history of the church, for instance, Catherine of Siena, Joan of Arc, and the great St. Teresa (to name only such whose particularly remarkable effectiveness departed from the usual paths of women). But it is not a special distinction of a chosen few whose names are preserved by world history to have a special vocation. Each human soul is created by God; each receives from God a stamp which distinguishes it from every other. This, her individuality, is to develop *with* her humanity and with her womanhood through her way of formation. And a vocation to a work corresponding to her is sketched out in her personal singularity. So the unfolding of this singularity must be taken up in the goal of girls' education.

One cannot sketch the image of the individuality as it is possible for the image of perfected humanity or perfected womanhood. One must only be clear oneself that pure humanity and pure womanhood cannot thoroughly determine the goal entirely, but can only develop in the concrete unity of an individual person. So that *genuine* humanity and womanhood becomes reality in the unstunted individuality, a flexible variety of educational ways and means is needed. Further and above all, the following is needed: faith in one's own being and courage to be oneself; likewise, faith in an individual vocation to a certain personal work, listening to the call, and readiness to follow it.

Thus, as the goal of individual formation work, we can denote the human being who is what *he* quite personally is supposed to be, who goes *his* way, and does *his* work. *His* way: that is not the way which he chooses in an arbitrary manner, but rather the way to which God leads him. Whoever wants to lead someone to the pure unfolding of his individuality must lead him to trust in God's providence and to the readiness to pay attention to its signs and follow them.

COMMUNITY AND INTERCONNECTION OF ALL HUMANITY

INTRODUCTION

Edith places great stress on the unique individuality of every human being. Each individual soul receives its own "stamp" from God and each is called to reflect God's image in an entirely personal manner. However, she places equal stress on the importance of community:

> The consideration of an isolated human individual is an abstraction. His existence is existence in a world, his life is life in community. And these are no external relationships which are added to one existing in and for himself, but rather, this being incorporated into a great whole belongs to the structure of the human person himself.[1]

Unlike angels, human beings unfold and develop as members of community. In fact, community is needed in order for the individual to unfold. The communities in which humans develop include the family, school, state, church, nation, race, and so forth.

In the first selection, taken from the final chapter of *Finite and Eternal Being*, Edith discusses the interplay between the individual and community. Community not only provides for the physical needs of the individual, but also offers spiritual sustenance for the soul by way of human works, such as cultural works and intellectual achievements that are passed on from one generation to the next.

This is a good example of how the term *spiritual* holds a much broader meaning for Edith than *religious*.

Edith highlights the uniqueness of the individual within community by comparing persons to flowers that bloom in a specific place but that, when fully unfolded, are to be placed in an eternally imperishable wreath. While the so-called average human beings (the "common blossoms" in the wreath) may all seem identical, especially when compared to the more distinguished persons (exquisite flowers), they are not the same. To make her point, she then switches the metaphor to a troop of marching soldiers. Although the assembled troops may all seem alike to indifferent observers, loved ones who are awaiting them recognize the differences.

Another significant part of Edith's discussion relates to the maturity needed for individuals to embrace humanity as a whole and to recognize their obligations to community. Perceiving humanity as a whole requires experiencing the common bond that links all people of all times and places, despite their differences. Likewise, our contact with persons whose backgrounds differ from ours enriches and perfects our own being. Such contacts are often misinterpreted and, as Edith remarks in a footnote, these misunderstandings can result in one-sided ideologies such as nationalism and internationalism. By the time *Finite and Eternal Being* was completed in 1937, she and her family were already among the many Jews personally affected by the ideology of Nazism.

The second selection presents Edith's entire lecture "The Theoretical Foundations of Social Formation Work," in which she addresses the question of how to educate and form children so that they are prepared to participate in the various types of human community. It must be noted that while the German word *Bildung* is often translated as "education," it conveys the idea of holistic education or the formation of the whole individual, not only intellectual education. *Bildung* can also be translated as "formation," which sometimes better imparts this understanding.

Formation [Bildung] is not an external possession of knowledge, but the shape [Gestalt] which the human personality takes on under the influence of various formative powers, or, the process of this forming. The material which is to be formed is, first of all, the body-soul predisposition which the human being brings to the world, and then the building materials which are continually taken in from the outside and must be incorporated into the organism. The physical body draws them from the material world, the soul from its *spiritual environment*—the world of persons and goods which are intended for its nourishment.[2]

Edith holds that the human being has a double nature—the nature of being an individual and the nature of being a member. Both the individual and the community are willed by God and founded in God, and the final goal of the human being—union with God—is not attainable without community. Thus, Christ established the community of the church to facilitate the salvation of souls. Edith uses the example of St. Benedict and centuries of the Benedictine lifestyle to illustrate some points about community.

A key point of this lecture is that both original sin and redemption would be incomprehensible if humanity consisted of completely separated individuals rather than being one body with head and members. Also, being a member of the one humanity finds its roots in human beings' having been made in the image of the Triune God. When explaining the ways human persons in community differ from the divine persons in the community of the Trinity, Edith nicely articulates the dynamic interplay between the human individual and community, both of which are in the process of becoming. She follows this with very practical examples of how people often do not find the place in community that matches their singular individuality and abilities, preferring instead to take refuge in their illusions and self-deceptions. From Edith's perspective, ever since human beings severed themselves from the first community—community with God in childlike obedience—human community came apart at the seams. She presents her view of this original idyllic community and believes that while a certain understanding of the original community remains, it is hindered by the isolating attitude of the individual. In contrast, she assesses the then current state of the specific communities of family, nation, church, and school. Her assessment finds

EDITH STEIN

decay at all levels of social structures and suggests that the solution is a return to the original meaning of human communities by a corresponding formation of its members. This is only possible through a restoration of the community with God, which was achieved by Christ's redemptive act. By her *fiat*, it was Mary who stepped back into the original community of humanity. Nevertheless, the way must be walked by everyone in a personal act and each community must be established anew in God and by God.

In the last segment of the lecture, Edith looks more specifically at the school community, concluding that the principle of social formation work is summed up in the command to love God and to love one's neighbor as oneself.

THE TEXTS

Finite and Eternal Being

Chapter VIII. §3.2. A Comparison between the Individual Particularity of Human Beings and of Angels[3]

...It pertains to the essence of the human being that the individual is a *member* of the human race and that this individual realizes himself as a whole (with all the possibilities implied therein) in a *humankind* in which the individuals inhere as "members of one another." To be a member of this totality, every individual must be an embodiment of "universal human nature." But this latter is only a frame which is to be filled with the manifold of the individual member beings. We may perhaps draw a comparison between this relationship and the one that exists between color and specific color gradations, since it pertains to the essence of specific color gradations to be *color*, and it pertains to the essence of color to be *a* color. And yet the latter relationship is quite different, since the individual human being is in his content not merely a particularization of something more universal, but a member of a whole that realizes itself as a *vital unity* and that can achieve its unfolding only in the vital context of the whole, in its particular place and in cooperation with the other members.

An important part in all this is played not only by the vital laws of propagation, the care and the division of labor required for providing the necessities of life—functions and activities which human beings have in common with the lower animate beings—but also by those laws of spiritual life by virtue of which all the products and creations of the human mind become the common property of humankind, "food" for the souls of contemporary and succeeding generations, or ways of life endowed with directive force and formative power. By virtue of its spirit nature, humankind is called to a communal life which—after having grown from a temporally, spatially, and materially determined soil—eventually annuls the limitations of time and space.

However, since the individual soul comes to bloom in a place prepared for it—prepared by the historical evolution of the people of its earthly homeland and by the generations of its earthly family—and since, after its pure and full unfolding at its [appointed] place, the soul is to be inserted as a flower in an eternally imperishable wreath, it does not seem fitting to see in its essence a *species* that can be *individualized* in a multiplicity of alike structures. Now in a wreath a rare and exquisite flower may well be surrounded by many insignificant small blossoms almost completely alike to each other and therefore mutually replaceable. Similarly, in the history of the human race as well as in the narrow circle of our own experience, we are able to distinguish the "great," "strong," "outstanding" personalities from those "average human beings" among whom we can hardly discover any significant differences. But we already know that only a superficial observer sees things in this way. When the troops who have been marching in rank and file disband, every soldier who was trotting along and was strictly keeping pace with the others, having perhaps almost forgotten that he is an individual, becomes once again a small, self-contained universe in his own right. And where the curious spectators along the way saw merely a homogeneous mass, the mother or bride was able to discern in the crowd him whom they were expecting, the individual, him whom none of the others resembled. The mystery of his being which their love divined is fully known only to the all-seeing eye of God before whom all human standards of "great" and "small," "significant" and "insignificant" come to naught.

There is no denying, of course, that in the kingdom of heaven, too, there are the "great ones" and the "little ones"—differences which may be traced back to preparation in earthly life: to the endowments of the individual person and to the use this person has made of his or her God-given "talents." Human beings may "find their own selves"[4] to a greater or lesser degree, but there is also the possibility of losing oneself. For those who do not find themselves do not find God either, and do not attain to eternal life. Or, more precisely, those who do not find God do not attain to their own selves—no matter how much they may be preoccupied with themselves—nor to that source of eternal life which lies in wait for them in their own innermost being.

To the dual meaning of the word *humanity*—which is now used to designate universal human nature, and then again to designate the living whole of humankind—corresponds a dual relationship of the individual human being to "humanity." The individual human being is an embodiment of the *universal*, and this human being is a member of the whole. The individual angel, too, is the embodiment of a universal "angelic nature," but the angel is not a member of a whole in the same sense as a human being. We are justified in speaking of an "angelic world" in which every individual angel represents a specific phase or stage of spiritual personal being and forms with others, as it were, a harmony of many voices. And, as was mentioned earlier, it is the opinion of the doctors of the church that angels communicate with each other and meaningfully to each other, inasmuch as they mutually illumine each other. But no angel owes its nature to another member of the angelic hierarchy,[5] and no angel needs any of the others for the unfolding of its nature. They form a unity as the "heavenly court" which surrounds the throne of the All Highest.

The human being's being a member is something which we experience as a fact. To be sure, individuals must be far advanced in their development to embrace humanity as a whole and to know of their obligations to this whole. At the time of the awakening of their reason, human beings discover themselves only as members of a more limited community (viz., the family and other cultural and educational communal associations), and they never gain a total and uninhibited perspective of the larger communities (not even of their township and much less of their tribe, nation, race, and humankind as a whole), although there are certain ways in which they experience the reality of these communal organisms. To become acutely aware of the integral unity of those more limited units of which we are members and to become conscious of our membership in them, it is of special importance that we experience their difference from other similar communities which yet strike us as *foreign*. On the other hand, to gain an acute awareness of humanity or humankind as of the totality which encompasses and sustains us, it is of signal importance for us to realize experientially that common bond which links us—notwithstanding all the differences—with people and individuals of every age and clime, and to be conscious of the fact that by our contacts with foreign members of the human race, our own being is enriched and perfected.

CHAPTER VIII.§3.3 THE UNITY OF THE HUMAN RACE. HEAD AND BODY, ONE CHRIST

This ever fragmentary, often misinterpreted, and sometimes completely misunderstood experience[6] receives firm support and a clear meaning from the doctrine of creation and redemption, which derives the origin of all people from one ancestor and which envisages as the goal of the entire evolution of the human race its union under one divine-human head, in the one "Mystical Body" of Christ.

Lecture: "The Theoretical Foundations of Social Formation Work"[7]

The school—and especially the elementary school—is given the task of educating the children of the nation to participate in its various formations—family, nation, state, church, etc.—as members who are competent and ready to serve. In this task lie certain presuppositions about the nature of individuality and community, and the relationship between the two. My goal today is to uncover these presuppositions, to examine them, and from the results of the

examination, to derive certain general guidelines for social formation work.

I. Presuppositions of the Demand for Social Formation Work

The first presupposition is: *Social formation work is possible*, i.e.,
it is not a meaningless undertaking to want to educate individuals for
community. The second: *social formation work is necessary*. To begin
with, this means: *individuals* are *not* already *finished members of community*, but first have to be raised, formed, and educated for it.
Moreover, going much deeper, it also means: *community is necessary.
Without community*, without social life, and therefore without the
education of individuals as members of the community, *the final goal
of the human being is not attainable*.

1. Let me begin with the last assertion because it is the fundamental one and because through it, we will also obtain the guiding
principles for the treatment of the others. If one wants to penetrate to
the theory of an art, i.e., to understand the foundation upon which it
is based, then one would do well to keep a close eye on a master of the
art at his work. Thus, if one wants to penetrate to the theoretical
foundations of educational work, one has to go to a great master of
that art. So, I went to the greatest teacher of the Western world, St.
Benedict, and watched how he began to lead to their goal, the men
who came to him and wanted to be educated by him for heaven. He
organized them into a monastic family, had them pray together and
work together, and placed them under obedience to an abbot—a
father who led them as the head leads its members, and who was
responsible for them before God. Only in very rare cases can a person succeed in finding the way to heaven all alone and dependent on
oneself. On average, even the persons who leave the world and choose
the work for heaven as their exclusive purpose in life will get lost if
they do not integrate themselves in a community under a fixed rule.

To begin with, that stands before us as a fact which we cannot
easily call into question because a practice of 1400 years builds on it.
Fourteen hundred years of Western religious life, with all its fruits for
the peoples of Europe, vouch for the fact that community leads to

heaven. But the fact is dark and mysterious. Can we succeed in penetrating to its comprehension? A simple reflection will lead us further. St. Benedict is the student of a greater master. The Holy Rule is only the practical interpretation of the Gospel of Christ. His monastic families are only particularly vigorous and well-formed groups of cells in the great body of the worldwide community which Christ himself established for the salvation of souls—the holy church. So, it was God's will that placed the human being in community. And if we look at sacred doctrine, we find further irrefutable proof for that. Through the fall of the first human being, destruction came over the entire race; and as we all fell in Adam, so in Christ we are all redeemed [cf. Rom 5:17; 1 Cor 15:22]. No one comes to the Father except through him [cf. John 14:16], i.e., through entrance into the community of the redeemed, by incorporation into the Mystical Body of Christ. So, in the mystery of redemption, we have fully valid evidence that *community* is necessary *in order to attain salvation*.

2. But with that said, we likewise have penetrated to a point from which light also falls on the first presupposition which we put forward: *social formation work is possible*. Social formation work is then only possible if *the human being is a member of community by nature*, because one can form nothing in the human being that is not in him. Furthermore, *original sin* and *redemption* would be fully incomprehensible if humanity were a sum of single, completely separated individuals and not one body with head and members [cf. Rom 12:5; 1 Cor 12:27]. Only because in Adam *humanity is created as one nature*, can its corruption be the corruption of all. Only because Christ grows in this organism as an organ, can the *grace of the head* overflow to all the members. That the human being by nature is a member of the great body of humanity, born out of community, in community, and for community, is a fact, but a mysterious fact—one which is joined with all the mysteries of Christianity and receives light from them; but precisely for that reason, it cannot be completely penetrated with the light of our natural reason. We could still pursue this fact a step higher or deeper to its root in the highest and ultimate mystery of faith: the *mystery of the Trinity*. God created human beings according to his image. But God is *one* in three persons. *One essence*, indivisible, perfectly simple, unique—therefore, an *individual* in the

most complete sense of the word—but an essence which is three persons as one and which joins them together in unity: unity of being and unity of life in knowledge, love, and action—therefore, *community* in the most complete sense of the word. Because the human being is created according to the image of the Triune God, he is an individual and member in essence at the same time. Because he is an *imperfect likeness of God*, he is for one, not an individual and member in essence in one, as is the Trinity, but rather, both are side by side in him. Thereupon, he is imperfect in both and he *is* not both from eternity, but he *becomes* both.

We will now examine these three points one after the other. The human being is an individual and a member of community at the same time, but not in one. *Individuality and membership* are *side by side* in him. Membership signifies that he shares in the one *human nature* which is one and the same in "all that bears the human countenance." It is the foundation for the *similarity in the life* of human beings: in their thinking, feeling, willing, and acting. And the foundation of the *common ground* is that wherever human beings come into contact, they always think, feel, will, and act *with one another*; i.e., they are able to *live in community* and *as community*. But the one human nature differentiates itself in *types* which realize themselves in *more narrowly defined communities*: race, nation, social position, professional class, family, etc. And so component organisms originate in the large organism of humanity which are closed in themselves and marked off from the others on the outside, though again, internally structured. Ultimately, however, each one is not only a human being and not only a representative of this or that type, but rather an *individual*, the only one of his kind, and thereby on his own and separate from all others.

The individuality of human beings places limits on the community. Because they are individuals, all human communities must be imperfect. Because each human being possesses something entirely for himself, communities are not able to become fully one as the divine persons are one through the unity of their essence. What the Father, Son, and Spirit do—creation, preservation, providence, judgment, whatever—is absolutely *one* act—nothing particular falls to one person. True, we can also say of human beings: *one* excitement took hold of the entire people. *One* sorrow filled the entire community. However, this "one" does not designate everything that occurs in the individuals. From each one something personal flows into the experience of the community which he does not share with the others. Each individual is still something other than what he is as a member of the community. No one comes into the community with his entire essence.

However, not only membership and community are imperfect, *the individuality of the human being is imperfect,* too. God's essence, which is one and indivisible—and which is imaged by all creatures and achieved by none individually or even by all of them together—is absolutely perfect. First of all, that means that God's essence is all encompassing—everything that is, is in God and from God. It further means that what God is, God is fully and entirely from eternity and without change in all eternity. The individual is imperfect—first of all, that means that according to his essence, he is a fragment; in each creature, a ray of the divine essence is imaged, and in each, a different ray. It further means that what the individual *is supposed to be* according to the purpose intended for him—precisely as the image of the divine archetype—he *is* not that from eternity and also not from the beginning of his existence. He is that according to his potentiality, but not in reality—he has to first *become* that. The becoming fills his existence.

Hence, we have arrived at the third point: *the individual as well as the community* are not something finished; they are understood as always *in the process of becoming,* in the process of development. The child steps into existence in the family. Through it the child receives his existence and grows in its custody and care. By thinking, feeling, acting *with* the others—the adults—that is, living in community, he learns to think, feel, and act, and grows as a community member. But at the same time, the child also grows as an individual because the individual nature which he brings into the world begins to stir, lives, and is active in actions which he carries out in and with the community and gives them its stamp [the individual nature's own distinctive character]. As a new member establishes himself in the community and develops as a member, the community itself experiences reorganization and development of action. So, the community, membership, and individuality grow and develop side by side and with one another, but at the same time, in conflict with each other. The more strongly the community draws the individual into its "operation" and forms him into its type, the greater is the danger that his individual nature will be hindered in its development. The more vigorously the individual nature unfolds, the greater is the danger that the individual becomes inwardly estranged from the community and possibly also separates from it outwardly. But one need not helplessly surrender to these threats. The individual who grows up in the community and the others with whom he lives in community and with whom he grows ever more closely together in community, are by nature *persons*; i.e., *rational and free beings*—beings who know and can act on the basis of knowledge—who also know themselves, and the other members, and the community, and are able to intervene in a formative way. The personality is the second root for the possibility of social formation work. Without it, only community *development* would be possible on the basis of natural membership, but not *work*. Certainly, the possibility of free intervention likewise means new dangers for the development of the individuals and communities. We will soon return to that threat.

With the last considerations, we have already arrived at the second presupposition of social formation work which we uncovered at the beginning. *Social formation work is necessary* because the human being does not come into the world as a finished member of community. It is necessary because membership and community first have to develop. And—as we are now able to add—it's necessary because in the double nature of the human being (the individual nature and the nature of being a member) lie the possibilities of conflict and dangers which may perhaps be avoided through appropriate formation work. Dangers arise during purely natural development without systematic intervention; perhaps still greater dangers arise with systematic intervention on the basis of perverse theories.

The human being brings along strengths into the world—the strengths of human nature and of his individual nature—which are meant to be and want to be unfolded in the course of one's life. They can only unfold through activity, and this actuation takes place predominantly under the guidance of, and in community with, already developed persons, with "grown-ups." The guidance does not need to be any systematic or actual [formal] education. The child joins in "with" whatever the grown-ups do, and does whatever they ask of him. And they act in front of him and demand of him many times without any preceding pedagogical reflection, without thinking whether the activity which they consciously or unconsciously lead him to do is appropriate for his individual and social development. In the family, and also in larger communities, it is assumed "without a second thought" that the individual can "join in," that he thinks and feels as the others. And he is placed where it is useful for the aims of the community. As far as the general human nature and the particular community type are dominant in him, he goes along without resistance and lets himself be "employed" here and there. However, as the individual nature develops and asserts itself in the actuation of his strengths, it can bring him into conflict with the outside influences and demands. The individual nature possibly causes an essentially different way of feeling and thinking than that of the others, and it demands a different actuation than that which was expected of him in the service of the community. For the time being, we assume that the individual—just like the community—acts "naively"; i.e., that which is in him takes effect without his thinking about himself and without his working on himself. If the individual is a "strong" nature, then conflict will result and possibly a break with the community. He will give expression to his different way of feeling and thinking, will refuse the demands which confront him if they conflict with his nature, and will seek the place in life which corresponds to his own strengths, unconcerned about what becomes of the community. Let's imagine that this is not an isolated but rather a common course of development, then all social structures would be broken apart and humanity shattered.

Nature has provided that it does not come to this and that, in general, social structures are able to come into being and maintain themselves because, on average, the social strengths in the human being surely prevail over the individual ones. For the majority of human beings, the danger is more likely that their individuality will suffocate in community than that it will break apart the community. That which they have in themselves as their "own" is too weak to assert itself against that which is different and opposes it from all sides. It does not venture to actuate itself and therefore must become stunted. And that also cannot be regarded as a more fortunate course of development—not for the individual and also not for the community which is dependent on the strengths of the individuals.

A healthier process of development must lead to a harmony of the individual and social strengths. And because left to itself, *fallen* human nature does not reach this harmony, it needs a systematic intervention of *formation work*. This formation work, however, will only reach its goal if it is based on genuine knowledge—on a correct theory of social life. A false theory means new threats.

The conflicts between the individual and community themselves give cause for reflection about the essence of both and about their appropriate relationship. This reflection has led to two counter errors, two one-sided theories whose disastrous effects on practical life we are able to perceive everywhere. *Individualism* emphasizes solely the right of the individual to free unfolding. It recognizes no original natural community but only social groups which serve the needs of individuals and which, by free choice, are founded by them for their purposes and are just as freely dissolved again. According to linguistic usage of recent sociology, we call these *associations*. This individualism which began to gain ground at the start of modernity as one of its characteristic features, and which has had a mighty effect since the French Revolution, to a great extent has led to the dissolution of the organic communities which dominated social life in antiquity, as well as during the Middle Ages. It has led to the decline of the family, the division of the church, and the shattering of the nation. The opposite view, which we can designate as *socialism* (without thereby limiting it to the particular viewpoint of the party), places the individual fully in the society and subordinates him fully to the society. Socialism acknowledges no individuality but only the same human nature everywhere, and it does not allow any life outside of the community and without profit for it. (Socialism, like that which we encounter in the party programs and in the practice of our socialistic parties, is not a pure example of what we are speaking about because historically, it has developed out of liberalism and therefore, is interspersed with individualistic tendencies.) We see the results in the lack of vigorous and independent personalities, the lack of great and original achievements, in the dominance of manufactured goods and stereotypes—not only in commodities, but also in the spiritual realm: run-of-the-mill people, run-of-the-mill views—empty and untrue, without their own stamp, without soul.

If false theories have led to the destructive illnesses of our social life, then a good theory for recovery will be necessary—a reflection on the eternal "foundations of being" of the individual and community as I tried to indicate with some strokes at the beginning. The individual and community are both willed by God and founded in God. Whoever wants to emphasize one of the two at the expense of the other harms both because community builds itself from individuals as one organism from its diversely formed members. Whoever injures one member harms the entire organism. And detached from community, no member can exist. Thus, the formation work which is demanded has to reckon with both and form both together, and for each other.

But there is still much more to it than a correct view about what the individual and community are in general; namely, the knowledge of the *particular* individuals and communities with whom one deals at any one time and to whom it is necessary to lend a hand. Whoever has a good theory of social life can still always cause damage in practice if he misjudges the particular individuals and the needs of the specific community. Think, for instance, about modern formators of youth and the nation who take into account the individuality and through education, want to pave the way for the entire nation through the advancement of powerful leadership personalities. Now, if they presuppose something for an average student which is found only in rare, exceptional persons, then they breed arrogance and presumption—human beings who offer big words and big gestures instead of a simple deed.

We can now summarize the results of our critical considerations. We have found that three presuppositions are involved in the demand for social formation work:

- Community is necessary.
- Social formation work is possible.

- Social formation work is necessary.

We have examined everything and recognize the following as justifiable:

- The foundational mysteries of our faith pointed out to us that the attainment of the eternal goal is tied to community.

- In the natural integration into community and in the freedom of the human being we saw the possibility established of educating the human being to become a capable community member.

- The human being's nature of becoming, the disharmony between his individual and social predisposition, as well as the dangers which threaten social practice by the influences of false theories and inadequate knowledge of the prevailing, concrete circumstances, showed us the necessity for social formation work structured on a good theoretical foundation. The theoretical foundation is good if we have general insight into the nature of the individual and community, if we are clear about the meaning of different types of community, and if we correctly judge the capabilities of concrete individuals with whom we have to carry out practical formation work. Finally, the theoretical foundation is good if we know the means which are able to lead to correct integration of the individual into the community.

II. THEORETICAL FOUNDATIONS FOR CONSTRUCTIVE SOCIAL FORMATION WORK

We are now trying to lay the foundation—the theoretical—the basis of knowledge upon which the structure of social formation work can arise.

1. First of all, we will summarize what we have already established about the general relationship between the *individual and community*, and supplement it as far as the objective demands. The

human individual is equipped with a general human predisposition and by nature stands in connection with his equals so that, in general, wherever human beings meet, an understanding emerges and a commonality of life in which they grow together into certain concrete social structures which we call communities. But moreover, they are provided with an individual predisposition, a unique singularity which limits the common ground of feeling, thinking, and acting. Nevertheless, the individuality has a positive significance for social life. Through it the position is sketched out for which the individual is intended in this or that more narrowly defined community, and possibly in the development of the whole of humankind. The community is a body with various members, and the diversity of the individualities corresponds to the diversity of functions in the large body. One individual is capable of these member functions, another of those; no arbitrary exchange of the individuals or members is possible. Furthermore, the individual is a *free person*, and as soon as he has attained the use of his freedom, he is no longer simply at the mercy of the community, but can give himself to it or shut himself off from it, and can take on this or that role in it, or refuse to take it on. The existence and the special nature and organization of the particular community are thus dependent upon the free will and individual predisposition of the individuals who belong to it. If human nature were pure and free of dross, as it came from the hands of the Creator, and human life proceeded purely according to the laws of reason, then the integration of the individual in community would take place smoothly. Each person would know by his individuality in which place he belongs and would willingly take this place; and the others, also led by correct knowledge, would likewise willingly grant him the place. We all know how little the reality corresponds to this beautiful picture. It is difficult to gauge what is more inadequate—our self-knowledge or our knowledge of other human beings. People constantly strive for positions and jobs for which by their nature they are not at all qualified. Constantly, on the basis of inadequate knowledge about their individuality, demands are placed on them by others to which they do not measure up. The most diverse applicants enter into competition with one another for the same place. Thus, quite a few ruin themselves struggling for a goal which, with rational insight, they would not set for themselves. Many are at variance with themselves and with the community in which they live because their nature is not granted adequate leeway. And even where there is insight, or there could be insight considering personal abilities, action is not guided by it. The human being takes refuge in illusions and self-deceptions because he does not *want* to see the truth which contradicts his wishes. He sees his enemy in whoever enlightens him on the basis of better insight and wants to guide him to other paths. And the repeated failures to which his irrational striving leads can have the effect that he wants nothing more to do with any community, becomes entirely wrapped up in himself, and shuts himself off from all others. After that, the ways by which help could come to him are completely cut off. Conflict on all sides, a solitary traveler going astray without a path, driven off course from his own destination and of use to no one—these are the images of social life as we can observe daily. Ever since the first human beings tore apart the first community and first social order in which they were placed—the community with God in childlike obedience—all human community came apart at the seams along with human nature. Everyone is at loggerheads with themselves and all others. In the original community with God, the human being was completely secure. He did not know himself but he was known and knew himself known. He did not take care of himself and did not worry about himself, yet he was taken care of. His gaze rested on God, not on himself. On his side, his community with God was neither absolute nor perfect. As God's image he was able to comprehend just as much of God so as to abandon himself to God with all his strength. Yet, as an imperfect image in infinite distance, he saw himself face to face with God as the incomprehensible and impenetrable One who infinitely transcends all human knowledge and love. Known and loved by the immeasurable One and secure in him, he must summon up all the knowledge and love of which he is capable in order to approach God. Before the mystery of God's immensity, he must bow in reverence and obedience. In God and by the power of God, he comprehends and embraces all creatures. As God's creatures, they are good and an object of his love. He knows himself one with them in the glorification of God, especially with those who, like himself, approach God spiritually in knowledge and love. He is in harmony with himself and with all others. Torn away from God, he is on his own. Grace carries him no more; he has to take care of himself. He has to seek to know himself and the rest of creation, test his strengths, and see how he can thus get through the world. And because each seeks his own way for himself, each has a different goal, and often the ways intersect. As a result, one looks at the person next to him to see how he can serve his own goal—just as one does with material things—and as the case may be, one makes common cause with him or opposes him. That is the "societal" attitude, the rationally deliberating attitude directed toward practical gain. The original community of human beings is not abolished. A certain understanding still exists and is presupposed for "societal" life itself. Communities continue to be formed but their formation is hindered and thwarted by that isolating attitude of soul. As the human being broke away from God, he also separated from his fellow human beings. Fratricide followed after original sin. [Cain killed Abel.]

2. We can become aware of the consequences of the fall [original sin] in all human communities if we bring to mind their original meaning and contrast this with their current average shape. Here we want to do this for the communities which play a special role in social formation work: *family, nation, church,* and *school.* Not only community in general, but every particular community type is willed by God and has its own meaning in the context of humanity. The organic character of community is nowhere clearer than in the family. God created human beings as male and female and wanted that both be "one flesh." The continued existence of humankind is tied to the fact that they who are separate individuals and independent persons function as a single organism, and that they care for and watch over the new life which arises from this organism—the individuals newly coming into being—until they are able to take care of themselves. And like all of God's creatures, alongside its natural meaning, the family also has a meaning related to salvation. The common life in marriage ought to be a means of sanctification for the spouses and through them, the children ought to be led on the way of salvation. In comparison with that, we place the average picture of the modern family. For some, marriage is an economic matter—a business which

one revokes when it doesn't turn out to be profitable; for others, it is an arrangement in which one can satisfy his drives under the protection of the law. The one party uses the other to this end and pushes him aside like a worn-out toy when the goal is no longer achieved. With the second type, it appears as an unfortunate accident when children come. With the first type, it is a matter of calculation of whether one can afford children and how many. Both are a degeneration. Here and there, the natural meaning of marriage and the family has gotten lost and the sacramental meaning entirely silenced.

The human being, who grew up in the family and finally *outgrew* it, is still not able to stand entirely on his own. His individual predisposition stamps him as a fragment, or more correctly, as a member or organ that is called to play a constructive role in one great totality and to secure his own existence therein. The totality is not only there for the sake of the existence of the individual, but has its own tasks. It brings forth goods which outlive the co-creating individuals and entire generations and are passed on to distant generations. We call the great organism which is capable of existing relatively independently and engendering a self-contained world of goods (i.e., a culture), a nation. A common possession of species, language, work, and destiny ties a narrow band around the nation's people which sets them off from the entire organism of humanity—certainly not outside of it, but again, as a member *in* it. The individual is born into the community of the nation and is carried by it; it is natural for him to love and serve it. That it also has a meaning related to salvation is demonstrated to us most clearly by the nation which God chose for himself specifically to be a holy nation. To the *entire nation*, God gave the *law* which is to show each individual the way through life, and God gave it to *one* nation in order to protect it and continually hand it down for all others, for the entire humanity. God gave it to the entire nation but through chosen individuals—through leaders, excellent organs of the whole—who had to announce, guard, and take care of its implementation. The organism of the nation differentiated between head and members, authority and subjects—it took on the form of the *state*. The nation is called to lead the individuals to salvation and, at the same time, to serve the salvation of all humanity. The individual is guarded by the nation and is integrated into an appropriate place as a constructive member. That is the eternal meaning of all nationhood, even if it is stamped in a special way "God's people," because in its organization, church and state are both prefigured. In contrast, let's again look at the average picture of the present life of the nation. No doubt, there are statesmen who administer their office properly, i.e., in accordance with its meaning; also such who perform it as a sacred service to the nation. But alongside these stands the multitude of those to whom the office is a feeding trough and likewise a temptation to a community-dissolving craving for power and its satisfaction that is contrary to God. And then there is the great mass of "citizens" for whom the national community as such has lost every meaning, who have interest in the state's institutions only as far as a personal advantage may be gained or a disadvantage avoided. The shattering of nationhood has progressed so far that it is hardly possible to recognize any clearly defined national character, or to bring about hardly any great actions by the entire national body.

In the Old Testament, the natural community of the people of Israel was organized into a divine institution of salvation. The church of the New Testament is primarily a divine institution of salvation and presupposes no other natural community than the universal human community. The church is the guardian and teacher of the truths of salvation, the steward and dispenser of the means of salvation. Through both she is meant to lead human beings back into community with God. At the same time, the church is the Mystical Body of Christ whose members constitute the faithful. Everyone who accepts the goods of grace offered by her enters as a member into the organism, the Communion of Saints. Because the church has not come to be from below, but rather was founded from above, there is no parallel degeneration with her as with other natural communities. It is only possible that her institutions become neglected or abused by her members. Precisely for this reason, they leave the organism and stop being living members. They are either also outwardly cut off or wither away and are used only like dead tools—as how the unworthy priest is able to mediate graces without having a share in them himself.

If we now proceed to the social structure which specifically concerns us—the *school*—then first of all, we see that the original meaning here is not automatically obvious. The school is not a natural community like the family and nation. It is a "social institution," systematically created for specific purposes. But these purposes are purposes of natural and supernatural communities, respectively. Thus, the school receives its meaning from these communities and if it fulfills this meaning, it then becomes a community—but yes, in order to fulfill the meaning, it has to be a community. The school stands in service of the nation and humanity as far as its task is to hand down the cultural goods—to hand down for the future what the past and present have created. For this purpose, it requires a vibrant contact between generations; i.e., between mature persons who take part in cultural life—creatively or at least with understanding—and young people in whom understanding and participation ought to be initiated. The fact that particular institutions were created for this contact presupposes that the family, the natural ground for the handing down from one generation to the next, was not sufficient. Obviously, the family's participation in cultural life is not comprehensive enough and will suffice less and less, the greater the wealth of cultural goods becomes. Thus, the professional teacher and formator became necessary, who on the basis of natural talent and systematic studies, actively masters certain cultural areas and is able to make them accessible to others. Merely to be able to achieve that, it is necessary for teachers and students to form a community. This is still more necessary for yet another purpose. The more the dissolution of the family progresses, the more urgent becomes the desire for a different *place of education*—a place where the individual and social strengths of children are able to unfold and form under appropriate care and protection instead of wasting away or degenerating, and where they are formed for their earthly and eternal goal. So it has become almost self-evident to us today to see in the school, especially in the elementary school, an *educational community*. As far as possible, it ought to substitute for home and family for the homeless or orphaned child, for the child who has no parental home, or whose parental home does not deserve this name. Where the family still fulfills its natural duties in relation to the child but does nothing more in order to incorporate the child into the community of Christ, the school can step in as a leader toward the church. And where the parental home carries out its work appropriately, it ought to be supported in it by the school. Education and passing on the faith tradition and cultural tradition are therefore its double task. If we measure the average school operation against its meaning and purpose, then one will be inclined to find the picture less bleak than the situation of the family and nation. In any case, one may say that more earnest striving can be found among those who are actively involved with the school operation—among faculty and administrative bodies who give an account to themselves of the meaning and purpose of the school and in practice, proceed accordingly as within other communities. It may further be said that the typical deviations from the original meaning and purpose are less widespread today than they were still a few decades ago. To begin with, that includes the abuse of the teaching profession purely as a source of income, a striving for it and practicing it without questioning one's own inner suitability and vocation, and without a practical willingness to serve. Then there is the megalomania of the schoolmaster who exercises a brutal command over the children and abuses their souls instead of serving them. Aberrations have by no means disappeared, but nevertheless, more earnest and selfless occupational zeal is seen along with these. In contrast, a danger different from earlier ones has probably increased in the last years and decades—the danger of a perverse organization of schools under the influence of false pedagogical theories. Individualism and socialism, which we recognized as dangers for the formation of the entire social life, have recently been able to have especially strong effects in the school system in the area of pedagogical experimentation. Loners, actual or alleged characters, presumptuous and arrogant or oversensitive people—in any case, such people who don't smoothly fit in any community—draw upon the individualistic principle: socialists are sheep without backbone, or rebels. And the influence of religionless circles on the organization of the school system has led, already to a large extent, to the secularization of schools and strives to carry it out thoroughly.

3. Thus, degeneration and decay of all social structures is the conclusion of our critical view. Only the return to their original meaning in knowledge and deed can bring recovery. Soon we will still discuss ways and means for that. Before that, we still have to

consider the last theoretical requirement which must be fulfilled for successful social formation work—the knowledge and correct assessment of the materials on hand at any given time. This is a known fact about which already more than enough has been said in the pedagogical field. Even if the teacher has the correct theoretical understanding of the individual and community, and if he himself is clear about the meaning and task of the social structure of the school in which he is placed, nevertheless, he will not achieve any successful social formation work with his students if he does not recognize in them their particularity and does not know how to deal with it accordingly. This is because the student is not completely formless matter which one can mold into any form whatever and which each immediately and willingly accepts, but rather, the student carries an inner form in himself which stipulates guidelines and sets limits for any formation from outside. Only the one who respects these naturally given guidelines will be able to form a community from the human beings who are given into his hands in which individual and social aptitudes come into their own in harmonious balance. And in that way, he likewise meets the requirements which are placed on his educational work by other communities.

III. Means of Social Formation Work

1. We have recognized how communities in general, and especially the communities in which and for which we work, ought to be constituted according to their original meaning and how they have deviated from that. Subsequently, it is clear what *social formation work* must consist of: *in returning communities back to their original meaning through corresponding formation of the community members.* And if the dissolution of human community life has its root in the breaking off of the community with God, then a recovery is possible only through *a restoration of the community with God.* This restoration is achieved by Christ's redemptive act for all of humanity. And as human freedom was at work in the fall that broke the bond, then it also takes part in tying it anew. With the words of the Virgin, "Behold, I am the handmaid of the Lord. May it be done to me according to your word!" [Luke 1:38], humankind grasped the outstretched hand of God's grace

and returned to the relationship of childlike obedience. Mary, who forgets herself in God and makes God's concern her own, by that very fact stepped back into the original community of all humanity; she encompassed everyone in God with her love and saving will. But the way which is thereby opened for all must be walked by everyone in a personal act, and every individual community must be established anew in God and by God. How that is to be achieved within other communities, we need not discuss here. We only want to obtain clarity about how it is possible in the school.

2. We'll take an entirely concrete situation: a teacher and her elementary school class—forty children who are together in a school room for the first time. Here, social formation work means: these children are to be formed into a community in which each takes the place which corresponds with his own individuality. And thus, they ought to become capable of likewise incorporating themselves appropriately into the communities to which they additionally belong, or into which they will still grow. How is that to be achieved? We have seen that the character of the community depends on the nature of the individuals and from them, the community is able to arise. The individuality of each individual must be recognized insofar as possible, in order to discover the place which befits him in the community. Moreover, each must be ready to take this place and generally participate in community life, and also to make the sacrifices which that demands of his individuality. First of all, only *one* individual is known to the teacher. It is likewise the only individual for whom it is certain from the outset which place befits her—that is she herself. She is called to be the head of this organism which is to become. Through her, all of it is to be organized. Whether it succeeds depends, first of all, on her bringing along the correct attitude which we have made clear earlier. She must know that she is not there in order to rule but rather, to serve—the children, the nation, and God. She must stand in a childlike relationship to God, forgetting herself in reverence and love for God. Then she brings into the school reverence and love for the children as God's creatures and already *stands* in community with them even before the community life begins outwardly. The ground is laid for that. Love awakens love in return and trust. Reverence raises the child to the feeling of his own dignity as God's

child and allows him all the more to look up to the human being who teaches him to feel this nobility. That is perhaps his first living contact with the kingdom of God. Love and reverence thus become the atmosphere in which the school community develops. While the teacher brings them [love and reverence] to all, love and reverence meet the children as the basic attitudes of the soul which befit all of them and which each child has to bring to all the others. In this atmosphere the community life can now unfold; the community can organize itself and every individual can form itself as its member. Where love and trust reign, the child's heart opens itself up easily and gives a first insight into the particularity of the individual.

This knowledge progresses further along with the formation of the community in the *work* which the school community is given as its principal raison d'être by the original purpose of the school—the cultural tradition. The children are to be brought so far as to be able to participate in the cultural life constructively and with understanding. Certain skills and knowledge by all are necessary for that. Thus, there are general teaching goals which ought to be achieved by all, as far as possible. But we know that not all are able to accomplish the same, that everyone brings with them different gifts and that even later, their tasks outside in life will be very diverse. So we will pay attention to what the individuals do well and gladly, what gives them trouble, and what is possibly unachievable. That way we recognize individual gifts and strengths. As far as possible, we will then give each the opportunity to cultivate his particular talent and at the same time, make it available for the community. There is a mathematical genius who finds by himself what must be taught to others with difficulty. One will provide him special assignments and possibly appoint him already to co-teaching. He is perhaps weak in German composition and needs tutoring by his fluent companions. A little artist accomplishes the necessary drawings on the board better than the teacher. There are found leaders of gymnastics and leaders of song. In games during recess and while on field trips, organizational talents are discovered. If one allows these strengths to come into their own, then an active and joyful life unfolds. Small personalities develop of firmly stamped individuality and a strong sense of community. Everyone feels in possession of his strengths and values those of others. Each knows himself as a member of the whole which needs his strengths and he joyfully serves the whole. When he has left the school, he will be socially formed to the extent that in the communities in which he newly enters, he will look around for the place which he is able to fill and will adapt easily and surely.

We had already seen at the beginning that community building in the school starts with the "head." And it requires leadership continually—the tasks must be provided or, at the very least, the opportunity for activity must be given so that the strengths manifest themselves. These strengths must be recognized and utilized in the right place. To do this requires no domineering manner and no instrument of power, only an interior superiority which becomes perceptible by itself. Whoever possesses it has authority; whoever does not possess it will not be able to "gain respect" by any means of coercion. Outer submission can be forced, but not interior, willing subordination which is necessary for correct community building. The one who is superior, who does not brag about his superiority, who does not emphasize it at all, finds joyful obedience because undeveloped strengths of themselves long for support from one who is stronger and for leadership. He finds respect and obedience precisely because he does not demand either. In any case, he does not claim it *for himself.* The teacher who is the head—in its genuine meaning—of her small community, certainly belongs to the community herself. Each one feels that she serves the whole and only desires what is beneficial for it. And while she commands, she obeys a Higher One from whom she has received her authority and to whom she leads her community.

Social education ultimately has its meaning in that it leads the community to God and is founded in God. The teacher receives the children's souls from God's hands, is to lead them to God, and is responsible for them before God. The community life itself is a help to her as well. In the school, the children are introduced to religious doctrines and the practice of the life of faith. Some show themselves as more receptive than others. Natural religious leaders develop who pull the others along. On the other hand, the community receives its firmest ground only through the life of faith. The community prays with each other and the members know that being heard is promised precisely to *common* prayer [cf. Matt 18:19]. The children are pre-pared together for the reception of the sacraments and are most inti-mately united in the common reception. They also become acquainted with the importance of the prayer of petition and feel responsible before God for one another. And every child who has been led so far so as to enter into the genuine child relationship with God, thereby gains that universal openness, that genuine brotherliness which gives him the correct attitude for *every* community.

And that is the comforting conclusion to which our investiga-tion leads: the correctly led school achieves social formation work which makes the human being suitable for every possible commu-nity. It develops competence and community spirit, the willingness for taking one's place and for subordination, which will prove effec-tive in the family, as well as in public life. And the school is able to lead to a loving community with all people in God. I believe that the teacher—and specifically the elementary school teacher—in his social formation work is more favorably placed than others who work at the same goal—government officials, reform writers, and reform preachers who seek to gain influence over the family and national life. He has fewer badly formed human beings, he has them much stronger in hand, and is disturbed less in his work by other influences. If he so practices his vocation, as its meaning demands, then he has the best chance to prepare the way for a recovery of the family and nation. And should it be too late for that today, then in any case, he works for the Communion of Saints.

Certainly, such social formation work requires a faculty which represents, so to speak, an elite troop of the holy church—firmly established in the faith, led by a knowledge that is enlightened by supernatural light, and strengthened by the church's means of grace and a constant, powerful, and sound inner prayer life toward the utmost surrender and willingness to make sacrifices for the cause of Jesus Christ, for the kingdom of God. The principle of all social formation work can be summed up in very few words: you shall love the Lord your God above all, and your neighbor as yourself [cf. Lev 19:18, Matt 19:19].

MYSTICAL BODY
OF CHRIST

INTRODUCTION

As the last chapter showed, Edith maintains the importance of both the individual and the community.

Every individual has his place and role in the one great development of humanity. Humanity is to be regarded as a single great individual (only by this presupposition can salvation history be understood). Every individual human being is a member of this whole. The structure of the essence of the whole becomes apparent in each member, but at the same time, everyone has his own member-character and must unfold it if the whole is to come to full unfolding. The human species will only realize itself completely in the process of world history, in which the great individual— humanity—becomes concrete.[1]

In the final pages of *Finite and Eternal Being*, Edith turns her attention to the relationship between humanity and Christ. She understands the fullness of humanity as being actualized both in the person of Christ and in the entire human race. Her discussion presents some interesting assumptions regarding Adam having had knowledge of Christ as the future divine-human head of the human race prior to the fall, but not having knowledge of Christ as the Redeemer. These statements strike contemporary readers as quite unusual. But while Edith does not refer to any specific source, possible sources for these notions include St. Jerome, John Duns Scotus, and Thomas Aquinas.[2]

However, another statement will resonate with most contemporary readers as being very much on target—that since Adam needed the complement of a female companion, he alone did not embody the fullness of humanity. In an earlier section in *Finite and Eternal Being*, Edith writes the following:

God created Adam and Eve in his image as spiritual personal beings. And this is why it was "not good" that such a creature be alone, since the most sublime meaning of all spiritual-personal being is mutual love and the union of a plurality of persons in love. The Lord gave Adam "a helpmate like unto himself" (*adiutorium simile sibi*, in the translation of the Vulgate; the Hebrew *eser kenegdo* places stronger emphasis on the equality)—a companion who was to Adam as one hand is to the other, almost completely his likeness and yet a trifle different, and who was thus capable in body and soul of a complementary activity of her own.[3]

The fullness of humanity could only be realized in the entire human family.

Edith also makes the interesting point that God creates us without our cooperation but did not want to save us without our cooperation, and so made the reception of sanctifying grace dependent on each human being's free assent and involvement. Thus, it is through the cooperation of nature, freedom, and grace that the Body of Christ is built up.

While the title *Mystical Body of Christ* may be familiar to some contemporary Christians, a brief look at the background of this terminology seems to indicate that Edith's familiarity with it possibly stems from Aquinas. John Hardon traces the historical origins of ascribing the term *mystical* to the church back to writings of Peter and Paul that convey the idea that the members are bonded in spirit and that the church is a spiritual home. The church fathers began referring to the church as the spiritual body. Augustine and Pope Leo I (440–461) used the phrase *sacrament of the Body of Christ* to refer to the church, with "sacrament" deriving from the Greek *mysterion* to designate something visible that symbolically confers invisible grace. William of Auxerre (d. 1231) used the name *Mystical and gratuitous Body of*

Christ to distinguish the church from Christ's natural body. Aquinas followed suit in writing about the Mystical Body of Christ, paving the way for the terminology in theological thought. The title became more popular when Pope Pius XII issued his encyclical on the Mystical Body, *Mystici Corporis Christi*, in 1943,[4] a year after Edith died.

From the perspective of ecclesiology, Edith anticipates Vatican II's recognition that both non-Catholic Christians and non-Christians are related to the "people of God" (Mystical Body of Christ) in various ways;[5] she clearly states that every individual human being is created to be a member of this Body of Christ. Moreover, she asserts that redeemed humanity united in Christ is the temple in which the Triune God dwells. Her anticipation of Vatican II's teachings surfaces again a year after completing *Finite and Eternal Being* when she writes, "It has always been far from me to think that God's mercy allows itself to be circumscribed by the visible church's boundaries. God is truth. All who seek truth seek God, whether this is clear to them or not."[6]

Edith certainly recognizes the validity in what she calls the narrower sense of relating the Mystical Body of Christ to humankind and states the reasons for this. However, she goes beyond this sense. After agreeing with Aquinas that the angels could be considered part of this body, Edith posits that all of creation can also be considered part of the Mystical Body of Christ and gives the following rationale: (1) everything was created in the image of the Son of God (the Logos); (2) by his incarnation, Jesus entered into the entire context of the created universe; (3) grace flows from the head into all creatures, not just human beings; (4) just as all subhuman nature was involved in the fall of the human being, it will share in the human being's restoration through redemption.

THE TEXTS

Finite and Eternal Being

Chapter VIII. §3.3. The Unity of the Human Race. Head and Body, One Christ[7]

...The entire human race is the race of Christ, although humanity as a whole is related to the person of the divine Word in a different way than that individual human nature which the Word assumed when it was born of the Virgin, and this humanity begins its existence in the first human being.

I shall now make an attempt to gain some understanding of the relationship that exists between Adam and Christ. The first man has, like every creature, his paradigm in the divine Word. As a spiritual person, Adam was, like every human being, a more perfect image of God than all nonpersonal creatures, and he was capable of being personally united with God. Moreover, he was, again like every human being, related in a special manner to the *humanity* of Christ. But Adam's *special* relationship to Christ distinguished him, nonetheless, from all other human beings. He was destined to be the *representative of Christ* as the head of the human race. We must assume, therefore, that no other human being was in his nature as Christlike as was Adam. (The Mother of God occupies an incomparable position, since her close intimacy with her son was of a different kind.)

The humanity of Christ was distinguished from that of all other human beings not only by his being free from all sin but by the fact that there was in him the "total plenitude of humanity." In him the entire specific essence of the human race was not only partially, as is the case with all other human beings, but fully actualized. And of his plenitude we all have received our share, not only "grace for grace" (John 1:16), but even in our nature, so that each of us in our own particular individuality might imitate the original prototype in the manner in which every member of a living structural unit embodies in its own particular way the essence of the whole, and in which all members together build up the total structure.

This is what makes the figure of the Savior, as it is depicted in truthful simplicity in the Gospels, so mysterious and unfathomable. He is "wholly human" and precisely for this reason unlike any other human being. He cannot be apprehended and comprehended as a "character" like Peter or Paul. Any attempt, therefore, to bring us into intimate contact with our Lord by depicting his life and character in the manner of a biographical portrait means really an impoverishment and a narrowing down of his life to some particular aspects, and in some instances it even means a distortion and falsification.

We see then that the fullness of humanity is actualized in a dual manner: in the person of Christ and in the entire human race. In the person of Christ it appears veiled during the course of his earthly life, but radiantly unveiled in the glory of the resurrected Savior, sitting at the right hand of the Father. And the road of the human race is a way that has its first beginning in Christ and that leads back to Christ in the end. He created the human being in his image, an image which he had designed from the beginning, to realize it eventually in his own person.

In his inviolate nature Adam was the purest image of this original prototype, and he possessed, moreover, the generative power to produce an even more comprehensive image in the totality of his descendants. Divinity and humanity were not united in him, as they are in Christ, in one person. But Adam was united with Christ by grace (in the manner in which one person may enter into union with another person), and he had been elevated to a participation in divine life. In this union the free descending of God and the freely ascending self-surrender of humanity meet. Because Adam possessed a more perfect knowledge of God and of creatures than did people after the fall, and because his will was still unimpaired, we may well imagine that Adam received the first infusion of grace with a lucid consciousness and a free resolve (i.e., not in the manner in which sanctifying grace is received in the baptism of infants, but rather in the manner grace is received by the created pure spirits). We may also assume that Adam had a knowledge of Christ as the future divine-human head of the human race and as the Son of Man in his flesh, and that he therefore freely responded to the call of grace as a token of his union with the God-Man and as a free assent to his own vocation as the chosen ancestor of the human race, which was to be generated for Christ and for the sake of Christ.

The recognition of the *Redeemer* cannot, on the other hand, have preceded that "knowledge of good and evil" which is linked with the fall. This latter knowledge is, rather, due to the revelation which followed upon the judgment that was pronounced after the fall (Gen 3:15).

Although we may justly ascribe to Adam a richer endowment with the gifts of nature and grace than was given to all his descendants (excepting the "Son of Man" and his mother), he cannot have been in possession of that plenitude of all gifts which we attribute to Christ. For only the God-Man was to bring to perfect fulfillment what had been initiated in Adam. Moreover, the fact that Adam needed as a complement a female companion and that Adam and Eve were destined to generate a race of human beings, seems to indicate that Adam did not in and by himself embody the fullness of humanity, but that this fullness was to be realized in and through the entire human family.

Christ does not generate according to the body, since he is the Creator prior to all time, the one who is perfect and who leads to perfection in the temporal order. Although he was born in time, like a human being, and as a descendant of Adam, his being-human is not a received being like that of all the other children of human beings: he was not "thrown into existence" as are all other human beings—but he came into the world because he so willed it just as he died because he willed it, and at the time he willed it. And all human being that precedes and follows his earthly life is oriented toward his being and is called forth by his being as by its final cause. But because God "created us without our cooperation, but did not want to save us without our cooperation," he made dependent on our free assent and willing collaboration not only the reception of sanctifying grace in every human being, but even the incarnation of the Redeemer, from whom grace emanates and flows into us.

In the covenant of the Old Testament this cooperation consisted in the trusting expectation of the promised Messiah, in being mindful of the task of propagation for the sake of this promise, and in the obligation to prepare the ways of the Lord by faithful obedience to his commandments and zeal in his service. All of this finds its crowning fulfillment and its most perfect expression in the *Fiat!* of the Virgin, and it finds its continuation in every efficacious action that serves the spreading of the kingdom of God by working for our own salvation and for the salvation of others.

In this manner, by the cooperation of nature, freedom, and grace, the Body of Christ is built up. Every individual human being is created to be a member of this body. And this is the reason why even on the purely natural level no human being is like the other—we recall that these reflections on the Mystical Body were to aid our understanding of the meaning of human individuality—but every human individual is a variation of the common human essence, and individual structural unit, and simultaneously a constructive part of a structural totality.

However, it is of the very essence of the human being that every individual as well as the entire human family are to become what, according to their nature, they are destined to be in a process of temporal unfolding, and that this unfolding depends on the cooperation of each individual as well as on the common effort of all. The corruption of human nature after the fall is the reason why a pure unfolding and a corresponding pure activity of the will is made possible only by redemptive grace. This grace also initiates the future fulfillment of the original ordination of the natural being of people: their participation in divine life by means of free, personal self-giving. Redeemed humanity united in Christ and through Christ is the temple in which the Triune God dwells.

So far we have spoken of the Mystical Body of Christ only in a narrower sense. However, it is possible to conceive of the Mystical Body in a broader sense. St. Thomas calls Christ—not only with respect to his divinity but also with respect to his humanity—the "head of the angels," because both angels and human beings are ordained to the same end, the fruition of divine glory, and they therefore form one body. According to St. Thomas, Christ is the head of this body, set by God the Father (Eph 1:20) not only above all people, but also above all dominations, principalities, virtues, and powers.[8]

We may go even one step further and may comprise in the Mystical Body the entire creation: in its natural order, because everything was created in the image of the Son of God and because the Son, by his incarnation, entered into the total context of the created universe; and in the order of grace, because grace flows from the head into all the members: not only into human beings, but into all creatures. As the entire subhuman nature was implicated in the fall of the human being, it is also to share in the restoration of the human being wrought by redemption. And though in the case of angels we cannot speak of *redemption*, since for them there is no possibility of a return or a conversion after their fall, it may nevertheless be assumed that those angels who persevered in their allegiance to God were able, by virtue of the grace merited by Christ, to give resplendent proof of their loyalty, and that they owe their glory to Christ.

Notwithstanding this possibility of a broader interpretation of the doctrine of the Mystical Body, we may and must continue to see in humankind the Mystical Body of Christ in the narrower sense. For humankind is the portal through which the Word of God entered into the created world. Human nature has received the Word, and the Word is linked in a special way with human beings, by virtue of a unity of common descent—not with subhuman nature and not with angels. As the head of humankind, which combines in itself the higher and the lower reaches of being, Christ is the head of creation in its totality.

SCRIPTURE, PRAYER, EUCHARIST

INTRODUCTION

Once when asked by a friend for the name of some books that she would enjoy, Edith listed a number of church fathers, commenting that "there is no healthier nor more nourishing spiritual fare than the Sacred Scriptures and the Fathers."[1] As evidenced in her writings and correspondence, she was well versed in Scripture. From the time of her baptism, she attended daily Mass and prayed the full Liturgy of the Hours of the Roman Breviary.[2] When teaching at St. Magdalena's in Speyer, Edith lived with the Dominican sisters and joined them for daily Mass and the Liturgy of the Hours. When her future was uncertain during the summer of 1933 in Münster, she found much comfort and joy in Romans 8:28: "We know that all things work together for good for those who love God" (NRSV).[3] She also wrote, "What an immeasurable treasure trove we have in Holy Scripture."[4] Noting elsewhere that John of the Cross counsels one to read Scripture, she maintains that the lives of both Teresa and John were "a translation of Sacred Scripture into life."[5] Her comment calls to mind a statement of Pope Francis in his apostolic exhortation *The Joy of the Gospel* that aptly applies to Teresa, John, and Edith: "Jesus wants evangelizers who proclaim the good news not only with words, but above all by a life transfigured by God's presence."[6]

The first selection, "Blessed Are the Poor in Spirit," stands out among Edith's writings as one in which she focuses entirely on a particular Scripture verse. She observes that external poverty does not guarantee poverty in spirit since the desire for material goods can still control the heart. The poor in spirit are those whose heart is free of attachment to earthly goods. This does not require relinquishing all of one's possessions but, rather, learning to carry one's possessions loosely in one's hands with the readiness to give them away. Being poor in spirit also means being humble and God-fearing and does not only entail a right relationship with "material" goods. As an intellectual herself, and possibly writing this essay for a publication of a secular institute of professional women, she points out that the possession of intellectual gifts can also bind the mind. Not only can the intellectually gifted consider themselves superior to those less gifted, but the great trust in human reason can turn one away from supernatural sources of faith. Thus, it can be difficult for those who are rich in earthly wisdom to enter the kingdom of heaven. But just as in the case of material goods, lacking intellectual goods does not imply that one has freedom concerning them. Likewise, those who are intellectually gifted need to learn the right relationship to intellectual goods, be ready to acknowledge the limitations of earthly knowledge in light of heavenly wisdom, and use their gifts as God desires.

Contrasting the Pharisee who valued his merits and the publican who, trusting in God's mercy, acknowledged his sinfulness, Edith states that we are all such beggars before God who depend on God's fatherly kindness. Here she inserts her theme of living in God's hands and being in a child relationship with God. When life's events make us aware of our human frailty, Edith's advice is to look the nothingness of our own existence in the eye in order to see that we are being held by eternal being; then we need to grasp God's hand and allow ourselves to be led by this hand of such a benevolent Father. Doing so results in a deep sense of security, certainty, rest, and peace—this is a share in the kingdom of heaven in this life. Edith states that the kingdom of heaven is, above all, living in a child relationship with God, knowing that one is cared for by a God of infinite kindness and love. Our blessedness on earth consists of experiencing God's kindness in ever new and undreamed-of ways.

Edith fully embraced the sacramental and liturgical life of the church. Her appreciation for the celebration of the sacraments comes through in a comment she made regarding the baptism of two children for whom she was the sponsor. Disheartened by the way the baptism was carried out, she wrote to a catechumen, "There was so little that was festive about it—five minutes in our sacristy—that it pained me greatly. I recalled with what holy seriousness and with what rich liturgy my own was carried out."[7] In a later letter to the same catechumen, Edith expressed her hope for this person's baptism:

> With all my heart, I wish the day to be one of truly new birth. Then the grace of your baptism and the ever new reinforcement through the holy sacraments will give you strength to bear with the difficulties, the arguments with your relatives, and your final year in college with its small and trivial daily cares.[8]

The second selection, "The Prayer of the Church," demonstrates Edith's grasp of the beauty of the liturgy and the need for both public and private prayer. In her autobiography, she notes that the church's liturgy has evolved from the Jewish liturgy composed of psalms and Scripture readings.[9] In "The Prayer of the Church," she makes further comparisons with Jesus' participation in Jewish worship and conveys the new meaning given by Jesus to the Passover seder at the Last Supper. Calling attention to a cosmic aspect of liturgy, Edith highlights how Jesus gave thanks to the Father throughout his life and calls on all creation to render thanks to the Creator. Moreover, she also makes symbolic comparisons between the tent of meeting and the Holy of Holies in Solomon's temple and the temple of living stones—the Communion of Saints—with Christ as the eternal high priest and all creation being drawn into the liturgy. While such understanding about the development of the Catholic liturgy became more widespread after Vatican II,[10] it followed on liturgical research and reform begun by Benedictine monks in the nineteenth century, including monks who had lived at Edith's beloved Beuron Abbey. While a few of her comments refer specifically to the Mass as it was celebrated prior to Vatican II, Edith demonstrates, here and elsewhere, a clear awareness of the growing understanding of the liturgical development, including another important aspect that has been stressed since Vatican II—the participation of the laity. She emphasizes that all Christians, not just those in religious orders, are called to give solemn praise to God.

Regarding private prayer, Edith notes that Jesus not only participated in public worship services but also practiced solitary, interior prayer. Focusing on Jesus' high priestly prayer (John 17), she makes insightful comparisons with the role of the high priest in ancient Israel on the Day of Atonement. Moreover, she believes that this prayer that Jesus spoke aloud in the presence of his disciples provides a window into his interior dialogue with the Father. Likewise, Edith notes the role of solitary prayer in the Christian tradition that has continued throughout the centuries. She strongly believes in the power of prayer and places special emphasis on women such as Bridget of Sweden, Catherine of Siena, and Teresa of Avila whose solitary prayer helped prepare for events in church history that aided in renewing the face of the earth. She provides excerpts from Teresa's *Way of Perfection*, written for her Carmelite sisters, to show how Teresa considered their lifestyle of prayer to be their contribution to countering the apostasy of her day. Edith believes that anyone who surrenders unconditionally to God will be used as an instrument in building God's kingdom, even if only God knows the effects. In fact, she calls the solitary mystical prayer that has flowed through the centuries the deepest life of the prayer of the church.

Edith rejects the distinction between personal inner prayer as subjective piety and liturgical prayer as the objective prayer of the church. She maintains that all authentic prayer is prayer of the church, for it is the Holy Spirit who prays within each member. Above all, prayer is an act of love. "What could the prayer of the church be, if not great lovers giving themselves to God who is love!" Those who totally surrender to God in love are gifted with union with God. Edith offers the example of Marie Antoinette de Geuser as a model for the laity in this regard. Two years before this essay, Edith had written a book review of a compilation of Marie's letters. In addition to taking part in traditional forms of prayer and public worship, Edith encourages those who have not yet reached such a unity of life in God to take time for silent listening and to allow the Word of God to act on them. Christ is the way to the interior life.

Witnesses have attested to Edith's great love for the Eucharist as evidenced by her daily participation at Mass and frequent prayer before the Blessed Sacrament. In addition, her own principle that leading others to the Christian mysteries can only be accomplished by those whose own lives are penetrated and formed by these mysteries[11] indicates that the practices that she recommends to others convey her own practices. The third selection, "Eucharistic Education," is an address to a women's group at the 1930 Eucharistic Congress for German-speaking countries. In it, Edith poses the question, "How can we ignite the love for the Eucharistic Savior in the hearts of others?" She refers to this as "teaching eucharistically," which requires setting an example by living eucharistically. Doing so is related to the dogmatic truths that Jesus is present in the Blessed Sacrament, that he renews his sacrifice on the cross at Mass, and that he wants to be intimately united with us in Holy Communion. These truths demand that one prays before the Blessed Sacrament, attends Mass, and receives Communion as often as possible. On his part, Jesus awaits us in order to comfort and guide us as a faithful friend. Jesus allows us to live his life, death, and resurrection together with him when we participate in liturgy.

Ever attentive to practicalities, Edith recognizes that daily Communion places demands on the body and one's lifestyle. It's obvious that making time for Mass in one's schedule involves sacrifice, and during Edith's era, one was required to fast from food and liquids from midnight in order to receive Communion. Perhaps less obvious is the fact that daily Communion also weans the soul from sin, and Edith also perceives this as a sacrifice for human nature. However, such sacrifices should come as no surprise since life with the crucified Savior means participation in his suffering. Yet, Edith's focus goes beyond the idea of sacrifice to encouraging her audience to find their home and center of life in the Eucharistic Savior.

The final selection is taken from a letter that Edith wrote to a former student who was apparently disturbed by something she had read concerning eucharistic adoration. Edith reassures her that knowing our need for personal nearness, Christ is present in the Blessed Sacrament for our sake, not his, and that a thoughtful and sensitive person will feel drawn there often. The letter also alludes to

Edith's own interest in liturgical correctness by conveying her dismay that a high choral Mass was sung during the time of adoration. In this regard, she even includes a mild admonishment given to her by her own spiritual director, Raphael Walzer. Also, writing this letter after having lost her position at the German Institute for Scientific Pedagogy in Münster because of Nazi policy, but still before she knew that she would enter Carmel, Edith expresses her confidence that God has something in mind for her.

THE TEXTS

Essays

"BLESSED ARE THE POOR IN SPIRIT"[12]

In the Beatitudes from the Sermon on the Mount, the Lord has sketched for us the image of the perfect Christian toward which the human soul must strive on earth to become ready for heaven. And at the beginning—as that which is apparently fundamental—he placed the *poor in spirit.*

The Savior repeatedly and vividly emphasized that freedom from external possessions is advisable for those who want to gain the kingdom of heaven. He advised the rich young man to give all of his possessions to the poor [Matt 19:16–26]. He expressed the dangers of wealth in the graphic image that a camel would sooner pass through the eye of a needle than a rich person would enter the kingdom of heaven [Matt 19:24]. The danger always exists that external goods— the striving to acquire them, the joy of possessing them, the worry of maintaining them—capture the heart and hinder its rising up toward God; for "no one can serve two masters" [Matt 6:24, Luke 16:13]. But it is not said that actual external poverty already means freedom of the heart. On the contrary, it can be a great danger for the soul if the external goods are not at the same time relinquished inwardly, if the desire for them still controls the heart. It's possible that they will then occupy and determine one's thoughts and wishes a lot more and give rise to more serious sin.

For that reason, the poor in spirit are praised—those whose heart is free of all attachment to earthly goods. Such poverty in spirit is also attainable for the one who has not outwardly given up all of one's possessions. The main point is only "to have as if one did not have" [1 Cor 7:29–31]. Carrying what one has loosely in one's hands, with the constant readiness to give it away, has to be learned. But the correct relationship to external goods is not the only meaning of "poor in spirit."

The liturgy of the church uses the Beatitudes as the Gospel text on All Saints' Day. And the liturgy elucidates the text in the Office of Readings for the third nocturne through a homily of St. Augustine on the Sermon on the Mount. In it the Beatitudes are related to the gifts of the Holy Spirit; the poor in spirit is related to the fear of God which is the beginning of wisdom. He relates the striving for earthly goods to the words of the preacher: "Everything is vanity and presumptuousness of spirit" [Eccl 1:2]. But presumptuousness of spirit means brazenness and pride. It is usually even said about the proud that their spirit is inflated, and rightly so, because *spiritus* also means "wind." But who wouldn't know that the proud are called "puffed up," filled as by the wind? Hence, also that word of the Apostle: Knowledge inflates, but love builds up [1 Cor 8:1]. That's why here, by the poor in spirit, we will rightly understand the humble and God-fearing; i.e., those who are not inflated spirits. Also, blessedness may begin with nothing whatsoever other than with poverty of spirit if it is to attain the highest wisdom. However, the beginning of wisdom is the fear of God [Prov 1:7] because, yes—as the counterpart to that—it is written that pride is the beginning of all sin [Sir 10:15 in the Vulgate]. But the proud strive for and love earthly dominion.

According to this understanding, the poor in spirit are those who do not imagine themselves great in the possession of earthly knowledge, human science, and human cleverness. As with external possessions, it also holds true for these natural intellectual gifts that they easily shackle the mind and do not let it rise to the supernatural and eternal; striving for knowledge always holds the danger of readily and wholly seizing the person. It is something which drives the person tirelessly forward so that he can find neither rest nor peace. And the one to whom natural knowledge seems to be something great will easily imagine himself great in its possession and superior to those who are "intellectually poor." The enormous trust in human reason easily leads to the turning away from the supernatural sources of faith which (according to Thomas Aquinas) is the beginning of eternal life in us. And so it is difficult for the "rich" in earthly wisdom to enter into the kingdom of heaven. In contrast, the simple-hearted who know that they know nothing and are able to know nothing of their own accord will humbly raise their eyes to heaven in order to receive as a gift from above, what they cannot obtain by themselves. For that reason, Christ praised the Father because the Father has revealed the mysteries of the kingdom to the poor and little ones.

But again, as with external possessions, it holds true that the actual not-having of intellectual goods—abilities and knowledge—is not synonymous with freedom from them. The riches of the spirit shackle whoever worries that he is not "able to keep up with" those more favorably placed because of insufficient aptitudes or lacking educational possibilities no less than the one who possesses them, and they obstruct his upward glance to eternal light which could make his spirit richer than all earthly wisdom and science is able to do. On the other hand, here there is also a "having as though one did not have." The one touched by the ray of grace knows that all human knowledge is patchwork [1 Cor 13:9] and not capable of giving us information about the one thing necessary. He can no longer be proud of his possession of knowledge and no longer direct his striving exclusively toward it. He will gladly be willing to relinquish all the science of the world in order to attain a glimmer of heavenly wisdom. But he will be just as willing, if it is God's will, to use his gifts and knowledge further in the field of natural research and teaching, or in another field of intellectual work and creativity for God's honor and the salvation of humankind. If only he sets his eyes unwaveringly on the *unum necessarium* [one thing necessary] and lets himself be led by it in everything he does, then the greatest scholar can be just as humble and simple-hearted, and hence truly poor in spirit like the uneducated peasant woman.

There were two kinds of people with whom the Savior surrounded himself during his earthly life: the poor and simple-hearted, and repentant sinners as well. There were two kinds of people whom he most sharply opposed: the Scribes and the Pharisees, i.e., the proud of knowledge and proud of virtue who are inflated with the supposed possession of "righteousness." The riches in which they trust and to which they ascribe endless value are their "merits," so that they believe to be certain of heaven and no longer fear God. They do that which, according to tradition, applies to the good and right, and with contempt, look down on those who act otherwise [Mark 7:5–9; Luke 18:9]. Jesus sketched their image with relentless sharpness: they pray and fast to be seen by the people, they make donations to the temple and let their poor parents live in want [Matt 6:5, 16; Mark 7:10–12], and they step before the Lord, not to praise him or even once to call upon his mercy because in their self-assurance, they don't feel needy at all. Grace finds no acceptance with them. On the contrary, the publican who, bowed down by the weight of his sins, does not dare to raise his eyes to heaven and knows nothing other to say than "Lord, be merciful to me, a sinner," goes home justified [Luke 18:13]. He is truly poor in spirit, a beggar before the Lord. He finds nothing at all in himself which he could show other than the misery of his sins. For this misery, there is no other remedy than God's mercy. Trusting in it, he dared to enter the temple. "A contrite and humbled heart, O Lord, you will not despise" [Ps 51:19]. And into this heart which is held out to God like an empty bowl, grace can pour forth. We are all such beggars before God. Even if the One who searches the heart [Ps 7:10] should find in us something which would be pleasing to him, we still could not boast of it because we have nothing which we have not received. If even the acquisition and possession of external goods and intellectual abilities is not due to one's effort alone but rather presupposes God's fatherly kindness anticipating all of our own doing, then all the more in our life of grace is God the first and the last who bestows the willing and the completion [Phil 2:13]. It is his gift when we call anything of our own good. We owe it to his assistance when we succeed in preserving his gifts. Therefore, in truth, we are all poor. It only depends on recognizing this, our poverty, and spiritually making it our own, so that it may open up the kingdom of heaven for us.

It's indeed a difficult realization for human pride to recognize that of oneself, one is nothing and has nothing. When someone who grew up in wealth loses his fortune overnight, when rulers are thrust from the throne [Luke 1:52], when a serious illness suddenly tears a person of flourishing health and energy from his sphere of activity and sentences him to inactivity, when a man of high moral standards who believed himself a match for every temptation unexpectedly falls—in all these cases, knowledge of one's own poverty and frailty may lead to the verge of despair. But whoever dares to look the nothingness of one's own existence straight in the eye will see the towering rock of infinite and eternal being appear behind it. The powerful hand which hurled him down from his supposed height is strong enough to raise him up again and is rich enough to compensate a thousandfold for what it took from him. If he brings himself to grasp this hand, then he will experience that it is the hand of a benevolent Father. He will become a child who willingly lets himself be led because the Father knows the way which he himself doesn't know. He will entrust the care for his life to the Father because he has certainly experienced that he himself is incapable of caring for himself in the right way. And with ever new admiration and gratitude, he will experience how he is now cared for in the best possible way. Thus, a deep sense of security, certainty, and rest will come over him, a peace like he has never known. The kingdom of heaven is his—not only as something promised him for future life, but rather, as something which has already now dawned, a preliminary stage and a guarantee of future glory. The more thoroughly he renounces everything of his own and the more he immerses himself in the child relationship to God, the more he will "taste and see how sweet the Lord is" [Ps 34:8].

The kingdom of heaven in which the poor in spirit already share on earth is peace. Because they desire nothing other than what God has intended for them, and since they have no other will than God's will, there can be no more conflict between them and God, no rebellion, no separation. And so they have already entered into his rest. Since they have no desire for other people's possessions, they rather gladly let others have whatever is placed in their hands. And since they do not consider themselves wise and are not inclined to express their view which is contrary to others, they are also above all human disputes. Certainly, they can be put in the position of having to refuse something to others—but if they deny a request, reject a strange view as erroneous, then it doesn't happen for their own sake, but rather because they act on behalf of God's truth and God's will. And at the same time, because they may be convinced that what they do is also the best for the one who opposes them, they still remain deeply in peace with him despite external opposition.

The kingdom of heaven consists in the fact that although they have nothing, they nevertheless possess everything. As God's children, they have a share in everything that belongs to the Father. They experience it in that they lack nothing, that they are nourished like the birds of the sky and clothed like the lilies of the field [Matt 6:26, 28]. At some point, it can surely be that they don't know on what they will live the next day. But at the right time, it will again be provided for them. And the riches of the heavenly Father are inexhaustibly at their disposal for others also. Hundreds of thousands [in currency] have passed through the hands of people and flowed to those in need who had no penny to call their own. And from the eternal spring of love and joy, they have raised up countless numbers of those bowed down and made them strong and happy.

The kingdom of heaven is above all, living in the state of being a child of God: the blessed certainty of being cared for by One of infinite and unchangeable kindness and love—the love of the Father who knows all of our needs and has a remedy ready for everyone by which we find comfort in every sorrow, whose infinite mercy never tires of forgiving us for what we have done wrong, and who compensates us in abundance for everything that people do to us. Experiencing this kindness of the Father in ever new and undreamed of ways—that is our blessedness on earth. Now we do not yet see God face to face, as it is promised to us. But that God lets himself be found by those who seek him with their whole heart—that we already experience in this life. God always makes himself more richly and deeply known to those who have emptied their heart of everything that can block the way to the Lord of heaven. God himself takes his dwelling in their heart and makes it his realm [John 14:23]. Those who seek the Lord meet him along all their ways. The entire creation carries his footprints; human fate and world events reveal his hidden workings. But the soul who has learned to look into one's own heart finds God most surely within himself. This inner way is the way of all mystics.

St. Teresa has incomparably described it in *The Interior Castle*. St. Augustine called for it with the words: "Do not go outside, come back into yourself. It is in the inner self that Truth dwells."[13]

"THE PRAYER OF THE CHURCH"[14]

"Through him, with him, and in him in the unity of the Holy Spirit, all honor and glory is yours, Almighty Father, forever and ever." With these solemn words, the priest ends the eucharistic prayer at the center of which is the mysterious event of the consecration. These words at the same time encapsulate the *prayer of the church*: *honor and glory to the Triune God through, with, and in Christ*. Although the words are directed to the Father, all glorification of the Father is at the same time glorification of the Son and of the Holy Spirit. Indeed, the prayer extols the majesty that the Father imparts to the Son and that both impart to the Holy Spirit from eternity to eternity.

All praise of God is *through, with, and in Christ. Through* him, because only through Christ does humanity have access to the Father and because his existence as God-man and his work of salvation are the fullest glorification of the Father; *with* him, because all authentic prayer is the fruit of union with Christ and at the same time buttresses this union, and because in honoring the Son one honors the Father and vice versa; *in* him, because the praying church is Christ himself, with every individual praying member as a part of his Mystical Body, and because the Father is in the Son and the Son the reflection of the Father, who makes his majesty visible. The dual meanings of *through, with*, and *in* clearly express the God-man's mediation.

The prayer of the church is the prayer of the ever-living Christ. Its prototype is Christ's prayer during his human life.

1. The Prayer of the Church as Liturgy and Eucharist

The Gospels tell us that Christ prayed the way a devout Jew faithful to the law prayed.[15] Just as he made pilgrimages to Jerusalem at the prescribed times with his parents as a child, so he later journeyed to the temple to celebrate the high feasts there with his disciples.

Surely he sang with holy enthusiasm along with his people the exultant hymns in which the pilgrim's joyous anticipation streamed forth: "I rejoiced when I heard them say: Let us go to God's house" (Ps 122:1). From his last supper with his disciples, we know that Jesus said the old blessings over bread, wine, and the fruits of the earth, as they are prayed to this day.[16] So he fulfilled one of the most sacred religious duties: the ceremonial Passover seder to commemorate deliverance from slavery in Egypt. And perhaps this very gathering gives us the most profound glimpse into Christ's prayer and the key to understanding the prayer of the church.

> While they were at supper, he took bread, said the blessing, broke the bread, and gave it to his disciples, saying, "Take this, all of you, and eat it: this is my body which will be given up for you."
>
> In the same way, he took the cup, filled with wine. He gave you thanks, and giving the cup to his disciples, said, "Take this, all of you, and drink from it: this is the cup of my blood, the blood of the new and everlasting covenant. It will be shed for you and for all so that sins may be forgiven." (Matt 26:26–28)

Blessing and distributing bread and wine were part of the Passover rite. But here both receive an entirely new meaning. This is where the life of the church begins. Only at Pentecost will it appear publicly as a Spirit-filled and visible community. But here at the Passover meal the seeds of the vineyard are planted that make the outpouring of the Spirit possible. In the mouth of Christ, the old blessings become *life-giving* words. The fruits of the earth become his body and blood, filled with his life. Visible creation, which he entered when he became a human being, is now united with him in a new, mysterious way. The things that serve to sustain human life are fundamentally transformed, and the people who partake of them in faith are transformed too, drawn into the unity of life with Christ and filled with his divine life. The Word's life-giving power is bound to the *sacrifice*. The Word became flesh in order to surrender the life he assumed, to offer himself and a creation redeemed by his sacrifice in praise to the Creator. Through the Lord's last supper, the Passover meal of the old covenant is converted into the Easter meal of the new covenant: into the sacrifice on the cross at Golgotha and those joyous meals between Easter and Ascension when the disciples recognized the Lord in the breaking of bread, and into the sacrifice of the Mass with Holy Communion.

As the Lord took the cup, he *gave thanks*. This recalls the words of blessing thanking the Creator. But we also know that Christ used to give thanks when, prior to a miracle, he raised his eyes to his Father in heaven.[17] He gives thanks because he knows in advance that he will be heard. He gives thanks for the divine power that he carries in himself and by means of which he will demonstrate the omnipotence of the Creator to human eyes. He gives thanks *for* the work of salvation that he is permitted to accomplish, and *through* this work, which is in fact itself the glorification of the Triune Godhead, because it restores this Godhead's distorted image to pure beauty. Therefore the whole perpetual sacrificial offering of Christ—at the cross, in the holy Mass, and in the eternal glory of heaven—can be conceived as a single great thanksgiving—as *Eucharist*: as gratitude for creation, salvation, and consummation. Christ presents himself in the name of all creation, whose prototype he is and to which he descended to renew it from the inside out and lead it to perfection. But he also calls upon the entire created world itself, united with him, to give the Creator the tribute of thanks that is his due. Some understanding of this eucharistic character of prayer had already been revealed under the old covenant. The wondrous form of the tent of meeting, and later, of Solomon's temple, erected as it was according to divine specifications, was considered an image of the entire creation, assembled in worship and service around its Lord. The tent around which the people of Israel camped during their wanderings in the wilderness was called the "home of God among us" (Exod 38:21). It was thought of as a "home below," in contrast to a "higher home."[18] "O Lord, I love the house where you dwell, the place where your glory abides," sings the Psalmist (Ps 26:8), because the tent of meeting is "valued as much as the creation of the world." As the heavens in the creation story were stretched out like a carpet, so carpets were prescribed as walls for the tent. As the waters of the earth were separated from the waters of the heavens, so the curtain separated the Holy of Holies from the outer rooms. The "bronze" sea is modeled after the sea that is contained by its shores. The seven-branched light in the tent stands for the heavenly lights. Lambs and birds stand for the swarms of life teeming in the water, on the earth, and in the air. And as the earth is handed over to people, so in the sanctuary there stands the high priest "who is purified to act and to serve before God." Moses blessed, anointed, and sanctified the completed house as the Lord blessed and sanctified the work of his hands on the seventh day. The Lord's house was to be a witness to God on earth just as heaven and earth are witnesses to him (Deut 30:19).

In place of Solomon's temple, Christ has built a temple of living stones, the Communion of Saints. At its center, he stands as the eternal high priest; on its altar he is himself the perpetual sacrifice. And, in turn, the whole of creation is drawn into the "liturgy," the ceremonial worship service: the fruits of the earth as the mysterious offerings, the flowers and the lighted candlesticks, the carpets and the curtain, the ordained priest, and the anointing and blessing of God's house. Not even the cherubim are missing. Fashioned by the hand of the artist, the visible forms stand watch beside the Holy of Holies. And, as living copies of them, the "monks resembling angels"[19] surround the sacrificial altar and make sure that the praise of God does not cease, as in heaven so on earth. The solemn prayers they recite as the resonant mouth of the church frame the holy sacrifice. They also frame, permeate, and consecrate all other "daily work," so that prayer and work become a single *opus Dei* [work of God], a single "liturgy." Their readings from the holy Scriptures and from the fathers, from the menologies of the church and the teachings of its principal pastors, are a great, continually swelling hymn of praise to the rule of providence and to the progressive actualization of the eternal plan of salvation. Their morning hymns of praise call all of creation together to unite once more in praising the Lord: mountains and hills, streams and rivers, seas and lands and all that inhabit them, clouds and winds, rain and snow, all peoples of earth, every class and race of people, and finally also the inhabitants of heaven, the angels and the saints. Not only in representations giving them human form and made by human hands are they to participate in the great Eucharist of creation, but they are to be involved as personal beings—or better, we are to unite ourselves through our liturgy to their eternal praise of God.

"We" here refers not just to the religious who are called to give solemn praise to God, but to all Christian people. When these stream into cathedrals and chapels on holy days, when they joyously participate daily in worship using the "people's choral Mass" and the new "folk Mass" forms, they show that they are conscious of their calling to praise God. The liturgical unity of the heavenly with the earthly church, both of which thank God "through Christ," finds its most powerful expression in the preface and Sanctus of the Mass. However, the liturgy leaves no doubt that we are not yet full citizens of the heavenly Jerusalem, but pilgrims on the way to our eternal home. We must always prepare ourselves before we may dare to lift our eyes to the luminous heights and to unite our voices with the "holy, holy, holy" of the heavenly chorus. Each created thing to be used in the worship service must be withdrawn from its profane use, must be purified and consecrated. Before the priest climbs the steps to the altar, he must cleanse himself by acknowledging his sins, and the faithful must do so with him. Prior to each step as the offertory continues, he must repeat his plea for the forgiveness of sins—for himself and for those gathered around him as well as for all to whom the fruits of the sacrifice are to flow. The sacrifice itself is a *sacrifice of expiation* that transforms the faithful as it transforms the gifts, unlocks heaven for them, and enables them to sing a hymn of praise pleasing to God. All that we need to be received into the Communion of Saints is summed up in the seven petitions of the Our Father, which the Lord did not pray in his own name, but to instruct us. We say it before Communion, and when we say it sincerely and from our hearts and receive Communion in the proper spirit, it fulfills all of our petitions. Communion delivers us from evil, because it cleanses us of sin and gives us peace of heart that takes away the sting of all other "evils." It brings us the forgiveness of past sins[20] and strengthens us in the face of temptations. It is itself the bread of life that we need daily to grow into eternal life. It makes our will into an instrument at God's disposal. Thereby it lays the foundation for the kingdom of God in us and gives us clean lips and a pure heart to glorify God's holy name.

So we see again how the *offertory*, *Communion*, and the *praise of God* [in the Divine Office] are internally related. Participation in the sacrifice and in the sacrificial meal actually transforms the soul into a living stone in the city of God—in fact, each individual soul into a temple of God.

2. Solitary Dialogue with God as the Prayer of the Church

The individual human soul a temple of God—this opens to us an entirely new, broad vista. The prayer life of Jesus was to be the key to understanding the prayer of the church. We saw that Christ took part in the public and prescribed worship services of his people, i.e., in what one usually calls "liturgy." He brought the liturgy into the most intimate relationship with his sacrificial offering and so for the first time gave it its full and true meaning—that of thankful homage of creation to its Creator. This is precisely how he transformed the liturgy of the old covenant into that of the new.

But Jesus did not merely participate in public and prescribed worship services. Perhaps even more often the Gospels tell of *solitary* prayer in the still of the night, on open mountain tops, in the wilderness far from people. Jesus' public ministry was preceded by forty days and forty nights of prayer (Matt 4:1-2). Before he chose and commissioned his twelve apostles, he withdrew into the isolation of the mountains (Luke 6:12). By his hour on the Mount of Olives, he prepared himself for his road to Golgotha. A few short words tell us what he implored of his Father during this most difficult hour of his life, words that are given to us as guiding stars for our own hours on the Mount of Olives. "Father, if you are willing, take this cup away from me. Nevertheless, let your will be done, not mine" (Luke 22:42). Like lightning, these words for an instant illumine for us the innermost spiritual life of Jesus, the unfathomable mystery of his God-man existence and his dialogue with the Father. Surely, this dialogue was life-long and uninterrupted. Christ prayed interiorly not only when he had withdrawn from the crowd, but also when he was among people. And once he allowed us to look extensively and deeply at this secret dialogue. It was not long before the hour of the Mount of Olives; in fact, it was immediately before they set out to go there at the end of the Last Supper, which we recognize as the actual hour of the birth of the church. "Having loved his own…, he loved them to the end" (John 13:1). He knew that this was their last time together, and he wanted to give them as much as he in any way could. He had to restrain himself from saying more. But he surely knew that they could not bear any more, in fact, that they could not even grasp this little bit. The Spirit of Truth had to come first to open their eyes for it. And after he had said and done everything that he could say and do, he lifted his eyes to heaven and spoke to the Father in their presence (John 17). We call these words Jesus' great *high priestly prayer*, for this talking alone with God also had its antecedent in the old covenant. Once a year on the greatest and most holy day of the year, on the Day of Atonement, the high priest stepped into the Holy of Holies before the face of the Lord "to pray for himself and his household and the whole congregation of Israel" (Lev 16:17). He sprinkled the throne of grace with the blood of a young bull and a goat, which he previously had to slaughter, and in this way absolved himself and his house "of the impurities of the sons of Israel and of their transgressions and of all their sins" (Lev 16:16). No person was to be in the tent (i.e., in the holy place that lay in front of the Holy of Holies) when the high priest stepped into God's presence in this awesomely sacred place, this place where no one but he entered and he himself only at this hour. And even now he had to burn incense "so that a cloud of smoke…would veil the judgment throne…and he not die" (Lev 16:13). This solitary dialogue took place in deepest mystery.

The Day of Atonement is the Old Testament antecedent of Good Friday. The ram that is slaughtered for the sins of the people represents the spotless Lamb of God (so did, no doubt, that other—chosen by lot and burdened with the sins of the people—that was driven into the wilderness). And the high priest descended from Aaron foreshadows the eternal high priest. Just as Christ anticipated his sacrificial death during the Last Supper, so he also anticipated the high priestly prayer. He did not have to bring for himself an offering for sin because he was without sin. He did not have to await the hour prescribed by the Law, and nor to seek out the Holy of Holies in the temple. He stands, always and everywhere, before the face of God;

his own soul is the Holy of Holies. It is not only God's dwelling, but is also essentially and indissolubly united to God. He does not have to conceal himself from God by a protective cloud of incense. He gazes upon the uncovered face of the Eternal One and has nothing to fear. Looking at the Father will not kill him. And he unlocks the mystery of the high priest's realm. All who belong to him may hear how, in the Holy of Holies of his heart, he speaks to his Father; they are to experience what is going on and are to learn to speak to the Father in their own hearts.[21]

The Savior's high priestly prayer unveils the mystery of the *inner* life: the circumincession of the Divine Persons and the indwelling of God in the soul. In these mysterious depths the work of salvation was prepared and accomplished itself in concealment and silence. And so it will continue until the union of all is actually accomplished at the end of time. The decision for the redemption was conceived in the eternal silence of the inner divine life. The power of the Holy Spirit came over the Virgin praying alone in the hidden, silent room in Nazareth and brought about the incarnation of the Savior. Congregated around the silently praying Virgin, the emergent church awaited the promised new outpouring of the Spirit that was to quicken it into inner clarity and fruitful outer effectiveness. In the night of blindness that God laid over his eyes, Saul awaited in solitary prayer the Lord's answer to his question, "What do you want me to do?" (Acts 9). In solitary prayer Peter was prepared for his mission to the Gentiles (Acts 10). And so it has remained all through the centuries. In the silent dialogue with their Lord of souls consecrated to God, the events of church history are prepared that, visible far and wide, renew the face of the earth. The Virgin, who kept every word sent from God in her heart, is the model for such attentive souls in whom Jesus' high priestly prayer comes to life again and again. And women who, like her, were totally self-forgetful because they were steeped in the life and suffering of Christ, were the Lord's preferred choice as instruments to accomplish great things in the church: a St. Bridget, a Catherine of Siena. And when St. Teresa, the powerful reformer of her order at a time of widespread falling away from the faith, wished to come to the rescue of the church, she saw the renewal of true interior life as the means toward this end. Teresa was very disturbed by the news of the continually spreading movement of apostasy:

...As though I could do something or were something, I cried to the Lord and begged him that I might remedy so much evil. It seemed to me that I would have given a thousand lives to save one soul out of the many that were being lost there. I realized I was a woman and wretched and incapable of doing any of the useful things I desired to do in the service of the Lord. All my longing was and still is that since He has so many enemies and so few friends that these few friends be good ones. As a result I resolved to do the little that was in my power; that is, to follow the evangelical counsels as perfectly as I could and strive that these few persons who live here do the same. I did this trusting in the great goodness of God.... Since we would all be occupied in continual prayer for those who are the defenders of the Church and for preachers and for learned men who protect her from attack, we could help as much as possible this Lord of mine who is so roughly treated by those for whom He has done so much good; it seems these traitors would want Him to be crucified again....

O my Sisters in Christ, help me beg these things of the Lord. This is why he has gathered you together here. This is your vocation.[22]

To Teresa it seemed necessary to use:

...the approach of a lord when in time of war his land is overrun with enemies and he finds himself restricted on all sides. He withdraws to a city that he has well fortified and from there sometimes strikes his foe. Those who are in the city, being chosen people, are such that they can do more by themselves than many cowardly soldiers can. And often victory is won in this way....

But why have I said this? So that you understand, my Sisters, that what we must ask God is that in this little castle where there are already good Christians not one of us will go over to the enemy and that God will make the captains of this castle…, who are the preachers and theologians, very advanced in the way of the Lord. Since most of them belong to religious orders, ask God that they advance very far in the perfection of religious life and their vocation….

These persons must live among men, deal with men…, and even sometimes outwardly behave as such men do. Do you think, my daughters, that little is required for them to deal with the world, live in the world, engage in its business…, while interiorly remaining its strangers…; in sum, not being men but angels? For if they do not live in this way, they do not deserve to be called captains; nor may the Lord allow them to leave their cells, for they will do more harm than good. This is not the time for seeing imperfections in those who must teach….

Is it not the world they have to deal with? Have no fear that the world will forgive this deficiency; nor is there any imperfection it fails to recognize. It will overlook many good things and perhaps not even consider them good; but have no fear that it will overlook any evil or imperfect things. Now I wonder who it is that teaches people in the world about perfection, not so much that these people might seek perfection…, but that they might condemn others…. So, then, do not think that little help from God is necessary for this great battle these preachers and theologians are fighting; a very great deal is necessary….

So, then, I beg you for the love of the Lord to ask His Majesty to hear us in this matter. Miserable though I am, I ask His Majesty this since it is for His glory and the good of the Church; this glory and good is the object of my desires….

And when your prayers, desires, disciplines, and fasts are not directed toward obtaining these things I mentioned, reflect on how you are not accomplishing or fulfilling the purpose for which the Lord brought you here together.[23]

What gave this religious, who had been living prayerfully in a monastery cell for decades, the passionate desire to do something for the church and the keen eye for the needs and demands of her time? It was precisely that she lived in prayer and allowed herself to be drawn ever more deeply by the Lord into the depths of her "interior castle" until she reached that obscure room where he could say to her, "that now it was time that she consider as her own what belonged to him, and that he would take care of what was hers."[24] Therefore, she could no longer do anything more than "with zeal be zealous for the Lord, the God of Hosts" (words of our Holy Father, Elijah, which have been taken as a motto on the shield of the order). Whoever surrenders unconditionally to the Lord will be chosen by him as an instrument for building his kingdom. The Lord alone knows how much the prayer of St. Teresa and her daughters contributed to protect Spain from dissenting from the faith, and what power it exerted in the heated battles regarding the faith in France, the Netherlands, and Germany.

Official history is silent about these invisible and incalculable forces. But they are recognized by the trust of the faithful and the carefully balanced judgment of the church after extensive investigations. And our time is more and more determined, when all else fails, to hope for ultimate salvation from these hidden sources.

3. Inner Life and Outer Form and Action

The work of salvation takes place in obscurity and stillness. In the heart's quiet dialogue with God the living building blocks out of which the kingdom of God grows are prepared, the chosen instruments for the construction forged. The mystical stream that flows through all centuries is no spurious tributary that has strayed from the prayer life of the church—it is its deepest life. When this mystical stream breaks through traditional forms, it does so because the Spirit that blows where it will is living in it, this Spirit that has created all traditional forms and must ever create new ones. Without him there would be no liturgy and no church. Was not the soul of the royal psalmist a harp whose strings resounded under the gentle breath of the Holy Spirit? From the overflowing heart of the Virgin Mary blessed by God streamed the exultant hymn of the "Magnificat."

When the angel's mysterious word became visible reality, the prophetic "Benedictus" hymn unsealed the lips of the old priest Zechariah, who had been struck dumb. Whatever arose from spirit-filled hearts found expression in words and melodies and continues to be communicated from mouth to mouth. The "Divine Office" is to see that it continues to resound from generation to generation. So the mystical stream forms the many-voiced, continually swelling hymn of praise to the Triune God, the Creator, the Redeemer, and the Perfecter. Therefore, it is not a question of placing the inner prayer free of all traditional forms as "subjective" piety in contrast to the liturgy as the "objective" prayer of the church. All authentic prayer is prayer of the church. Through every sincere prayer something happens in the church, and it is the church itself that is praying therein, for it is the Holy Spirit living in the church that intercedes for every individual soul "with sighs too deep for words" (Rom 8:26). This is exactly what "authentic" prayer is, for "no one can say 'Jesus is Lord' except by the Holy Spirit" (1 Cor 12:3). What could the prayer of the church be, if not great lovers giving themselves to God who is love!

The unbounded loving surrender to God and God's return gift, full and enduring union, this is the highest elevation of the heart attainable, the highest level of prayer. Souls who have attained it are truly the heart of the church, and in them lives Jesus' high priestly love. Hidden with Christ in God, they can do nothing but radiate to other hearts the divine love that fills them and so participate in the perfection of all into unity in God, which was and is Jesus' great desire. This was how Marie Antoinette de Geuser understood her vocation. She had to undertake this highest Christian duty in the midst of the world. Her way is certainly a very meaningful and strengthening model for the many people who, having become radically serious about their inner lives, want to stand up for the church and who cannot follow this call into the seclusion of a monastery. The soul that has achieved the highest level of mystical prayer and entered into the "calm activity of divine life" no longer thinks of anything but of giving itself to the apostolate to which God has called it.

> This is repose in orderliness and, at the same time, activity free of all constraint. The soul conducts the battle in peace,

because it is acting entirely from the viewpoint of eternal decrees. She knows that the will of her God will be perfectly fulfilled to his greater glory, because—though the human will often, as it were, sets limits for divine omnipotence—that divine omnipotence triumphs after all by creating something magnificent out of whatever material is left. This victory of divine power over human freedom, which he nevertheless permits to do as it pleases, is one of the most wonderful and adorable aspects of God's plan for the world.[25]

When Marie Antoinette de Geuser wrote this letter, she was near the threshold of eternity. Only a thin veil still separated her from that final consummation that we call living in glory.

For those blessed souls who have entered into the unity of life in God, everything is one: rest and activity, looking and acting, silence and speaking, listening and communicating, surrender in loving acceptance and an outpouring of love in grateful songs of praise. As long as we are still on the way—and the farther away from the goal the more intensely—we are still subject to temporal laws, and are instructed to actualize in ourselves, one after another and all the members complementing each other mutually, the divine life in all its fullness. We need hours for listening silently and allowing the word of God to act on us until it moves us to bear fruit in an offering of praise and an offering of action. We need to have traditional forms and to participate in public and prescribed worship services so our interior life will remain vital and on the right track, and so it will find appropriate expression. There must be special places on earth for the solemn praise of God, places where this praise is formed into the greatest perfection of which humankind is capable. From such places it can ascend to heaven *for* the whole church and have an influence *on* the church's members; it can awaken the interior life in them and make them zealous for external unanimity. But it must be enlivened from within by this means: that here, too, room must be made for silent recollection. Otherwise, it will degenerate into a rigid and lifeless lip service.[26] And protection from such dangers is provided by those homes for the interior life where souls stand before the face of God in solitude and silence in order to be quickening love in the heart of the church.[27]

However, the way to the interior life as well as to the choirs of blessed spirits who sing the eternal "*Sanctus*" is Christ. His blood is the curtain through which we enter into the Holiest of Holies, the divine life. In baptism and in the sacrament of reconciliation, his blood cleanses us of our sins, opens our eyes to eternal light, our ears to hearing God's word. It opens our lips to sing his praise, to pray in expiation, in petition, in thanksgiving, all of which are but varying forms of adoration, i.e., of the creature's homage to the Almighty and All-Benevolent One. In the sacrament of confirmation, Christ's blood marks and strengthens the soldiers of Christ so that they candidly profess their allegiance. However, above all, we are made members of the Body of Christ by virtue of the sacrament in which Christ himself is present. When we partake of the sacrifice and receive Holy Communion and are nourished by the flesh and blood of Jesus, we ourselves become his flesh and his blood. And only if and insofar as we are members of his Body, can his Spirit quicken and govern us.

> It is the Spirit that quickens, for the Spirit gives life to the members. But it only quickens members of its own body.... The Christian must fear nothing as much as being separated from the Body of Christ. For when separated from Christ's Body, the Christian is no longer his member, is no longer quickened by his Spirit.[28]

However, we become members of the Body of Christ "not only through love..., but in all reality, through becoming one with his flesh: For this is effected through the food that he has given us in order to show us his longing for us. This is why he has submerged himself in us and allowed his body to take form in us. We, then, are one, just as the body is joined to the head...."[29] As members of his Body, animated by his Spirit, we bring ourselves "through him, with him, and in him" as a sacrifice and join in the eternal hymn of thanksgiving. Therefore, after receiving the holy meal, the church permits

159

us to say: "Satisfied by such great gifts, grant, we beseech you, Lord, that these gifts we have received be for our salvation and that we never cease praising you."[30]

Lecture: "Eucharistic Education"[31]

The marvelous tribute paid to the Eucharistic Savior in the declarations of these days and in the preceding weeks—with the Feasts of Corpus Christi and the Sacred Heart of Jesus and their octaves—should not be a one-time and passing thing, but rather bring forth a lasting effect in us. For that reason, we ask ourselves in silent reflection, "How can we ignite the love for the Eucharistic Savior in the hearts of others?" For that is what is meant by *teaching eucharistically*. It is understood that we, as women, are able to cooperate in a special way in this work and that all of us, regardless of the differences of our positions in life—as wife and mother, religious sister, or single, professional or self-employed woman—bring to it something we have in common. And what could that be other than the feminine heart with its desire for unlimited, self-sacrificing dedication—the heart which, in a way, has a natural kinship with the divine heart which beats for all in the tabernacle and which, for that reason, ought to be particularly receptive to the impulses of this divine heart? So we want to consider what can qualify us for the work of eucharistic education and how we can achieve it. *One* principle applies to all of us who want to teach eucharistically: we are able to do so only if we *live eucharistically*. We want to lead others to a eucharistic life, and we are able to do that only by setting an example for them. Thus, our first question will be

I. What Pertains to a Eucharistic Life?

Eucharistic living means *allowing the eucharistic truths to become effective in practice*. These truths concern essentially three simple statements of faith: 1. The Savior is present in the Blessed Sacrament; 2. he daily renews his sacrifice of the cross on the altar; 3. he wants to unite every single soul most intimately with himself in Holy Communion. First, we will ask,

1. What Do the Eucharistic Truths Demand of Us?

It's the Savior's delight to be among the children of humanity [Prov 8:31] and he has promised to be with us until the end of the world [Matt 28:20]. He has made this promise true through his sacramental presence on the altars. He waits for us here and one would think that people would throng to the sacred places. The simple meaning of this truth of faith demands that we have our home here, that we move away from here only as far as our tasks require, and that we daily accept these tasks from the hands of the Eucharistic Savior and put the accomplished day's work back into his hands.

The Savior died for us on Calvary. But it didn't satisfy him to accomplish the work of salvation for us with this sacrificial death once and for all. He wanted to personally bring the fruits of his deed to every individual. For this reason, he daily renews the sacrifice on the altar and everyone who is present with a believing heart is washed clean in the blood of the Lamb and renewed in the soul. Every Mass is intended to bring this abundance of grace to the people it can reach, i.e., those who are able to be present and to make it fruitful for themselves and others. But whoever could be present and isn't, goes past the cross of the Lord with a cold heart and tramples on his grace. The Savior lays down the fruits of the grace of the sacrifice for us not only on the altar. He wants to come to every individual and, like a mother to her child, nourish us with his flesh and blood; to enter into us himself so that we will totally enter into him and grow into him as members of his Body. The more often the union takes place, the stronger and more intimate it becomes. Is it comprehensible that anyone would evade this strongest proof of divine love, or even *once* come less to the table of the Lord than is practically possible for him? So this is what the correctly understood meaning of the eucharistic truths demand of us: to seek the Savior in the tabernacle as often as we can, to be present at the holy sacrifice as often as we can, and to receive Holy Communion as often as we can. We will now further ask,

2. What Does the Savior Give Us in the Eucharistic Life?

He awaits us in order to take all of our burdens upon himself, to comfort us, to counsel us, and to help us as our most faithful and never-changing friend.

At the same time, he allows us to *live his life together* with him, especially when we join in the *liturgy*, and by doing so, experience with him his life, suffering, death, resurrection, and ascension, and the development and growth of his church. Because we are lifted out of the confines of our existence into the vastness of God's kingdom, his concerns become ours, we become ever more deeply united with the Lord, and in him, with all who belong to him. All loneliness ceases and we are unassailably secure in the tent of the king, and walk in his light.

II. Eucharistic Education

We can and should communicate to others the life which we ourselves lead. That happens through *example, instruction,* and *habituation.*

Through example: If the eucharistic life is effective and noticeable in us as strength, peace, love, and readiness to help, and, if, on the other hand, the Eucharist is clearly the center of our life and source of all we radiate, then it has to unfold a power of attraction.

Through instruction: Instruction in the eucharistic truths is necessary. Orthodox instruction is effectively supported by the additional word and corresponding practice of the mother and the rest of the child's surroundings. The young child appears to be especially receptive to these truths and their translation into action. With older children and adults, one has to be sparing with words and wait for the desire for instruction, but always be ready and prepared for it.

Habituation: Body and soul must be formed for the eucharistic life. The earlier the formation, the more receptive is the material [i.e., the person] and the easier the formation; therefore, *early Communion.* The more frequently, the stronger the formative effect; therefore, *daily Communion.* That places certain demands on the *body* and strongly influences one's *daily lifestyle.* It likewise carefully guards the soul, *weaning it from sin*—which means considerable sacrifice for human nature. It cannot be otherwise, because yes, the Eucharistic Savior is the *crucified* Savior, and life with him is a *participation in his suffering.* He revealed to St. Margaret Mary Alacoque how dear to him the *atonement* is which his faithful make. However, total consecration to the divine heart is reached only when we have in him our home, our daily abode, and the center of our life—when his life has become our life.

Letter

To Elly Dursy, May 7, 1933[32]

Pax!

Dear Elly,

As I have just come up from the chapel where the Most Blessed Sacrament is exposed (and where *coram Sanctissimo* [before the Most Holy] a choral High Mass was sung—a horrendous thing for an ultra-liturgist!) I would like to bring you greetings from our Eucharistic Savior, and at the same time, an affectionate reproach for letting yourself be led astray by a few printed words about something you have experienced before the tabernacle for so many years. Dogmatically, I believe the matter is very clear: the Lord is present in the tabernacle in his divinity and in his humanity. He is not present for his own sake but for ours: it is his delight to be with the "children of men." He knows, too, that, being what we are, we need his personal nearness. In consequence, every thoughtful and sensitive person will feel attracted and will be there as often and as long as possible. And the practice of the church, which has instituted perpetual adoration, is just as clear.

Furthermore, let me bring in a crown witness about whose liturgical expertise you can have no doubt: Father Archabbot [Raphael Walzer of Beuron]. Some years ago, he said to me: "It's a fact, isn't it, that you are not *liturgical*, you're Catholic!" (You see, he was so fed up with having people come to him to tattle about the liturgy.) Besides, remember that we are not meant to have heaven on earth. I believe if you were more aware how many thousands are now driven to despair, you would yearn to relieve them of some of that surfeit of need and pain.

Which brings me to your first question: the meeting in Karlsruhe cannot be held because of the great crisis now engulfing all of the Catholic educational system. Therefore I will not go either. Our institute has been drawn into the crisis. I am not permitted to give any lectures this semester (because of my Jewish descent). Provision has been made for me for the time being, because there is still some hope that my academic research activity may in some way continue to benefit the Catholic cause. I do not believe, however, in any return to the institute nor, for that matter, in any possibility of a teaching career in Germany. I will stay here for the time being until the situation is clearer. Don't worry about me. The Lord knows what he has in mind for me.

Most cordially, your

Edith Stein

CARMELITE MYSTICISM

INTRODUCTION

From the time of her baptism, Edith felt drawn to the Carmelite way of life but was dissuaded by her spiritual directors out of consideration for her mother and because of the good they believed she could accomplish in the active apostolate. She wrote, "I always had the Mount of Carmel before my eyes."[1] And so she did not hesitate to begin incorporating a contemplative life into her busy apostolic life. As stated in the introduction, Edith's spiritual director, Raphael Walzer, described Edith as "mystically gifted in the true sense of the word," without seeking extraordinary mystical experiences. Rather, she simply liked to be with God. Walzer and others noted her deep absorption in prayer, evidenced by her very still, motionless posture, whether during liturgy or before the Blessed Sacrament.[2]

Interested in the body-soul-spirit constitution of the human being from the time of her dissertation, Edith investigated and pondered the workings of the soul first from a phenomenological approach, and later through the theological writings of Aquinas as well as the writings of spiritual masters such as Augustine, Pseudo-Dionysius, Teresa of Avila, and John of the Cross. In the selections taken from *The Science of the Cross* we particularly reap the benefit of her study and assimilation of the works of Teresa of Avila and John of the Cross.

The first selection from *Finite and Eternal Being* succinctly sketches John of the Cross's depiction of the ascent to Mount Carmel. It highlights the difficulty known to all who have taken time for quiet prayer—trying to become silent within oneself. Yet, led by the truth of faith, those who seek God will set out for that place within where the mystics were drawn, lingering there in dark faith with a simple loving glance of the spirit toward the God who dwells within, and remain there in deep peace. She does not say so, but the latter may very well be descriptive of Edith's own prayer experience.

The second selection, taken from *The Science of the Cross*, focuses on John of the Cross's treatment of spirit and faith, neither of which can be captured in static definitions. Edith first elucidates John's understanding of the soul as comprising both sensual (referring to the senses) and spiritual (referring to the intellect, will, memory) faculties whose activities are closely intertwined. Since the spirit's calling is to direct its gaze to the Creator, it needs to surrender itself to God with all its faculties. This occurs progressively by means of education and detachment. Faith teaches the intellect about God's qualities and works. In this connection, faith signifies the revealed truths or doctrinal content offered to the intellect. The intellect's acceptance of these truths is its first step into the dark night of faith, and here, faith denotes the personal act of belief. By the life of faith, the spirit raises itself above its natural activity without separating itself from it. In fact, the world of faith provides the natural spiritual activities with new material for engagement by means of meditation. Through this engagement of both the sensual and spiritual faculties, the soul comes to love and know God more deeply. After lengthy practice in the spiritual life, the soul is content to remain in loving surrender in God's presence. This form of acquired contemplation is also a form of the personal act of faith. The point of such surrender to God in faith places one on the threshold of the mystical life, at the entry to the transformation brought about by the night of the spirit. Here, the soul needs to detach itself even from God's supernatural communications and gifts in order to gain God, the giver, not the gifts. God's intervention is required for this by means of the dark, mystical contemplation in which the soul realizes that human salvation came about by Christ's extreme humiliation and annihilation on the cross. The soul then understands that the midnight darkness of faith experienced in the annihilation of everything sensory, as well as everything spiritual, will also lead to her union with God.

In the third selection, also from *The Science of the Cross*, Edith delves into the distinctions made by John of the Cross regarding the three kinds of union with God and compares John's thought with that of Teresa of Avila. Crucial to her discussion is Edith's understanding of "person" as a being who is conscious of his or her own being as distinct from all others and is a free, self-determining "I." Within her exposition, she also describes living faith as a firm conviction about God's existence, an acceptance of what God has revealed, and a loving readiness to be led by God's will. Living faith is placed in us as a seed that we need to care for so that it will lead us to union with God in this life and in the future life of glory. Edith then tries to delineate the difference between indwelling grace and the union of love by analyzing Teresa's description of her experience of the "prayer of union." Teresa urged her sisters to strive for the highest level of the life of grace—perfect union of one's will with the divine will through the perfect practice of love of God and neighbor—and equally taught that it was useless to attempt to reach that type of union that only God can give. The prayer of union described by Teresa is only a step toward the union about which John speaks as the goal of the dark night. Edith's ability to point out and offer possible explanations for some apparent discrepancies between the two spiritual masters demonstrates her close reading and study of both writers.

After her analysis, Edith presents the objective differences between the three modes of God's indwelling presence. Love's highest fulfillment—the intertrinitarian divine life of being-one in free mutual surrender—is the model for the human being's yearning love that strives to ascend and God's merciful love that reaches down. She cleverly applies Augustine's comparison of catechumens who profess their faith in Christ but do not yet receive him in the Eucharist to the two modes of indwelling by grace and union. The indwelling by grace imparts the virtue of faith; in the indwelling of mystical election God grants a personal encounter through a *touch* in the soul's inmost being, granting enlightenment about God's nature and decrees. Edith also discerns a difference between the loving surrender in mystical marriage and the unconditional surrender of one's will to the divine will. In mystical marriage, the soul learns to know God and her inmost depths in a new manner. At this point, the soul has a greater knowledge of the God to whom she surrenders her will, what she surrenders, and what this surrender can demand from her.

EDITH STEIN

THE TEXTS

Finite and Eternal Being

CHAPTER VII. §9.4.
THE INTERIOR OF THE SOUL[3]

...If one really withdraws from all that into the interior of the soul, then there is certainly not nothing, but an unaccustomed emptiness and silence. Listening to the "beat of one's own heart," i.e., to the being of the inner soul itself, is not able to satisfy the craving for the life and action of the "I." And so it will not stay here for long if it is not held by something else, if the interior of the soul is not filled and moved by something other than the outer world. But that is what the experts of the "interior life" of all times have experienced. They were drawn into their innermost being by something which drew them more strongly than the entire outer world. They experienced there the onset of a new, powerful, higher life, of the supernatural, divine. "...If you are indeed searching for a high place, a holy place, then pray within yourself as the temple of God. 'Because the temple of God is holy, and you are the temple.' Do you want to pray in the temple? Pray in yourself. But first, you are to be God's temple, for God listens to the one praying in his temple."[4] "Call me back from errors: You are my guide—and I retreat into myself and into You."[5] The mystical grace bestows as experience what faith teaches: the indwelling of God in the soul. Whoever, led by the truth of faith, seeks God, will set out by his free effort precisely to there, where the mystically graced are drawn—withdrawing himself from the senses and the "images" of the memory, yes, even from the natural activity of the intellect and will into the empty solitude of his interior in order to linger there in dark faith—in a simple loving upward glance of the spirit to the hidden God who is presently veiled.[6] Here he will remain in deep peace—as at the place of his rest—until it pleases the Lord to transform faith into seeing. Indicated in a few strokes, this is the *ascent* to Mount Carmel as our holy father John of the Cross has taught it.[7]

The Science of the Cross

9. The Activity of the Spirit[8]

B. Reciprocal Illumination of Spirit and Faith

1) Retrospect and Prospect

Here the *Ascent of Mount Carmel* comes to an abrupt end. We do not know whether the work was ever completed or whether a completed manuscript was not preserved. The treatise on joy was never finished, and the other passions are not treated at all. The aforementioned sections on the passive purification are expounded in the *Dark Night*. Furthermore, it is remarkable that there are direct interpretations of the indicated poem only at the outset, then the exposition moves further and further away from the poem ever broaching new questions. Here, too, the *Dark Night* offers a completion. In the last sections, the verses actually serve as guides. In any case, at the third strophe of verse 1, the explanation breaks off as suddenly as does the *Ascent* in the very midst of the treatise on joy. One can probably understand the fragmentary and, when viewed at times in hindsight, rather discordant aspects of these writings when considering the circumstances and the manner in which they came into being. John did not write them as an artist who wishes to form a fully conceived and well-rounded whole. Nor did he want to construct, as a theologian, a system of mysticism nor, as philosopher and psychologist, a complete, extended doctrine on the passions. He wrote as a father and teacher for his spiritual sons and daughters. He wished to comply with their request that he explain his spiritual songs. He meditated on the inner experience that had found expression in this manner and wanted to translate the images into the language of intelligible thought. Probably he noticed only while at work what preparatory considerations were necessary, what had to be brought forward, step by step, in order to make it understandable. Thus he could be led farther along some sidetracks that he had not had in mind originally. However, he never lost the trend of his thought. With a firm hand on the reins, he held the lively movement of the spirit in check and repelled the onset of a plenitude of thoughts. It must also be noted that he wrote these treatises precisely in the years in which he was most overburdened with holding offices and dealing with external affairs. Certainly he had not the leisure to compose in peace and, subsequently, to proofread and to make comparisons. It could very well be that after a lengthier interruption, he did not pick up the thread where it had slipped from his grasp, but rather set the second discourse beside the first. All of this needs to be recalled in order to assess the saint's preceding explanations correctly.

We have repeated what John said in the *Ascent* about entrance into the night of the spirit in order to see clearly what he understands as *spirit* and *faith*. For faith leads the way through the night to the goal of union with God. In faith the spirit is painfully reborn; it is remodeled from the natural to the supernatural. The explanations of spirit and faith mutually elucidate each other. Faith demands the renunciation of the natural activity of the spirit. This renunciation constitutes the active night of faith, one's own active following of the cross. To comprehend this renunciation and, thereby, faith, the natural activity of the spirit must be discussed. On the other hand, the very presence of faith reveals the possibility of a spiritual being and activity surpassing the natural, thus an explanation of faith can cast a new light on the spirit. Consequently, it will be understood that the spirit may be spoken of in different ways, in different instances. Viewed superficially, this may seem to be contradictory and disproportionate. In truth it is a pertinent necessity. For insofar as spiritual being is life and change, it cannot be captured in static definitions, but must rather be a continual movement seeking fluid expression. This is true also of faith. After all, it is of itself a spiritual being and therefore movement: an ascent to ever less conceivable heights and a descent into ever more immeasurable depths. Therefore the understanding must seek to lay hold on it by means of manifold expressions, insofar as this is at all achievable.

2) Natural Spiritual Activity:
The Soul; The Soul's Parts and Faculties

In the first place then, the natural activity of the soul must be made clear. It is the result of the way that being itself is constructed of psyche and intellect. John seeks to grasp this through the concepts imparted by Scholastic psychology that were surely familiar to him from his student days in Salamanca. The soul is a reality that has many faculties: inferior and superior, or sensual and spiritual. In both the inferior and the superior *parts*, the faculties are divided into functions of knowing and of striving. (John does not express this but it is prerequisite for his descriptions.) The *senses* are bodily organs but at the same time, they are the *windows* of the soul through which it gains knowledge of the external world. *Sensuality* therefore is common to the body and soul, but John hardly considers the bodily aspect, relatively speaking. Sensuality includes, in addition to the impressions that mediate a knowledge of the sense world, the enjoyments and the desires called forth in the soul through sensory perceptions. As has already been said, the *night of the senses* is primarily concerned with sensuality in that second aspect. In the first night, the soul is to free herself, or as the case may be, to be purified from, craving or desiring sensory gratification. Such limitation is entirely justified because enjoyment and desire are already possible on the level of a purely sensory life of the soul (therefore, in animals as well). Knowledge, on the other hand, even in the inferior form of sensory perception, is impossible without intellectual activity. Furthermore, it is desire and enjoyment which actually captivate the soul.

Sensory knowledge is impossible without intellectual activity. This states the close connection between the *superior* and the *inferior* spiritual being. They are not constructed as one story over another. Talk of superior and inferior parts is but a spatial image for a being which has nothing spatial about it at all. John says expressly, that of "the soul, insofar as it is a spirit, one cannot speak of high or low…as one can regarding quantitative bodies."[9] In the natural sphere, sensory and intellectual activities are closely intertwined. Just as the *windows of the senses* do not provide any knowledge of the sensory world if the spirit does not peer through them, so, on the other hand, it has to make use of them in order to look out into the world. Expressed in another way: the senses deliver the matter with which the spirit occupies itself. In agreement with Augustine[10] and deviating from St. Thomas, John places the memory as the third spiritual faculty beside the intellect and the will. This is not to be seen as a seriously contrary technicality since it is not a matter of an actual partitioning of the soul, rather of varying operations and of the preparation of the *single* spiritual faculty to proceed in this or that direction. Good reasons can be adduced for both divisions. Without the original achievement of the memory—the *keeping in mind*—there would be no possibility of a sensory impression or of any spiritual activity.

This is because both have a temporally successive structure and therefore it is necessary that the respective momentary contents (roughly stated) not be annihilated but preserved instead. For the actual functioning of the intellect (comparing, generalizing, making conclusions, and so on), it can be demonstrated that the other exercises of the memory (recollections and free associations by the imagination) are also necessary. But it is impossible to pursue this further here. It was merely indicated to let it be understood that one can perceive sensory and spiritual activity in the memory and consider it in relation to the other faculties.[11] On the other hand, the memory's achievements are not really acts of knowledge, but merely assist the intellect. (The same may be demonstrated respectively for the relation between the memory and the will.) All of this entitles us to see the memory as a separate faculty. For Augustine, in any case, the consideration of the trinitarian structure of the spirit was decisive for the tripartite division. For John, it was the reciprocal relationship between the three spiritual faculties and the three theological virtues. Here we touch on the decisive point of his spiritual doctrine.

3) Supernatural Elevation of the Spirit. Faith and Its Life

The spirit is dependent on the senses for its natural activity. It accepts what they offer, keeps what it perceives to be true, recalls it to view on occasion, connects it to other things, changes it, and arrives at judgments and conclusions, through making comparisons, generalizations, deductions, etc., with its conceptual knowledge. This process constitutes the actual function of the intellect.

Likewise, the will naturally occupies itself with what is provided through the senses, finds in this its joy, seeks to take possession of it, feels pain over its loss, hopes for possession, and fears loss. But it is not the spirit's calling to recognize created things and to enjoy them. To be thus involved is a perversion of the spirit's original and actual purpose for existence. It must be liberated from this captivity and elevated to the true being for which it was created. Its gaze must be directed to its Creator. It must surrender itself to him with all its faculties. This will be achieved progressively, step by step, through *a work of education and detachment*. God gives the stimulus for this and completes it, but demands the person's own spiritual effort in collaboration. Everything with which the spirit naturally occupies itself must be *taken from it*.

It must be *educated* to know God and to rejoice only in him. First of all, this is achieved by offering to the natural faculties something that attracts them more powerfully and satisfies them more than what they naturally know and enjoy. *Faith* points the intellect toward the Creator who has called every last thing into being and who is, himself, infinitely greater, more exalted, and worthier of love than all of them. Faith teaches the intellect about God's qualities and about all he has done for humankind and what the human being owes to him.

What does faith signify in this connection? Apparently, *that which* is proffered to our faith, the entirety of revealed truths proclaimed by the Church: *fides, quae creditur* [the faith that is believed— the doctrinal content]. When the intellect accepts what is offered to it, what it could not know through its own capability, then it takes the first step into the dark night of faith. But this is nothing but the *fides, qua creditur* [the faith by which it is believed—the personal act of faith], a vital activity of the spirit and, correspondingly, a *durable attitude* (*habitus* or *virtue of faith*), the conviction that God exists (*credere Deum*) [to believe God exists], and the convinced acceptance of that which God teaches through the Church (*credere Deo*) [to believe God].[12] By means of this life-in-faith, the spirit raises itself above its natural activity, but in no way detaches itself from it. Rather, in the new world that faith reveals to them, the natural spiritual faculties receive plenty of new material with which to occupy themselves.

This occupation in which the spirit interiorly assimilates the content of faith is *meditation*. Here the imagination presents itself with images of events in salvation history, seeks to plumb their depths with all the senses, weighs with the intellect their general meaning and the demands they place on one. In this way the will is inspired to love and to resolve to form a lifestyle in the spirit of faith.

John knows an even higher form of meditation:[13] a spirit that is richly endowed and vibrant by nature penetrates by means of the intellect deep into the truths of faith. It carries on a dialogue with itself, investigating all sides, proceeding thought by thought and discovering their intrinsic connections. This activity becomes even livelier, easier, and more fruitful when the Holy Spirit gives the human spirit wings and bears it aloft. The spirit feels itself so thoroughly in the hand of a superior power and enlightened by this power, that it appears to itself to have ceased all activity of its own and to be, instead, receiving instruction through divine revelation.

Whatever the spirit has elaborated through this or the other manner of operating will be its permanent possession. And this is more than a treasure of stored truths that may be recalled from the memory on demand. The spirit—and this, if one understands it in a broad and objective way, means not only the intellect but also the *heart*—has gained confidence in God through continual engagement and has come to know and love him. This knowledge and love have become a very part of the spirit's being, somewhat resembling the relationship to a person with whom one has lived a long time and whom one trusts intimately. Such persons no longer need to gather information or to think about each other to arrive at mutual comprehension and love each other. There is scarcely any need for words between them.

Of course, every time they are together again there is both a new awakening and an increase of love, perhaps also a learning of new individual traits, but this happens almost of itself, one need not trouble oneself about it. This applies to the relationship of a soul with God after a lengthy practice in the spiritual life. She no longer needs to meditate in order to love and to come to know God. The path lies far in the past, she has arrived at her goal. As soon as she sets herself to pray she is with God and, in loving surrender, remains in his presence. Her silence is more precious to him than many words. This is known today as *acquired contemplation*. (John of the Cross does not use that term but it was well known to him.)[14] It is the fruit of one's own activity but, of course, is inspired and supported by the help of many graces. It is a grace when the message of faith, God's revealed truth, reaches us. It is grace that enables us to accept this message of faith and to become *believers*—even though we must actually do so by our own free decision. Without the support of grace, prayer and contemplation are impossible. Yet, all of this is achieved by our freedom and is completed under our own power. It also depends on us whether we give ourselves to prayer, whether and how long we remain in this *acquired contemplation*. If we examine this *contemplation* itself, the peaceful, loving surrender to God, we can also claim it as a *form of faith*, the *fides, qua creditur*, not as *credere Deum* (although faith in God's existence is a prerequisite and is included in it), nor as *credere Deo* (although it is the result of all God's revealed truths we have accepted with faith). Rather it is *credere in Deum*: belief "into" God, venturing into him by faith.

This is the pinnacle of what can be attained in the life of faith by dint of one's own activity, even if, as an appropriate consequence, one's own will is surrendered to the divine and all one's doing and leaving-undone is regulated according to the divine will. Also, it already raises the spirit far above its natural conditions of being. To be sure, at first, the truths of faith bring God near to us through images and parables and concepts that derive from created things. But more than that, they teach us that God far surpasses everything created and is beyond all that can be grasped and understood. Therefore we must leave all creatures behind as well as all those faculties by which we comprehend and understand creatures in order to raise ourselves in faith to God, the inconceivable and incomprehensible one. But neither the senses nor the intellect are capable of raising us to God if we understand that capability as thinking in tangible concepts.

When we surrender to the incomprehensible God in faith we are *pure spirit*, freed from all images and concepts—therefore in darkness, because the world we see by day is constructed of images and concepts—*detached* also from the mechanism composed of manifold powers, and *unified* and *simple* in a life that is at once knowledge, remembrance, and love. Herewith we are only at the threshold of the mystical life, at the entrance to the transformation that is to be reached through the night of the spirit. But we have reached something that was not touched when the faculties were suspended. For, after all, something must remain if union with God and transformation in God is still possible after a suspension of the faculties. And this something beyond [sensuality] and the intellect dependent on the sense must only then be what is, *in the proper sense, the spirit.* John also speaks of the *substance of the soul* in this connection.

In its substance, the soul is spirit and receptive in her inmost being for all that is spiritual, for God, the pure Spirit, and for all creatures that are also spiritual according to their inner essence. But she is buried in corporeality and has senses which are bound to the body as receptive organs for whatever is material. As a consequence of the fall, these servile organs have become ruling ones. In order to regain strength for a purely spiritual life and activity and to have mastery over the senses, the spirit must first be freed from their grasp. We have followed the action of faith in this liberating process to a certain point: how it directs the spirit toward God and finally raises it to a purely spiritual relationship with God. Something else must be added that will render our attitude to God more perfect: a turn away from all that is not God. This is the principal task achieved in the active night of the spirit.

4) Extraordinary Graces Imparted and Detachment from Them

It has been said that faith attracts the spiritual faculties and inspires them to be occupied with God and with divine things. But by no means does this signify that detachment from the created world has been achieved. Even persons who have seriously resolved to lead a spiritual life and who persevere in the effort, devote only a lesser or greater part of the day to prayer and meditation. For the rest, they have both feet firmly planted on the ground of the created world. They take pains to penetrate this world intellectually and to gain mastery over it, to acquire temporal goods and to enjoy them. They still succumb to the captivating magic of natural goods and do not yet reject that which satisfies the senses even though, perhaps influenced by their prayer life, they already set up extensive barriers in this direction.

So their intellect is occupied, to the point of exhausting its energy, with the things of this world, their imagination filled with these things, their will's efforts directed toward them, and their passions set on them. All of this inhibits the prayer life within and would, finally, completely annihilate it if God did not come to the help of the soul with the particular support of his grace. However, this happens, and indeed, not only through the message of faith but through extraordinary communications that are able to surpass the attractions of the natural world and to make them ineffective. Images are offered to the senses and to the imagination that excel all things terrestrial. The intellect is raised through supernatural enlightenment to insights it could never attain through its own intellectual endeavors. The heart is filled with heavenly consolation before which all earthly joys and satisfactions pale. In this way, the soul is readied to turn with all her might from earthly goods and to raise herself toward what is heavenly.

But this is only half the task. One would never reach the goal, union with God, if one were to stand still before these supernatural communications and wish to rest in their enjoyment. For visions, revelations, and sweet sensations are not God himself nor do they lead to him—with the exception of those most sublime, purely spiritual *touches*, in which God imparts himself to the substance of the soul and precisely in this way accomplishes that union. Therefore the soul must detach herself again, from all that is supernatural, from God's gifts, in order to win the giver, not the gifts. But what can induce her voluntarily to renounce such great goods? Here faith once more is active, teaching her that God is not anything that she is capable of grasping and understanding, and invites her to that dark way that alone leads to the goal.[15] But faith would achieve little were it only to turn to the intellect with instructive words. The powerful reality of the natural world and the supernatural gifts of grace must be upset by an even mightier reality. This takes place in the passive night.

Without this passive night—as John repeatedly insists—one would never arrive at the goal. The strong hand of the living God must intervene to free the soul from all the bonds of created things and draw her to himself. This intervention is the *dark, mystical contemplation*, joined to *detachment* from all that which so far has given light, support, and consolation.

10. Dark Contemplation

C. Death and Resurrection

1) Passive Night of the Spirit

A. FAITH, DARK CONTEMPLATION, DETACHMENT.

We already know from the *Night of the Senses* that a time arrives at which all taste for spiritual exercises as well as for all terrestrial things is taken away from the soul. She is put into total darkness and emptiness. Absolutely nothing that might give her a hold is left to her anymore except faith. Faith sets Christ before her eyes: the poor, humiliated, crucified one, who is abandoned on the cross even by his heavenly Father. In his poverty and abandonment she rediscovers herself. Dryness, distaste, and affliction are the "purely spiritual cross" that is handed to her. If she accepts it, she experiences that it is an easy yoke and a light burden. It becomes a staff for her that will quickly lead her up the mountain.

When she realizes that Christ, in his extreme humiliation and annihilation on the cross, achieved the greatest result, the reconciliation and union of mankind with God, there awakens in her the understanding that for her, also, annihilation, the "living death by crucifixion of all that is sensory as well as spiritual" leads to union with God.[16] Just as Jesus in the extreme abandonment at his death surrendered himself into the hands of the invisible and incomprehensible God, so will the soul yield herself to the midnight darkness of faith which is the only way to the incomprehensible God. Then she will be granted mystical contemplation, the "ray of darkness,"[17] the mysterious wisdom of God, the dark and general knowledge that alone corresponds to the unfathomable God who blinds the understanding and appears to it as darkness. It floods the soul and does this all the more easily the more the soul is free from all other impressions. This wisdom is something much purer, more tender, spiritual, and interior than all that is familiar to the intellect from the natural life of the spirit. Also raised above temporality, it is a true beginning of eternal life in us. It is not a mere acceptance of the message of faith that has been heard, nor a mere turning of oneself to God, who is known only from hearsay, rather it is an interior *being touched* and an *experience* of God that has the power to detach the soul from all created things, and to raise her, simultaneously plunging her into a love that does not know its object.

14. The Kinds of Divine Union[18]

E. THE DIFFERENT KINDS OF UNION WITH GOD

We must remember here that John has distinguished three kinds of union with God.[19] By means of the first, God dwells substantially in all created things and sustains their existence. By the second, we are to understand the indwelling of God in the soul through grace; by the third, the transforming union through perfect love that divinizes the soul. As John states at the quoted source, between the second and third kinds, there is only a difference in degree. If we look at other passages and evaluate the matter as a whole, there seems to be a difference in kind, and within each of the kinds, a series of steps. In the *Spiritual Canticle*, for instance, the saint mentions the same three categories, without speaking of only a degree of difference between God's presence by grace and that by love. Rather, he emphasizes the perceptible feeling of the presence of the highest good in the union of love and what it effects: the ardent longing for the unveiled beatific vision of God.[20]

Our holy Mother, St. Teresa, has also been greatly occupied with this question. In the *Interior Castle*,[21] she says that through the prayer of union, she came to know the article of faith that God is in everything through his essence, his presence, and his power. She had only known, before that, of the indwelling through grace. Now she consulted various theologians in order to gain clarity about her discovery. A "half-learned man" also knew only of the indwelling through grace. But others were able to confirm for her that the enlightenment she received through her experience of union was an article of faith. Perhaps if we attempt a comparison of our order's founders' presentations which differ so much from each other, it will help us gain greater objective clarity.

They agree on the article of faith, which was familiar to John, the theologian, while Teresa had to discover it at first: God the Creator is present in each thing and sustains it in existence. He has foreseen each, and knows it through and through with all its changes and destinies. By the might of his omnipotence he can do with each, at every moment, whatever he pleases. He can leave it to its own laws and the normal flow of events. He can also intervene with extraordinary measures. God dwells in this manner in every human soul, also. He knows each one from all eternity, with all the mysteries of her being and every wave that breaks over her life. She is in his power. It is up to him whether he leaves her to herself and the course of worldly events or whether, with his strong hand, he will interfere in her destiny. Such a marvel of his power is every rebirth of a soul through sanctifying grace.

John and Teresa again agree that God's indwelling through grace is different from the presence common to all creatures by which he maintains their existence. With "essence, presence, and power," God can be in the soul without her knowing or willing it even when she lives hardened in sin at the utmost distance from God. It is possible that she does not perceive the slightest effect of his presence. The indwelling by grace is possible only in personal-spiritual beings, for it requires the free acceptance of sanctifying grace by the recipient. (At the baptism of infants, this free acceptance is made by adults as proxy and is later personally ratified through the baptized person's whole life of faith, and expressly in words at the renewal of the baptismal vows.) Herein lies the implication that, in this second mode, God cannot dwell in a sinful soul who has turned away from him. *Sanctifying grace*, after all, is called that because it wipes out sin.

By reason of its own nature, the indwelling through sanctifying grace is impossible in non-personal, that is, subhuman beings. It denotes that divine being and life continually flow into the graced soul. Divine Being, however, is personal life and can only flow in where one personally admits him. For that precise reason, it is impossible to receive grace without its being freely accepted. It results in a being-within-each-other such as is possible only where a genuine *interior being*, that is, a spiritual one, is available. Only in that which lives spiritually can spiritual life be received. The soul in which God lives through grace is not an impersonal stage on which divine life appears, rather she is herself drawn into this life.

The divine life is tri-personal life. It is the overflowing love with which the Father begets the Son and surrenders to him his own being, while the Son embraces this being and surrenders it back to the Father, the love in which Father and Son are One, which they breathe out together as their Spirit. Through grace this Spirit is poured out into hearts. Thus the soul lives her life of grace through this Holy Spirit. In him she loves the Father with the love of the Son and the Son with the love of the Father. This sharing of life with the trinitarian life can take place without the soul's awareness that the divine persons dwell in her. Actually, only a small number of elect come to perceptibly experience that the Triune God is in their soul. For a larger number, an enlightened faith leads to a living knowledge of this indwelling and to a loving communion with the divine three in pure faith.

A person who has not yet arrived at this high level is still united to God through faith, hope, and love, even when he is not clearly aware that God lives in his inmost region and that he can find him there, that all of this life of grace and virtue is an effect of this divine life in himself and is his participation therein. Living faith is the firm conviction that God exists, the acceptance-as-truth of all that has been revealed by God, and a loving readiness to be led by the divine will. As supernatural knowledge infused by God, living faith is the "beginning of the eternal life in us"[22]—but it is only a *beginning*. Through sanctifying grace, it is laid within us as a seed; under our careful custody it is to burgeon into a great tree bearing glorious fruits. For it is the way that is to lead us to union with God even in this life, though the highest fulfillment belongs to the next life.

Now we face the hard task of determining how the union of love differs from the indwelling by grace. At this point there is a divergence between our holy Mother St. Teresa's delineation and holy Father St. John's. Our holy Mother believes she has discerned the *first* mode of the indwelling in the prayer of union, which differs from the indwelling by grace, while in the *Ascent*, the union through love is to be considered a higher degree of the union of grace. Besides this, St. Teresa knows a union with God that can be attained purely through untiring cooperation with grace, through a mortification of nature, and perfect practice of the love of God and neighbor. She stresses this with particular emphasis as consolation for those who do not attain to that which is called the *prayer of union*.[23] However, earlier, she explained with as much emphasis and with all desirable clarity that the *prayer of union* can in no way be attained through one's own effort.[24] The soul is so captivated by God that she is bereft of all feeling for the things of the world while she is fully awake for God. She is "as though out of her senses" so that she has no power to think of anything.... "Here she only loves, but...does not even know how she loves, nor what it is that she does love.... The intellect would want to be wholly occupied in understanding something of what the soul is feeling; but since its powers cannot achieve this, it is so stunned that it moves neither hand nor foot."

Here, God works within the soul "without anyone—not even we—disturbing him." And what he effects in it "exceeds all joy and all delights and all the happiness on earth."[25] This condition lasts only a brief time (scarcely more than half an hour). But the manner in which God remains in the soul during that time is such "that when she comes to herself again, she cannot doubt at all that she was in God and God in her. She holds to this truth with such security that she will never forget it nor can she ever doubt it, even when God does not again grant her such a grace for years. And this happens entirely apart from the effects that remain in the soul." As long as the mysterious incident lasts, she has no perception of God. But afterward she is certain he was present.

She did not see him clearly "but for her there remains a certainty that God alone can give." There is nothing corporeal about it as there is in the invisible presence of Christ in the Blessed Sacrament. The divinity alone is present. "But how can we have such certainty about what we cannot see? That I do not know; that is God's working; but I know that I tell the truth.... It is enough for us to know that he who is the cause of it is almighty. Since we have no part at all to play in bringing it about no matter how much effort we put forth, but it is God who does so, let us not desire the capacity to understand this union."

Without intending it, our holy Mother attempted all the same to suggest some explanations. It was one explanation when she interpreted God's indwelling that she experienced with such unshakable certainty as that indwelling which is common to all creatures. It was also an explanation when she remarked: "I would say that whoever does not receive this certitude does not experience union of the whole soul with God, but union of some faculty or that he experiences one of the many other kinds of favors God grants souls."[26] Granted, in true union, God is united with the substance of the soul.

It is extremely valuable for us that Teresa wrote about her experience with such artlessness. She was unconcerned about the possibility that there was a theoretical explanation of the experience and unconcerned, too, about the judgment her explanation might find. Her faithful depiction can perhaps help us to recognize which kind of indwelling is described and at the same time make it possible for us to evaluate her explanation. *The soul possesses certainty that she was in God and God in her.* This certainty remains hers after the experience of union with God. It was part of the experience itself, essentially helping to construct it, even though it can only be brought into relief afterward. The consciousness of union does not join the union from without; rather it belongs to the union itself. Where such consciousness and a subsequently prominent certainty are impossible— as would be the case with a stone or a plant—such a form of indwelling or union is also impossible. So what Teresa experienced in the prayer of union is actually a different form of indwelling than that common to all creatures. And this new form of indwelling is not always really available where it would basically be possible. Teresa expresses this when she says the soul is certain that she *was* in God and God in her. It was a temporary condition. The indwelling through "presence, essence, and power," however, does not cease for a moment as long as a thing exists. Its cessation would mean annihilation for the thing.

So we hold with John of the Cross that the indwelling of the union of love differs from that which sustains all things in existence. On the other hand, our holy Mother's explanation makes it penetratingly clear that an indwelling is meant here that differs in kind from the one by grace and not merely by degree.

She emphatically urges her daughters to endeavor with all their might to attain the highest level of the life of grace that is to be reached by faithful cooperation with grace: the perfect union of the human will with the divine through the perfect practice of the love of God and neighbor. But just as decidedly, she explains that it is senseless to try to attain that union which God alone can give. By one's own effort, even when this is supported by grace, one can never arrive at having, in living reality, a feeling of God's presence and union with him. The labor of the will undergirded by grace will never produce the wonderful effect that is brought about in the brief span of the time of union: a transformation of the soul so thorough that she can scarcely recognize herself anymore. The caterpillar is transformed into a butterfly. One's own work requires many years of hard struggle to achieve something similar.

The prayer of union is not yet *the* union John always has in sight as the goal of the *Dark Night*. It is the forerunner to that and its initial stage. It serves to prepare the soul to surrender completely to God, and to awaken in her a burning longing for the return of union and to possess it permanently. This is clearly expressed in the fifth and sixth dwelling places of the *Interior Castle* where the preparation for and the consummation of the *spiritual betrothal* are described. The corresponding explanation is to be found in the exposition on the thirteenth and fourteenth stanzas of *The Spiritual Canticle*. At the two passages, John and Teresa state in full agreement that the betrothal takes place in ecstasy. God wrests the soul to himself with such force that nature nearly succumbs. For this reason, our holy Mother emphasizes that great courage is demanded to enter this betrothal.[27] And in *The Spiritual Canticle*, the frightened bride begs her Beloved to turn his eyes away when, suddenly, after she has waited, longed, and begged for such a long time, he answers and looks at her.

It is with a certain kind of contradiction, then, that we read in another passage from John that possession by grace and the possession by union correspond to each other much as do betrothal and marriage. The one is said to mean what we can obtain through the will and grace—the perfect conformity of the human will with the divine will through the complete purification of the soul—the other, the mutual complete surrender and union.[28] This contradiction can be explained in part by reason of the terminology: the expression *betrothal* apparently is not used in the same sense in both cases.

Beyond that, there is an essential difference present: what is actually mystical in one case seems to be restricted to the highest stage, while in the other explanation it begins at an earlier stage.[29] What is predominantly decisive in all these considerations is that John clearly expresses a difference between what can be attained by outward means through grace and the will and what takes place through the mystical marriage. This, apparently, supersedes the explanation from the *Ascent* that purports to see only a difference in degree between the union by grace and mystical union. Furthermore, passages can be shown in all his writings that clearly show that the beginnings of what is actually mystical are to be sought at a much lower level. We but recall those *touches* in the substance of the soul of which there was talk in the *Ascent*.[30] It is said of them that they make the intellect experience God in an exceptionally sublime and delightful way that has no proportion at all to the works the soul has performed, that one can only prepare oneself to receive them but in no way can one produce them. They are produced passively in the soul and are intended to lead to union with God.

All of this indicates something that lies outside the *normal paths of grace*: a temporary union that gives a foretaste of the lasting one.

How are we to understand why John of the Cross does not express himself clearly and unequivocally in this decisive question? To answer that with certainty we would need to know more about the personal life of the silent saint than he has divulged through his writings or entrusted to his contemporaries. We can only express as possibilities what the history of his time and the latest research on the textual history of his works reveal.[31] The great religious battles of the time, the ever-widening spread of heresies, the dangers of an unhealthy mysticism had led to a strict supervision of religious literature. Everyone who wrote about questions of the interior life had to reckon that the Inquisition would lay hands on him and his work. It is conceivable that John, out of foresight, was careful to make a sharp distinction between his doctrine and that of the *Alumbrados* (as occurs obviously in some passages) and endeavored to connect the mystical process as closely as possible to the *normal path of grace*.

That such an intention determined the editions of his writings has been verified by the comparisons made between the older publications and the manuscripts, and of the manuscripts among themselves. *The Living Flame* and *The Spiritual Canticle* are available in two manuscript versions. The editing apparent in the later versions demonstrates that keen statements were softened and explanations inserted in an effort to prevent misinterpretation. Do these changes date back to the saint himself or were they undertaken by an anonymous hand? Only one manuscript version of *The Ascent* and one of *The Night* has come down to us. The difference between these manuscripts and all older printed versions down to the first critical one of P. Gerardo (as well as the difference between the old printed versions of *The Living Flame* and the first handwritten version on which they are based) is so considerable that the mutilation here by alien hands cannot be denied. *The Ascent* and *The Night* are available only in fragments. In both cases, those sections are missing in which union might be spoken of in detail and clarification found for the questions that preoccupy us now.

Were these sections never written or were they suppressed in the copies? (All four major treatises are extant only in copies; we do not have any original manuscripts; only one copy of *The Spiritual Canticle* contains corrections in the saint's own hand.) And was such suppression made at the direction of the author or did an alien will decree it? We have no answer to any of these questions.

Out of a desire to arrive at clarity, we have taken refuge in our holy Mother's unconstrained descriptions. They give us certitude where the differing formulations in John of the Cross allow doubts to arise. As totally authentic factual accounts, hers are not merely an invaluable documentation enabling one to arrive at one's own theoretical understanding. We also have a right to assume that the two saints were of one mind in their grasp of the essentials of the interior life—despite all their differences in character, in literary individuality, as well as of their types of sanctity, and their evaluation of nonessential mystical graces.

The Interior Castle and the writings of our holy Father St. John were composed after the two had lived in Avila for years exchanging their most intimate thoughts. Our holy Mother consequently called her youthful collaborator the "father of her soul,"[32] and John occasionally made reference to her writings to avoid having to write explanations that could be found there.[33] Therefore, if we find in her explanation of the different stages of mystical union something that can be unmistakably distinguished in kind from the union of grace, we may be convinced that what we have before us had John of the Cross's approbation. And so we come through the combination of the explanations of both parents of our order to a confirmation of the view that the three named modes of God's indwelling are not mere gradations but rather differences in kind. We will seek now to establish their objective differences more precisely.

It is the same one God in three persons who is present in each of the three modes, and his immutable being is the same in all three modes. Still the indwelling is different because that wherein dwells the one and same unchanged deity changes its mode of being each time. Thus the nature of the indwelling is modified.[34] The first mode of indwelling—or better, of the divine presence, since it is not yet strictly speaking a dwelling *within*—requires from that within which God is present nothing more than subjection to God's knowledge and might, as well as its dependence on the divine being for its existence. All this is common to all creatures. Divine and created being remain totally separate; the only relation between them is the unilateral dependence for existence, which does not signify an actual "in-one-another," and so no actual *in*dwelling. For, to be an indwelling, both sides must have an inner being, that is, a being that contains itself interiorly and can receive another being within itself, so that without the accepted and the accepting beings ceasing to be independent, a unity of being comes into existence. This is only possible in spiritual being: only what is spiritual is self-contained and can take within itself another being, again only a spiritual one. This alone is authentic indwelling. The indwelling by grace is already something of this kind.

Whoever is subject to God's being, wisdom, and power, not without his own knowledge and willingness, but indeed says yes to this, takes God into himself, and his being is penetrated by the divine being. But this is not complete penetration. It only extends as far as the recipient's capacity permits. In order to be completely penetrated by the divine being—this constitutes the perfect union of love—the soul must be detached from every other being: empty of all other creatures and of itself, as our holy Father St. John has so emphatically explained. Love's highest fulfillment is "being-one" in free mutual surrender: this is the inter-trinitarian divine life. The *creature's aspiring, yearning love* (*amor, eros*) that strives to ascend, and God's merciful, condescending love for his creatures (*caritas, agape*) aim for this fulfillment. Where these two meet, the union can progressively happen: at the expense of whatever still stands in its way, and in the measure in which this obstacle is destroyed. As we know, this happens both actively and passively in the *Dark Night*. Through its own efforts to purify itself, the human will enters more and more into the divine will, but in such a manner that the divine will is not felt as a present reality; rather it is accepted in blind faith. Here there is actually only a difference in degree between the indwelling by grace and the union of love. In the purification passively experienced through the consuming fire of divine love, on the contrary, the divine will penetrates the human will more and more by allowing itself to be felt simultaneously as a present reality. Here, in my opinion, there is a new mode of indwelling that differs not only in degree from that of the indwelling by grace. The difference is made clear in connection with the explanation that St. Augustine gives to the words in the Gospel of John: "Many believed in his name, ... Jesus himself, though, did not entrust himself to them."[35]

Augustine applies this to the catechumens: they already profess their faith in Jesus Christ, but he does not yet give himself to them in the Most Blessed Sacrament. We can also apply it to the two modes of the indwelling whose differences we want to grasp, and at the same time, to the difference between faith and contemplation. The indwelling by grace imparts the virtue of faith, that is, the strength to accept as real what one cannot perceive as present and to hold as true what one cannot strictly prove on rational grounds. It is like the case of a person about whom you have heard many good and great things. He has bestowed on you many benefactions and given many gifts. Therefore you are inclined to him in love and gratitude and have, increasingly, the desire to get to know him personally. But he has not yet *confided* himself to you, his protégé; not even in the very least degree of allowing a meeting. Even less has he revealed to you his inner thoughts or even made you a gift of his heart. But all of this is granted—again in an ascent by steps—to the human being by God in the third mode of indwelling, that of mystical election. God grants him a personal encounter through a *touch* in his inmost region. He opens to him his own inner being through particular enlightenment about his nature and his secret decrees. He gives him his heart—at first in a momentary transport by a personal meeting (in the prayer of union),[36] then as a permanent possession (in mystical betrothal,[37] and marriage[38]).

All of this is not a gaze from face to face—it is here that the image of the development of the attraction between human beings fails. But as far as a person-to-person encounter and therefore an experiential recognition is concerned, that already has taken place on the lowest step. God touches with his being the inmost region of the soul (which our holy Father St. John also calls her *substance*). God's essence however is nothing other than his *being* and himself. He is himself a person, his *being* is personal being; the inmost region of the soul is the heart and fountainhead of her personal life and at the same time the actual place where she meets other personal life. It is only possible for one person to touch another in their inmost region; through such a touch one person gives the other notice of his presence.[39] When one feels one has been touched interiorly in this manner, one is in lively *contact* with another person. This is not yet a union, but merely the point of departure thereto. However, compared to the indwelling by grace, it is already a breakthrough to something new. In the former, the soul is given participation in divine being, but God's personal fountainhead remains hidden and does not enter into the sharing of being. Here the fountainhead of the divine life (insofar as one can speak of it) makes contact with the fountainhead of the human-spiritual life and by that touch is manifested as distinctly present. But still the divine source remains in darkness and locked away. When the divine mysteries are illuminated, the *locked inner region* of God opens up. When the soul experiences the influx of the divine being into her own in the communication of grace, then she enters into divine life. In the union (with its various stages) a becoming-one is accomplished, proceeding from [their] personal fountainhead of life through mutual personal surrender.

Here some different things must be mentioned: the indwelling by grace is not necessarily a prerequisite for a simple touch in the inmost region. It can be given to a total unbeliever to cause an awakening of faith and as preparation for the reception of sanctifying grace. It can also serve as a means of making an unbeliever capable of serving as a tool for certain purposes. Particular illuminations may be given for either of these same reasons. Union, on the contrary, as mutual surrender, cannot happen without faith and love, that is, not without sanctifying grace. Were it to start within a soul that is not in the state of grace, its beginning would have to coincide with the gift of sanctifying grace and as a prerequisite for the latter, perfect contrition. These possibilities confirm the basic difference between union by grace and mystical union, and between the corresponding ways of indwelling. It is a matter of two different ways of gradual ascent. But it does not preclude the preparation of the way to mystical union through a life of grace.

That the inmost region of the soul is fundamentally the place of personal encounter and union makes it understandable—as much as it is possible to speak of understanding where divine mysteries are concerned—that God has chosen the inmost region of the soul as his dwelling. When union is the goal for which souls are created, then the condition which makes this union possible must, after all, exist from the beginning.

It is likewise understandable that this inmost region of the soul is given into the hand of the soul along with the freedom to dispose of it, since loving surrender is only possible for a free being. Is this loving surrender in mystical marriage on the side of the soul still something other than the unconditional surrender of her will to the divine will? Apparently yes. It differs according to the degree of *knowledge*: when God gives himself to her in mystical marriage, she learns to know God in a manner in which she had not known him earlier, and in which she cannot know him by any other means. Nor had she come to know, before this, her own inmost depths. So, until now, she had not at all really known, as she does now, to whom she surrenders her will, what it is that she surrenders, or what this surrender to the divine will can demand from her.

There is a difference according to the *will* also: in the *goal*, for the surrender of the will is the union of one's own will with the divine *will*, not with the heart of God, nor with the divine *persons*; in the *point of departure*, for only now is that deepest fountainhead attained, only now does the will involve itself fully because only now does it enfold the whole person from her personal center; in the *consummation*, for in the bridal surrender not only is one's own will subordinated and conformed with the divine one, but the divine surrender is also received. For this reason, in surrendering one's own person, one takes possession of God in a way so daring that it surpasses all human understanding. John of the Cross gives clear expression to this when he says that the soul can now give God *more* than she is herself: she gives to God, God himself in God.[40] So it is that there is something in *essence* that differs from the union of grace: a being drawn to the utmost limit within the divine being. This divinizes the soul herself. It is a union of persons that does not end their independence, but rather has it as a prerequisite, an interpenetration that is surpassed only by the circumincession of the divine persons upon which it is modeled.

This is the union that John unmistakably has as the goal before his eyes in all his writings, even though he often uses the word in a different sense and has not delineated its characteristics as sharply against the other modes as we have endeavored to do here. It has been said, in anticipation, that the mystical marriage is union with the Triune God. As long as God touches the soul only in darkness and hiddenness, she can only feel the personal touch as just that without also perceiving whether it is *one* person who touches or whether there are more. But once she is completely drawn into the divine life in the perfect union of love, it can no longer be concealed from her that it is a tri-personal life and she must establish contact with all three divine persons.[41]

RELIGIOUS/SPIRITUAL FORMATION OF THE HUMAN BEING

INTRODUCTION

In contrast to Eternal Being, the visible world of earthly reality is a world of becoming where "every formed thing bears within itself possibilities of future actualization" and is subject to "becoming and passing away, change and transformation."[1] Moreover, that which is living is "never finished. It is forever on the way to its own self, but it bears within itself—i.e., within its soul—the power of forming itself."[2] These thoughts from Edith's ontology, which emphasize that the process of becoming characterizes the created world, also underlie her holistic perspectives on the education and formation of the human being. She understands education to involve the "formation of the whole human being to that which he is supposed to be. This process includes body, soul, and spirit with all their faculties."[3] Edith addresses the needs of each of these aspects in several of her writings, but the selections here from her lectures focus on religious education or formation, or what today's reader would understand as spiritual formation in a religious sense. As already stated, for Edith, the notion of "spiritual" was not limited to a religious sense, but applies to the functions of the higher faculties of the soul—intellect and will.

As noted in chapter 7, the German word *Bildung* can be translated as both "education" and "formation." In the following selections, I have tried to choose the translation that best fits the context, although at times it seems that either would be appropriate. However, whenever "education" is used, the reader needs to keep in mind the idea of "holistic education" within the process of "becoming" what one was created to be, and not just intellectual learning.

In the first selection, "The Participation of Religious Institutions of Education in the Religious Education of Youth," Edith stresses the idea that education is a process of formation with the goal of helping to form children into God's children—God-formed, Christ-formed. Just as Vatican II emphasized the universal call to holiness in "The Dogmatic Constitution on the Church," (39–42), she is quick to point out that all Christians, not only those in religious life, are called to perfection.

Edith applies the metaphors of both the gardener and sculptor to the educator. She maintains that like a seed, an inner form lies in the human soul that must be activated so that the human essence may develop fully from within and to the outside. She further maintains that a natural striving toward God exists in every person and manifests itself as a longing for happiness and a desire for purity and goodness, even among those who have no knowledge of God. Those who are baptized also carry a seed of grace that can burst forth in supernatural life. Both of these seeds require care. More than simply positive reinforcement, Edith makes the interesting point that if naturally good behavior finds recognition, the resulting joy acts as a nutrient in the soul.

Essential to the process of religious formation is the introduction of Christ as the exterior form—the image of Christ portrayed in the Gospels, as well as the ever-living Christ found in the Eucharist who forms the soul from within. The image of Christ found in the Gospels is more powerfully portrayed by someone who has incorporated this image through long, intimate contact with Christ. By repeated reflection on the Gospels and immersion in the deeds and words of Christ, they become part of oneself, providing living strength and influencing one's decisions. The importance that Edith places on Scripture comes through beautifully when she states, "Whoever constantly attends the school of Scripture as a teachable student will take the Savior with him into *his* school, and the children will sense that he is present with them and assists with the work."

Edith believes that meditation before the tabernacle is especially fruitful. So, too, is consciously joining in Jesus' sacrifice and abandoning oneself to God during Mass so as to be transformed and offered with him. In order to understand the treasure to be found in the Eucharistic Savior, she maintains that it is essential to learn the truths of faith concerning the Eucharist. Here she names the same three truths that she notes in her lecture "Eucharistic Education," included in chapter 9. Questions about these truths can surface outside of religious instruction and the educator must be ready to respond well, but this requires the study of church teachings, the writings of the church fathers, and contemporary theological works. Edith recognizes that educators (including the religious at that time who taught in their institutions of education) have little time for that. But she stresses continuity, not quantity, in learning about the eucharistic truths. Moreover, the learning must be supported by one's own eucharistic living in which the Eucharist is the center of one's life. In some very practical examples, it is clear that Edith encourages positive means for enkindling love for the Eucharistic Savior, rather than any type of supervised or regimented practices.

The church itself also acts as a formative principle in religious education. Edith notes that numerous saints provide examples of Christian discipleship, and familiarity with church teaching enables one to respond to questions that surface when encountering other views. In addition, the church's prayer—Mass and the Liturgy of the Hours—is a powerful means of forming souls. Here, Edith displays her liturgical sensibilities regarding the celebration of the Mass during her time, but at the core stands her concern that people participate in the Mass as fully as possible. She also encourages the laity to take part in the Liturgy of the Hours.

For Edith, genuine religious formation encompasses the spirit of an apostle because the person formed in the image of Christ will love both Christ and souls. She finds no division between one's own sanctification and the apostolate. "Whoever aspires to perfection for the sake of God, seeks it not only for oneself, but rather for everyone." After her baptism, Edith herself gradually came to the conviction that the deeper one is drawn into God, the more one must go out of oneself and into the world to carry the divine life into it.[4] Or as she states elsewhere, "Penetration into the mysteries of Christianity must always lead to a transformation of one's way of life."[5]

EDITH STEIN

Taken from the lecture "The Foundations of Women's Education," the second selection is a segment focused on religious formation, which Edith considers the most important part of formation. For Edith, a living faith is a matter of the intellect, heart, will, and action. One who knows God will love God, and one who loves God will choose to serve God. Religious instruction that leads to the depths of the divinity, represents God's kindness to others, and is presented from the fullness of one's own religious life will awaken a living faith by enkindling love. In turn, love that is enkindled will want to take action through participation in Mass, the Liturgy of the Hours, and works of love.

Edith was later requested to expound on ways to attain the qualities that she attributed to woman's soul in this particular lecture— namely, wideness, stillness, emptiness of self, being self-contained, and warmth. Her response is presented in the third selection. She clarifies that it is not a matter of striving for certain qualities, but rather concerns a state of the soul that can only be brought about by grace. Our part is to open ourselves to grace by surrendering to God's will and placing our soul into God's hands. She points out that becoming empty and becoming still are closely related and then provides some practical suggestions for opening oneself to grace in daily life. In doing so, Edith demonstrates her familiarity with the demands of a very busy life. Her recommendations include attendance at Mass, Holy Communion, a brief time for silence at midday (if possible, before the Blessed Sacrament), and then at night, placing the day and all that it has held into God's hands in order to rest well and begin the next day like a new life. Notably, at Communion she recommends following Teresa of Avila's practice of asking God what God desires of us. Keenly aware of the individuality of every person, she stresses that each individual has to know how to apply her suggestions to her own circumstances. It is also important to note that Edith recognizes the need for adaptability and flexibility in terms of spiritual practices because the situation of the soul varies at different times and with different people.

The last selection includes excerpts from the lecture "The Life of Christian Women." Here again, Edith stresses that religious formation is the core of all human formation. Religious formation needs to convey the truths of faith in a manner that inspires action and promotes participation in the liturgy, an intimate relationship with God, and a eucharistic life. Only those who are themselves permeated and formed by the spirit of faith can carry out such formation work. But although Edith asserts the importance of religious formation, she is also a strong proponent of the need for a well-rounded education that includes all the various subject areas.

Like all teachers, Edith knew that despite one's best efforts, results are unpredictable. But while lack of results may keep one humble, she advises teachers not to overlook the possible positive results of their efforts that they may never know. Moreover, she reminds them that God is the first and most essential formator, not human beings.

Later in the lecture, she discusses how those called by God to the extraordinary must also endure extraordinary trials, including the dark night of the soul. In this situation, the best recourse is obedience to an enlightened spiritual director selected through God's guidance.

THE TEXTS

"The Participation of Religious Institutions of Education in the Religious Education of Youth"[6]

I was asked to speak about "Participation in the Religious Education of Youth." I found the topic in need of completion. It needs to be asked, participation *with whom* and *whose* participation? *With whom*? (Objectively), through its teaching office, the church is primarily called to the religious education of youth. It fulfills this task through Mass, the administration of the sacraments, through the word of the priest in the pulpit and in religious instruction, and through its entire pastoral activity. *Chronologically*, the first educational work usually falls to the parental home, and we all know that the most lasting effects generally come from here. In addition to the church and parental home, a third factor is the educational institution in which the maturing young people spend a major part of the period of development which is decisive for their entire life. Even if due to the failure of the first and second factors, the prospects for success for the third are extremely small, then, in any case, a large part of the responsibility still falls on the institution. Even if the child from the parental home attends school only for class time [i.e., as a day student], he can receive influences from there pointing the way for his entire life. Still greater is the possibility of an impact and hence, likewise the responsibility, when the entire education is placed in the hands of an institution. In that case, there are various possibilities, depending on whether the educational community has an interconfessional or confessional character, and whether it is secular (even if confessionally oriented) or religious. I consider it my task today to speak about the particular opportunities which are given especially to a religious institution of education for participation in the religious education of youth.

I. Religious Education

As an essential preparation for doing so, we have to address the question of what we understand by *religious education*. To shape [*bilden*] is to form a material. In common usage, education [*Bildung*] denotes both this process of forming and the result, the form which is imprinted on the material—the form which it has assumed. Four aspects pertain to educational work:

1. the form which *ought* to be achieved, that is, the *goal of education*;

2. the *material* which is to be formed, that is, the children who are entrusted to us;

3. the hands which are at work and the *tools* they employ;

4. the formation process or *educational process*.

1. The Goal of Education

First we will consider the *goal of education*. Which form are we to give the material? We are to help form the children into *God's children.* They are to become *God-formed* [cf. Lev 19:2, Matt 5:48], *Christ-formed* [cf. Rom 8:29]. In other words, they are to walk their life's journey in God's hand, unresistingly led by God's will. That automatically includes that this way will be the way of the imitation of Christ. They are to take off their own selves and put on Christ [cf. Rom 13:14, Gal 3:27], and be living members of the Body of Christ [cf. 1 Cor 12:12] through which the supernatural life of this mystical body flows. *Alter Christus*—another Christ—that is the form which is the educational goal which is to be attained. Frightening in its magnitude! But we may not reach for anything less. If one speaks of a state of perfection within the church, that doesn't mean that solely those in religious life are called to perfection. It is the distinction of religious that they have become aware of the vocation and have committed themselves to it; and indeed, in particular forms and with the particular means which the institute of consecrated life provides. However, every Christian is called to perfection.

2. The Material

Of what nature is the *material* which is to assume this form? Does it already possess an aptitude for it? Does it perhaps already carry it embryonically in itself—as an *inner form*—like the seed carries the form of the rosebush or the apple tree? Or must it be brought in from the outside like the clay of the sculptor? Children are to be formed as God's children. The work which we thereby have to achieve is, at the same time, that of both the gardener and the sculptor. In fact, an inner form lies in the human soul which must be made a driving force in order for the entire human essence to develop fully from within and to the outside. And that in a double sense. To begin with, a *natural striving toward God* lies in every creature of God, its origin and goal. It stirs in *every* human heart as a longing for happiness and as a desire for purity and goodness, even where no knowledge of God exists at all. And moreover, a seed is sown in the soul of the Christian child by the *grace of baptism* which can burst forth in supernatural life and raise its crown to the heavens. But both the natural striving for the good and that with which one is supernaturally equipped for eternal life are seeds which require care, and without care, can waste away. They are embedded in matter which puts up more or less resistance to the formation. In order to grow and make the matter compliant, they have to be made the driving force and maintained. Nutrients must be supplied and also a preformed outer form. The striving for the good grows and becomes robust if, for example, naturally good behavior finds just recognition. The joy in that is a nutrient which the soul has assimilated. Certain goals and tasks and moral role models are external forms which, first of all, give direction to the yet undetermined drive and for this reason, work formatively. The life of grace awakens and bursts forth if the image of God in its kindness and majesty steps before the awakening spirit and enkindles love and respect in the soul. It becomes formed from the outside through regular forms of prayer and worship which comply with the undetermined need for expression. That is the *positive* external care and formation which the inner forms require for their unfolding. In addition, as a *negative* complement, there is the battle against obstructive influences—wild shoots and pests, laziness and stubbornness of the matter. Thus, with the description of the educational material, the educational process is already sketched in broad outline as a growth and forming process from the interior outward which only needs certain kinds of assistance from the outside.

3. Educational Means

We have spoken in an introductory way about who is called to give the assistance. In our examples, we have only briefly touched upon the means which are to be considered for formation work. We now have to look more closely in order to see which of those are available to the religious institution of education.

The child is to become God's child; the human soul is to take on the form of Christ. Thus, *Christ himself* as the exterior form has to be introduced to the material; first of all, the *image* of Christ as of the Son of Man, as he walked this earth—the image which the Gospels portray. It is the example which the human soul can model itself on. After that, the *ever-living Christ*, who as a present reality abides among us—the Eucharistic Christ, who in the sacrament of love enters into the soul itself and then, in turn, forms it from within, and in closest relation, thereby forms the *Mystical Body of Christ*, the church with its *historical development* and its *liturgical life*, its prayer and sacrifice, which incorporates its children and imprints the form of Christ on the living members.

II. THE EDUCATIONAL WORK OF RELIGIOUS INSTITUTIONS

What is the religious institution of education able to do in order to facilitate the contact of the child's soul with Christ as the shaping form?

1. Formation through the Image of the Son of Man

Naturally, portraying the image of the Son of Man according to the Gospels is, first of all, the concern of religious instruction, and that can take place in any school. But *how* it takes place depends on the formative power of the image. It is a different matter whether someone simply reports the facts of Scripture like any other subject matter which he has made his own in terms of content, or whether someone tells of the Savior who, through long, intimate contact, has wholly assimilated his image and, to a certain extent, is permeated by him. Whoever again and again thoroughly reflects on the Gospels and with a loving soul immerses himself in the deeds and words of Christ, for him they become a part of one's self and a living strength which continually works in him. And what he then carries within will spontaneously press to his lips on this or that occasion. The teacher who so lives with the Savior will not only speak of him during religious instruction. Wherever a practical decision is concerned, his way of acting in this or that situation will appear before her and will be a guideline for the decision. With difficult, intellectual questions, as they arise, for instance, in discussions of essays, sometimes a teaching of the Savior will come to mind entirely unsought which sheds light. What especially matters for the pedagogical impact is that all of that happens entirely unsought. If the word of Scripture illuminates something which was previously obscure, then the children directly realize what living power lies hidden in the word of God. It will not be perceived as a "pious saying" if it thus surfaces in the middle of a lively thought process in an enlightening and fruitful way. Whoever constantly attends the school of Scripture as a teachable student will take the Savior with him into *his* school, and the children will sense that he is present with them and assists with the work. Thus, he will take hold of their souls. In this way, a good piece of religious educational work is achieved without being systematically planned. The soul formed by God's word works spontaneously in the same way, forming further. And where could there be better soil for such a formative effect as in a religious community whose members dutifully practice daily meditation? They only need to make this daily practice in a fruitful manner and let it take effect freely in their instructional activity—naturally, in the right place and at the right time. Then the effect on the receptive souls of the children will not fail to materialize. But it must be emphasized: never may something be drawn upon in an artificial and superficial way and in a connection where it is objectively wrong. Otherwise, the children sense an "intention which upsets"[7] and as a rule, the effect is repulsive instead of religiously formative.

2. Eucharistic Formation

The best help for attaining a living image of the Savior which forms the soul in the teacher as well as in the pupil is when contact with Christ who is present enters into the meditation on the historical Christ—first of all, *contact with the Eucharistic Savior*. Whoever has tried it knows that meditation is nowhere made more fruitful than before the tabernacle. Everyone surely knows that the same thing works quite differently at different times and under different circumstances. One may have read, heard, and spoken, and even understood a Scripture passage in a certain sense a hundred times, but it did not penetrate the interior. It lies on the surface like a seed on stony ground and cannot germinate. But someday it suddenly penetrates and in a flash becomes radiant light which shines on the mysteries of faith and illuminates one's own dark path of life. And that occurs most frequently near the Eucharistic Savior. He himself forms the soul of whoever seeks him and opens the soul to him, and places the soul in him, so to speak, like formable material in his hands. He opens the eyes of the mind so that they become clear-sighted for what is written, and the ears that they hear it, and the lips that they can announce it when and where and how it can fruitfully take place. That is only *one* of the effects which come from the Eucharistic Savior. He places his hand on us when we come to him; most strongly, naturally, when we participate in the holy sacrifice in the manner which the meaning of this sacrifice demands. That is, when we are not only present and see and hear, but rather join in the *sacrifice*, abandon ourselves entirely in order to be transformed and offered with him. In the most authentic way, the Savior can incorporate the person who comes to the altar with this disposition, making him a member of his body, a branch on the divine vine. It goes without saying that Holy Communion belongs to such participation at the sacrifice of the Mass as the fulfillment of the union. There is no stronger religiously formative effect. Here, the Savior himself is the formator and the task of the teacher is simply to lead the children to this formator.

Here the religious institution now has an immeasurable advantage over all others purely because it has the Savior in the building. Everyone who enters the enclosure of the convent surely feels something of the quiet effect which comes from this Lord of the house (even without knowing anything about the source). One sees that children are receptive to this effect if one has the opportunity to observe how many, in the course of a day, slip into the church for a few minutes for quiet conversation. Certainly, most must be given a little help so that the understanding of what they have in the Eucharistic Savior becomes apparent to them. That occurs, first of all, when it is taken to heart by them in a vivid and penetrating manner that: Christ is truly and really present in the Blessed Sacrament and only waits for us to come to him in order to allow him to shower us with his love; Christ truly and really offers himself in the holy sacrifice; Christ unites us with himself most intimately in Holy Communion. Whoever has a living faith in these truths must surely, at all costs, feel drawn to visits to the Blessed Sacrament, Mass, and Communion. Opening up these truths to the children is the task of dogmatic instruction, but the possibility is not limited to that. One also runs into such questions in other lessons—history, reading—or in conversation with the children outside of class, and then what matters is that one can instruct in the right manner. One discovers ambiguities, doubts, and difficulties about which perhaps the religion teacher has no idea at all, and for this or that reason, the children don't wish to express their views to him about them. Here, the right word can be a safeguard against grave errors. One will not always be able to find this right word on the basis of one's own unshakeable faith alone. An unsatisfactory answer can cause more damage than help. Thus, careful, thorough dogmatic education is necessary. That is, one must not only be ready to recall the truths of faith from memory, but rather, they must be inwardly comprehended in their organic relationship and meaning and, in turn, be an inner form of the spirit. That means to own them, so that at any time, one can be prepared for the particular demands of the moment. Naturally, one gains such a thorough dogmatic education only by continual study of doctrine—the dogmatic definitions themselves, the writings of the church fathers and teachers, and classical theological works of the modern era. From where can one take the time for that? This question will surely press itself on many and I know that it's not easy. But one certainly has one's entire life for it. It cannot and need not happen all at once, not even much at once. The main point is continuity. The inner forming of the spirit grows slowly and imperceptibly, but incessantly and surely if only one allows it daily bread. When no other time at all is available, perhaps it will be possible—similar to Scripture—to use the prescribed daily practices for it; instead of the usual books for meditation and edification, to occasionally use writings of the type mentioned. (Naturally, occupation with them may not be purely intellectual. As required for good reading or meditation, the right mindset must be maintained. But that is precisely also the right mindset in order to internalize and organically assimilate the truths of faith.) But still something else must enter into this thorough knowledge of dogmatic theology of the Eucharist that enables us in a given moment to give an account in order to truly lead the children to the Eucharistic Savior—that is one's own eucharistic living. Daily Mass and Communion are indeed a matter of course for religious women and the ordinary custom for most pupils at the convent school. But the children have to feel that this does not arise only from an established rule, but rather from the innermost promptings of the heart. Living consequences must follow from the belief in the eucharistic truths—that the Eucharist is truly the center of one's entire life and that in comparison to that, all earthly concerns shrink to something insignificant. Here is a very small, practical example. If I were a principal, I would never organize an excursion so that Mass and Communion would be omitted as a result. The joy and recreation of the children need not be shortchanged for that reason. If only one day is available, then one wouldn't entertain any thoughts of far away destinations, but rather would choose something beautiful in the vicinity. But if one once encounters the lively wish for a more distant trip, then I would find it appropriate to extend the trip to two or more days instead of forsaking the Most High for it. Naturally, not even this is meant as a fixed rule, but rather because one feels it as self-evident, and the children sense it too, that one gets strength, peace, and joy from the Eucharistic Savior and would like to undertake nothing without his blessing. If thus leading the young soul to the school of the Savior through teaching and example is successful, then the work of the teacher is done and he can take his leave as an intermediary. I believe if these positive ways would be utilized sufficiently, then one could do away with something else which always seemed to me to be a very questionable means—the control and supervision of church attendance and the reception of the sacraments. I well know the reasons which may be cited for this common practice and that one cannot immediately do away with them without hesitation. But I can understand when children perceive the supervision as policing which seems embarrassing and provoking toward the Most Holy and to the most fragile, and in their eyes, diminishes the supervisors themselves. I am convinced that many young shoots of the inner life are destroyed by such regimentation, especially in the delicately sensitive souls of children, and I don't know whether an adequate equivalent exists for that.

3. Formation through the Mystical Body of Christ

The Eucharist is the soul, the inner life principle of the church. People whom Christ makes his own through the Eucharist are members of his Mystical Body. This Body itself, the church, can now also be a formative principle in religious education. In this regard, there are three aspects to consider: the outward destiny of the organized

Christian community, dogma in which the teaching of Christ progressively unfolds, and finally, the prayer of the church.

a) Church History

It's easy to see how church history can function formatively. What more lively stimulus could be given young, receptive minds than the image of the saints who preceded us on the way of Christian discipleship and the heroic courage of faith and sacrifice of the early Christian communities and of the periods of great struggle in the church during the 13th, 16th, and 17th centuries. Again, what matters is that all of these are vividly brought before them; and in order to do this, it's necessary that we ourselves consistently participate in and live according to the development of the church. As it is, one in religious life is already guided in this by participating in the church year through the breviary.

Today, a whole range of good portrayals of great events and personalities of church history based on the sources are already available for the enrichment of the image. We can use them for ourselves and, where we find it appropriate, can also put them into the hands of the children.

b) Dogmatic Theology

As the little mustard seed of the small band of disciples shot up into the tree of the church overshadowing the world, so the concise teachings of Christ grew into the richly unfolded organism of ecclesiastical *doctrine*. The example of eucharistic truths has already shown what significance a thorough dogmatic education holds. Today, we must always think about how our children, at every step or turn, come into contact with views which bring them into doubt and difficulties and elicit uncertainty and confusion. Even when they come from good Catholic families and grow up in the convent school, they are not secure in the face of day students, people with whom they come into contact during vacation, newspapers, and books. Even textbooks which they get hold of in our schools bring the atmosphere of the time to their attention. And if during their time at the institute they happen to remain untouched by that, they come across it immediately afterward, as soon as they have left the gates of the convent. And it's good if we don't let them leave unprepared, but rather well equipped for this battle of the spirits [cf. Eph 6:12]. For this reason, it again means that we have to be well equipped. To begin with, we have to critically think through and treat the material which we ourselves must cover with the students according to the curricular requirements, and then be able to discuss objectively, faultlessly, and convincingly, questions which confront us unexpectedly. Thus, the spiritual organs of the children ought to develop gradually so that they themselves can cope with whatever confronts them when they are on their own.

c) Liturgy

The church struggles and teaches and forms her newly maturing members into soldiers and teachers when they look at the images of the past and listen to the teaching. And in addition, she has a powerful means to form souls—her *prayer*. Like the external structure and dogma, the prayer of the church has also richly and magnificently unfolded in her *liturgy*. Yes, in general, everything that is available for the purpose of religious education by way of formative strengths is summarized in it. We have spoken about the significance of the Holy Sacrifice and the appropriate participation in this offering. There is no better instruction for fitting participation than the words of the Liturgy of the Mass in which the sacred action has found its full linguistic expression. Their meaning must become alive in whoever joins in praying these words with an open mind and heart, and must impel them to participation. Word and meaning belong together like body and spirit; together, they are *one* living structure. For that reason, the words cannot arbitrarily be replaced with other ones. It's another matter whether I am in the church and praying spontaneously (which naturally has its worth and right and should not be taken from any soul who desires it), or whether I am following the sacrificial act with the prayers and songs of a German sung Mass,[8] or in the closest connection with the wording of the text of the Mass itself (and certainly, the Latin; because even the translation is still a "substitute" even if it's the best approximation of the original among all possible substitutes.) So one may indeed say, even if a different manner of prayer may be fruitful for particular souls according to their individual disposition or temporary state of mind, objectively, the sacrifice of the Mass is most complete when the faithful join in the liturgical prayers of the priest. The understanding of Latin would naturally be necessary for this to take place inwardly in a fully fruitful manner. And I must even call it the liturgical ideal that all the faithful know as much Latin as pertains to the understanding of the liturgy. The ideal image of a liturgical celebration now still requires a completion in another direction. According to its full nature, the word is, of course, not something written or printed, not even something silently thought, but rather a sounding and ringing word. And in turn, there are tones and sounds which quite intrinsically belong to it, corresponding to its meaning. Even the liturgical word has its tones which belong to it and those are the tones of the Gregorian chant. Everything else that is sung and played in church may be an expression of personal devotion and the strongest religious emotion, and may even incline the soul of singers and listeners accordingly— but liturgical music, i.e., objectively belonging to the sacred act—it is not. And so I would like to say that the ideal form of the celebration of Mass, which at the same time can work most strongly to form the participants as members of the church, is the High Mass in which the faithful join in prayer and where possible, join in singing. It is eucharistically formative through the prayers which refer to the sacrifice itself, dogmatically formative through the parts which contain a solemn confession (Gloria, Credo, Preface), and historically formative through the epistles, gospels, and the varying prayers.

The prayer of the breviary relates most intimately to the Liturgy of the Mass. What is initiated in the Mass, but is limited in scope by the concentration on the offering, can unfold itself more broadly here: the historical accounts, reflections on them, dogmatic deliberations on the readings, the conversation with God, and songs of praise and thanks in psalms and hymns. On the other hand, the solemn *Gotteslob* [commonly used German prayer- and songbook] stipulates, "in vain, one fails to sing to him fitting praise" which alone is appropriate for the Divine Majesty in accordance with the transition from word to deed, to the offering. Everyone who is familiar with the life of our Benedictine abbeys knows what significance the solemn Divine Office holds for the formation of the soul, not only for priests and monks, but also for all the faithful. Indeed, every day of the year, one sees silent worshipers in the nave when the monks take their place in the choir. And on the high feasts, large crowds flock from near and far so that the space hardly suffices. What draws them here? Isn't it the instinctive feeling that one is closest to heaven here, that this life consecrated to the praise of God represents the border where the Church Militant touches the Church Triumphant, and that from these sacred places, one takes strengths for the daily struggles of our earthly pilgrimage?

So I believe that there is no more comprehensive and effective means for religious education than the liturgy in its double form: Mass and the Divine Office. The majority of religious institutions entrusted with the education of youth probably have both in their own house. But do they make sufficient use of them? Two different things would be required for that: first, the appropriate fostering of the liturgy within religious life; then the participation of the children in it. Regarding the Mass, a number of things in this direction have, in fact, already been done: liturgical instruction for the children, training in choral singing, and practice of the choral offices, at least for some Sundays and feast days throughout the year. It's different regarding the Divine Office. It seems to me that its significance for religious education has not yet been sufficiently grasped. One frequently finds it difficult or not possible at all to join the Divine Office together with teaching. And one doesn't consider what strengths can be obtained for oneself from the prayer for the daily work in school— how here, one is always lifted out of the pettiness of earthly life and filled with the life of the church which one ought to bring to the children. This effect will be all the stronger, the more perfectly the Divine Office is formed in the liturgical sense. And now I believe in the possibility of also having this effect directly accessible to the children. Naturally, one cannot place them together [with the monks] in the choir. Even in Beuron, no stranger has his place there. But everyone can see and hear what happens there and the doors to the outside stand wide open. Whoever wants to join in prayer is warmly welcomed. In my opinion, in many women's convents, everything takes place too much "behind closed doors." Often, it has to do with the structure of the monastery churches which doesn't allow any view into the choir and will not easily be changed. However, there is still also a certain inner attitude in effect which considers the inner religious life as a matter of enclosure into which one is not allowed to peer. In the interest of religious education, I regret that. If children would be introduced to the spirit of the Divine Office and, as far as time allows and the desire for it is present, at least to be able to *hear* the Office, and if they were able to hear it in an arrangement which can awaken holy joy and enthusiasm, then they would take along with them something for their entire life. What has been said here about the Divine Office also applies to the rest of religious life. It shouldn't stand there as something mysterious that rouses curiosity. That's not in accord with its dignity and sacredness. Children who grow up in the convent school ought to know what genuine religious life is. I almost believe that the complaints about lacking new members would then stop because the attracting power of religious life rightly exemplified would be so strong. And after such a religious education, the pupils who are not called to live a religious life would be sent out as true apostles because genuine religious education encompasses the spirit of an apostle. The love of Christ and the love for souls must also be alive in whoever is formed according to the image of Christ. Fundamentally, there is no separation between self-sanctification and the apostolate. Whoever aspires to perfection for the sake of God, seeks it not only for oneself, but rather for everyone.

And so I come to the conclusion: religious education is formation through Christ toward Christ. Christ, how he lived and how he is depicted for us in the gospel, and Christ himself, who lives on in the Eucharist and in the struggles, teachings, and prayers of the church, must form the soul. No one is as much called to establish the connection between him and the children as the religious communities whose entire life is dedicated to him. Facilitating religious education is the specific vocation of religious institutions of education. If they were not able to do that, then they would have no right to exist. But they will be able to do it all the more fully, the more fully they live up to their religious vocation and set about their apostolic work accordingly.

"The Foundations of Women's Education"[9]

III. External Formation Work

...The *actual* task of the school would be to see to it that the girls come to know and understand the world and people, and learn to deal with them. It has become strikingly clear to us that the correct knowledge and treatment of creatures is only possible if it comes from a correct relationship to the Creator.

So we are led back to the point that religious formation is the most important part of formation. Opening up a door to God for the child is the most urgent task. We can also say that to be religiously formed means having a *living faith*. Having a living faith means to know God, to love him, and to serve him. Whoever knows God (in the sense and measure in which knowledge of God is possible through natural and supernatural light) cannot do otherwise than love him. Whoever loves God cannot do otherwise than serve him. Thus, living faith is a matter of the intellect and heart, an achievement of the will, and action. Whoever understands how to awaken it trains all the faculties. However, one can only awaken a living faith by calling upon all faculties, not through dry, rational instruction, but also not through instruction "appealing to the emotions" which generates enthusiasm. Rather, one can awaken it through religious instruction which, from the fullness of one's own religious life, knows to lead into the depths of the divinity and represent God in his kindness, which enkindles love and demands—and may demand—that the learner proves herself through action since the instructor renders such proof herself. Where love is enkindled, there love itself desires action and eagerly reaches for the practical forms of the life of faith which God and the church have provided: participation at Mass which makes the life of faith an offering in union with the Eucharistic Savior, solemn Liturgy of the Hours, and all works of love in which Christ is served in the members of his Mystical Body. In this way, the entire fullness of the supernatural world of the spirit is opened up to the soul and with it, an inexhaustible amount of formation materials which can enter it, build it up, and transform it.

Supplement to the Lecture, "Foundations of Women's Formation"[10]

St. Lioba, Jan. 12, 1932

In the lecture on the Foundations of Women's Formation which I held in Bendorf in November 1930, I tried to sketch the image of the soul of women as it would correspond with the eternal destiny of the woman and named the attributes: *wide, still, empty* of its self, *warm,* and *clear.* Now you ask me to say something about how one could attain possession of these qualities. I believe it's not a matter of a variety of qualities which one could individually tackle and work for; rather, it's a matter of a simple state of the soul in its entirety which is comprised of different aspects of these attributes. We cannot volitionally work for this state; it must be brought about by grace. What we can and must do is open ourselves to grace. I.e., *fully renounce our own will* and surrender it to God's will—*to place our entire soul, receptive and ready for forming, into God's hands.* Hence, to begin with, *becoming empty and still* are closely connected. By nature, the soul is variously filled; so much so that one thing always supplants the other and it is in constant motion, often in tumult and turmoil. When we awake in the morning, the duties and worries of the day already want to press themselves upon us (in case they have not already driven away our night's rest). There rises the uneasy question: How shall all of this be accommodated in one day? When will I do this, when will I do that? And how shall I tackle this and that? One would like to start up as though pursued and rush forth. Then it's the time to take the reins in hand and say: Easy! Nothing of all this may now get hold of me. My first hour of the morning belongs to the Lord. I will tackle the day's work which he entrusts me with and he will give me the strength to accomplish it. So I will go to the altar of God. Here it is not a matter of me and my tiny little concerns, but rather a matter of the great sacrifice of reconciliation. I may participate in that, allow it to cleanse me and make me glad, and at the offertory place myself on the altar with all my doings and sufferings. And then when the Lord comes to me in Holy Communion, I may ask him, "What do you desire of me, Lord?"

(St. Teresa). And after quiet conversation, I will go to that which I see before me as my next task. When I enter into my workday after this morning's celebration, a solemn calm will fill me and the soul will be empty of that which would assail it and weigh it down, and be filled with holy joy, courage, and energy. The soul has become large and wide because it has gone out of itself and has entered into the divine life. Love as a quiet flame which the Lord has enkindled burns in it and the soul presses to prove its love and to enkindle love in others. "Let charity be enflamed with fire, and ardor enkindle our neighbors."[11] And it sees clearly the next little piece of the path before it; it does not see very far, but it knows that when it has arrived there where now the horizon cuts off, a new view will open itself up.

Now begins the day's work. Perhaps teaching—4–5 lessons consecutively. Then it means being attentive to a different subject for each lesson. In this or that lesson, perhaps in all of them, one cannot achieve what she wanted. One's own tiredness, unforeseen interruptions, lack of receptiveness of the children, all sorts of annoyances, and outrageous and frightening things. Or office work: communication with unpleasant superiors and colleagues, unattainable demands, unjust reproaches, human wretchedness, and perhaps even needs of the most diverse kind.

The noon hour arrives. Exhausted and worn out, one goes home. Perhaps new challenges await you there. Where is the morning freshness of the soul now? Again, rebellion, irritation, and regret would like to seethe and rage. And still so much to do until evening. Doesn't one have to proceed further immediately? No, not before entering into silence, at least for a moment. Everyone must know or learn to know herself in order to know where and how she can find rest. Preferably, if possible, again take a short time before the tabernacle to pour out all your cares. Whoever cannot do that—whoever perhaps also very much needs a bit of physical rest—can take a respite in her own room. And if no outer rest at all can be attained, if there is no space in which to retreat, if pressing duties prohibit a quiet hour, then at least for a moment, inwardly close off everything else and flee to the Lord. He is certainly there and in a single moment can give us what we need. Thus the rest of the day will continue, perhaps with great tiredness and toil, but in peace. And when night comes and looking back on the day shows that everything was patchwork and much of what one had planned remains undone, when so much rouses deep humiliation and regret, then take everything as it is, place it in God's hands, and surrender it to God. In this way, you will be able to rest in God, really rest, and begin the new day like a new life.

This is only a small hint of how the day could be shaped in order to create space for God's grace. Each individual will know best how it needs to be applied to her own circumstances. Furthermore, it would be necessary to show how Sunday must be a great gateway through which heavenly life can enter everyday life and provide strength for the work of the entire week, and how the great feasts, festive seasons, and times of penance lived in the spirit of the church allow the soul to mature from year to year toward the eternal Sabbath rest.

It will be an essential task of each individual to consider how she must shape her daily and yearly schedule according to her disposition and her respective circumstances in order to prepare the way of the Lord. The external arrangement must be different for everyone and also different in the course of time, and must flexibly adapt to a change in circumstances. But even the situation of the soul is different at different times with different people and individuals. Of the means which are suitable for establishing, keeping alive, or even giving new life to a relationship with the Eternal—like contemplation, spiritual reading, and participation in the liturgy and popular devotions, etc.—all are not equally fruitful for every person, nor for all times. For example, contemplation cannot be practiced by all and not always in the same way. It is important to find what is most effective at any given time and to make use of it. It will be good to be knowledgeable about what is necessary for oneself and especially to listen to experienced advice before undertaking changes in a proven routine.

"The Life of Christian Women"[12]

II. Women's Formation

...For that reason, the core of all women's formation (as of all human formation in general) must be religious formation—a religious formation which knows how to impress the truths of faith in a manner that stirs the emotions and inspires action and, at the same time, is suited to practicing all the ways of practical activity in the life of faith in a manner forming the soul for the entire life: life and prayer with the church by fostering the liturgy, paving the way for a close personal relationship with the Lord, above all by opening up the meaning of the Holy Eucharist, and a genuine eucharistic life. Such religious formation work can naturally only be achieved by personality types who themselves are quite thoroughly permeated by the spirit of faith and whose life is formed accordingly. To this religious formation is to be added paving the way for human knowledge and human action in all of girls' education to which instruction in history and literature, biology, psychology, and pedagogy (naturally, in a simple form suitable to their capacity) can contribute. But such instruction will only become fruitful if it provides guidance and opportunity for observation and activity in the practical life.

...Thus, if the uncertainty of all natural formation work serves the purpose of teaching the educator to think humbly about his work, then it may still not allow him to become fully skeptical and despairing of the entire meaning of his efforts. Efforts remain an important factor and the educator must not only take into account the impact in a negative sense, but also in a positive sense which he can't overlook, and of which perhaps he will have no knowledge at all. Above all, he may never forget that the first and most essential formator of human beings is not the human being, but rather God. God provides the nature as well as the living conditions under which the nature can unfold. God also has the power to transform the nature from within and everywhere to make use of his work there where human power fails. If religious formation is developed to the point that no more resistance is offered to the divine work of formation, then one may be at peace about the rest. And beyond that, one may take into account that in the divine economy of salvation, no sincere efforts remain without fruit, even where human eyes can perceive nothing but failures....

IV. Life of Women in the Light of Eternity

...Everyone who is familiar with the interior life knows that precisely the ones who are called by God to the extraordinary must also undergo extraordinary trials, not only external difficulties and afflictions, but also enduring much more difficult sufferings and trials of the soul. That is what mystical theology calls the dark night of the soul. Without the purity of its will being marred, the soul falls into the utmost anxiety and confusion. It loses the taste for all pious practices and is led into temptation by an aversion to church institutions and by doubts of faith. The soul falls into the danger of regarding its entire way as a wrong way and fearing that it is irretrievably lost. In order not to lose the right way in such afflictions of the soul, there is no better protection, as experience shows, than obedience to an enlightened spiritual director. That such obedience possesses this power against the powers of darkness is itself a *mysterious* fact—just as it is by the special guidance of God's grace that God sets aside such a director for the tested soul—but it is a *fact*. God is not bound to this way of mediation but he has bound himself to us on inexplicable grounds; moreover, he has also ordered certain ways of mediating graces, although his possibilities which work toward salvation are infinite. Whoever wants to find the right spiritual director will also let God's providence, not his own arbitrariness, direct his choice, as inner and outer direction must always go hand in hand all along the way. To which tasks the direction might appoint the individual person—that, only life itself can teach.

12

THE CROSS

INTRODUCTION

The cross held significance for Edith long before she entered Carmel. She first encountered what she refers to as the "power of the cross" when she experienced Anna Reinach's faith-filled acceptance of her husband's death in battle in 1917. The cross undoubtedly had a formative effect on Edith's life, as she describes in the introduction to her final book, *The Science of the Cross*. There she writes that a theology of the cross is

> a living, real and effective truth. It is buried in the soul like a seed that takes root there and grows, making a distinct impression on the soul, determining what it does and omits, and by shining outwardly is recognized in this very doing and omitting…. From this living form and strength in one's innermost depths, a perspective of life arises, the image one has of God and of the world, and therefore one can find expression for it in a mode of thinking, in a theory.[1]

Edith believes that joining one's own suffering with Christ's suffering bears fruit for oneself and for others. In the summer of 1933, after she had lost her position in Münster, Edith wrote to Anneliese Lichtenberger, a former student who had a serious illness. After first expressing regret that she was unable to visit her, Edith continued,

> For now I want to wish you very much patience in your suffering, and the ultimate consolation that I have often had to point out to you: that the way of suffering is the surest road to union with the Lord. The saving power of joyfully

borne suffering is particularly necessary in our time. I beg you especially for your prayer for my relatives.[2]

The young woman died two years later at age twenty-three.

In a letter written in 1938, Edith explains that she brought her choice for her religious name with her when she entered Carmel and received exactly the name she requested—Teresa Benedicta of the Cross (Teresia Benedicta a Cruce). In the escalating suffering inflicted on her own Jewish people, she saw the suffering of Christ. This must not be misconstrued as any sort of anti-Semitic view. Very simply, Edith identified the suffering of the Jews with the suffering of Christ. This perception moved her to a willingness to help bear this cross of suffering.

> By the cross I understood the destiny of God's people which, even at that time, began to announce itself. I thought that those who recognized it as the cross of Christ had to take it upon themselves in the name of all. Certainly, today I know more of what it means to be wedded to the Lord in the sign of the cross. Of course, one can never comprehend it, for it is a mystery.[3]

By Palm Sunday 1939, Edith felt an even stronger call to be united with Jesus' sacrifice. Having lived through World War I, she wanted to contribute her own efforts to help prevent another war by appealing to the heart of Jesus with her self-offering. Five months before the outbreak of World War II, she formally asked permission of her superior in writing to offer her life as a sacrifice.

> Dear Mother: please, will [you] allow me to offer myself to the heart of Jesus as a sacrifice of propitiation for true peace, that the dominion of the antichrist may collapse, if possible, without a new world war, and that a new order may be established? I would like it [my request] granted this very day because it is the twelfth hour. I know that I am a nothing, but Jesus desires it, and surely he will call many others to do likewise in these days.[4]

Edith considers the title, "of the Cross," to be a noble one, but one that bears consequences. In a 1940 letter to Sister Johanna a Cruce, Edith writes, "After all, one cannot wish for a deliverance from the cross when one bears the noble title 'of the Cross.'"[5]

The first selection, "Exaltation of the Cross—*Ave Crux, Spes Unica!*," is a meditation that Edith wrote for the prioress of the Echt Carmel to be used for the Carmelites' renewal of vows on the Feast of the Exaltation of the Cross celebrated on September 14, 1939. Germany's invasion of Poland just two weeks before (September 1, 1939) triggered World War II. Three times in the meditation Edith repeats that "the world is in flames" and states that the conflagration could also reach their convent. She knew the horrors of war from her own experience as a Red Cross volunteer during World War I, as well as from the loss of friends who died in that war. Nevertheless, the cross rises above all flames. She encourages the sisters to faithfully live their vowed life and to embrace the cross in faith, hope, and love, for it will lift them into the heart of the Trinity.

The first of the letter selections was written six years before Edith entered Carmel. In it she recognizes that everyone bears a cross and that watching another bear their cross is more difficult than carrying one's own. The second letter was written to Anneliese Lichtenberger a year before the letter to her mentioned above. In it she talks about the vocation to suffer with Christ as a member of the Mystical Body. Edith's letter to Gertrud von le Fort in 1935 expresses her view that having had to postpone her entrance into Carmel in the past was more of a sacrifice than the life she was now living. However, she writes that she awaits the time when she will be allowed to feel more of her vocation to the cross. The last letter selection is actually a note written to the prioress in the Echt Carmel where Edith was then living. In 1941, after the required three years since her transfer, the question of Edith's canonical incorporation into the monastery in Echt arose just at the time when the Nazis declared non-Aryans in the Netherlands stateless, ordering them to report for emigration. Meanwhile, efforts were already being made to transfer Edith to a convent outside of the Netherlands. Without this procedure of incorporation, a transfer to yet another Carmel could simply be processed through the Cologne Carmel where she first entered. The ever increasing anguish caused by the evils of Nazism brought Edith to a radical encounter with the cross. Typical of her stance of surrender to God's will and the importance she placed on obedience, she left the matter in the hands of her superiors. Along with the note, she attached a letter from a Jesuit giving his opinion about the matter.[6]

The last selections include two of Edith's poems. Edith begins the first poem, "Sign of the Cross," with the first line of the fourteenth stanza of the sequence, *Stabat Mater*. In the next line, she mentions a "booklet." Her prioress, Sister Teresa Renata of the Holy Spirit, wrote a commemorative booklet for the three-hundred-year celebration of the founding of the Cologne Carmel, Queen of Peace, which was celebrated September 30–October 3, 1937. Edith mentions the booklet in four letters written between August 18 and November 14, 1937.[7] It seems plausible that she wrote this poem for Sr. Teresa Renata, who perhaps wrote the line *Juxta crucem tecum stare!* (To stand beside the cross with you!) in a copy of the booklet for Edith.

On December 12, 1937, Edith wrote a letter to Mother Petra Brüning, OSU, thanking her for sending a picture of the face of Jesus from the shroud of Turin. Edith states that she took it as a gift from the Lord as a means of preparation for her final vows and placed it on the table in her room so that she could look at it often. She further writes that she has written something about it and was enclosing it for Mother Petra as her thanks. The poem, "The Holy Face," is apparently what she had sent her.[8]

THE TEXTS

Meditation

"Exaltation of the Cross—*Ave Crux, Spes Unica!*"[9]

September 14, 1939

"Hail, Cross, our only hope!"—this is what the holy church summoned us to exclaim during the time for contemplating the bitter suffering of our Lord Jesus Christ. The jubilant exclamation of the Easter Alleluia silenced the serious song of the cross. But the sign of our salvation greeted us amid the time of Easter joy, since we were recalling the discovery of the One who had passed from sight. At the end of the cycle of ecclesiastical feasts, the cross greets us through the heart of the Savior. And now, as the church year draws toward an end, it is raised high before us and is to hold us spellbound until the Easter Alleluia summons us anew to forget the earth for awhile and rejoice in the marriage of the Lamb.

Our holy order has us begin our fast with the Exaltation of the Holy Cross. And it leads us to the foot of the cross to renew our holy vows. The Crucified One looks down on us and asks us whether we are still willing to honor what we promised in an hour of grace. And he certainly has reason to ask. More than ever the cross is a sign of contradiction. The followers of the antichrist show it far more dishonor than did the Persians who stole it. They desecrate the images of the cross, and they make every effort to tear the cross out of the hearts of Christians. All too often they have succeeded even with those who, like us, once vowed to bear Christ's cross after him. Therefore, the Savior today looks at us, solemnly probing us, and asks each one of us: Will you remain faithful to the Crucified? Consider carefully! The world is in flames, the battle between Christ and the antichrist has broken into the open. If you decide for Christ, it could cost you your life. Carefully consider what you promise. Taking and renewing vows is a dreadfully serious business. You make a promise to the Lord of heaven and earth. If you are not deadly serious about your will to fulfill it, you fall into the hands of the living God.

Before you hangs the Savior on the cross, because he became *obedient* unto death on the cross. He came into the world not to do *his* own will, but his Father's will. If you intend to be the bride of the Crucified, you too must completely renounce your own will and no longer have any desire except to fulfill God's will. He speaks to you in the Holy Rule and constitutions of the order. He speaks to you through the mouth of your superiors. He speaks to you by the gentle breath of the Holy Spirit in the depths of your heart. To remain true to your vow of obedience, you must listen to this voice day and night and follow its orders. However, this means daily and hourly crucifying your self-will and self-love.

The Savior hangs naked and destitute before you on the cross because he has chosen *poverty*. Those who want to follow him must renounce earthly goods. It is not enough that you once left everything out there and came to the monastery. You must be serious about it now as well. Gratefully receive what God's providence sends you. Joyfully do without what he may let you to do without. Do not be concerned with your own body, with its trivial necessities and inclinations, but leave concern to those who are entrusted with it. Do not be concerned about the coming day and the coming meal.

The Savior hangs before you with a pierced heart. He has spilled his heart's blood to win your heart. If you want to follow him in holy *purity*, your heart must be free of every earthly desire. Jesus, the Crucified, is to be the only object of your longings, your wishes, your thoughts.

Are you now alarmed by the immensity of what the holy vows require of you? You need not be alarmed. What you have promised is indeed beyond your own weak, human power. But it is not beyond the power of the Almighty—this power will become yours if you entrust yourself to him, if he accepts your pledge of troth. He does so on the day of your holy profession and will do it anew today. It is the loving heart of your Savior that invites you to follow. It demands your obedience because the human will is blind and weak. It cannot find the way until it surrenders itself entirely to the divine will. He demands poverty because hands must be empty of earth's goods to receive the goods of heaven. He demands chastity because only the heart detached from all earthly love is free for the love of God. The arms of the Crucified are spread out to draw you to his heart. He wants your life in order to give you *his*.

Ave Crux, Spes unica!

The world is in flames. The conflagration can also reach our house. But high above all flames towers the cross. They cannot consume it. It is the path from earth to heaven. It will lift one who embraces it in faith, love, and hope into the bosom of the Trinity.

The world is in flames. Are you impelled to put them out? Look at the cross. From the open heart gushes the blood of the Savior. This extinguishes the flames of hell. Make your heart free by the faithful fulfillment of your vows; then the flood of divine love will be poured into your heart until it overflows and becomes fruitful to all the ends of the earth. Do you hear the groans of the wounded on the battle-fields in the west and the east? You are not a physician and not a nurse and cannot bind up the wounds. You are enclosed in a cell and cannot get to them. Do you hear the anguish of the dying? You would like to be a priest and comfort them. Does the lament of the widows and orphans distress you? You would like to be an angel of mercy and help them. Look at the Crucified. If you are nuptially bound to him by the faithful observance of your holy vows, *your* being is precious blood. Bound to him, you are omnipresent as he is. You cannot help here or there like the physician, the nurse, the priest. You can be at all fronts, wherever there is grief, in the power of the cross. Your compassionate love takes you everywhere, this love from the divine heart. Its precious blood is poured everywhere—soothing, healing, saving.

The eyes of the Crucified look down on you—asking, probing. Will you make your covenant with the Crucified anew in all seriousness? What will you answer him? "Lord, where shall we go? You have the words of eternal life."

Ave Crux, Spes unica!

Letters

To Sr. Callista Kopf, OP, October 12, 1927[10]

Dear Sister Callista,

...But let me tell you something encouraging now that the new semester is beginning. Sr. Agnella visited me several times even after the Newman manuscript was completed.[11] She bears a cross like everyone else, but it has borne fruit for her, and she knows that and so would not wish to give it up. We too, dear Sister, have to learn to see that others have a cross to carry and to realize that we cannot take it from them. It is harder than carrying one's own, but it cannot be avoided....

Many good wishes and best regards, and these for Srs. Immolata and Theophana, as well, from your

Edith Stein

EDITH STEIN

To Anneliese Lichtenberger, December 26, 1932[12]

Dear Anneliese,

From the cloistered solitude (at the Ursulines' in Westphalia, with whom I have been allowed to celebrate Christmas) I return your good wishes most cordially. Before all else, I would like to answer your question. There is a vocation to suffer with Christ and thereby to cooperate with him in his work of salvation. When we are united with the Lord, we are members of the Mystical Body of Christ: Christ lives on in his members and continues to suffer in them. And the suffering borne in union with the Lord is his suffering, incorporated in the great work of salvation and fruitful therein. That is a fundamental premise of all religious life, above all of the life of Carmel, to stand proxy for sinners through voluntary and joyous suffering, and to cooperate in the salvation of humankind.

With cordial wishes and greeting, your
Edith Stein

To Gertrud von le Fort, January 31, 1935[13]

Pax Christi!
Dear Baronness,

...You cannot imagine how embarrassed I am when someone speaks of our life of "sacrifice." I led a life of sacrifice as long as I had to stay outside. Now practically all my burdens have been removed, and I have in fullness what I formerly lacked. Of course, there are sisters among us who are called upon to make great sacrifices daily. And I do await the day when I shall be allowed to feel more of my vocation to the cross than I do now, since the Lord treats me once more as if I were a little child....

In caritate Christi, your
Teresa Benedicta a Cruce, OCD

To Mother Ambrosia Antonia Engelmann, OCD,
[presumably December 1941][14]

Dear Mother,

Once [you have] read the letter from Father Hirschmann,[15] you will know his opinion. Now I would like to do nothing more at all about the matter of my stability.[16] I put it in [your] hands and leave it to [you] whether to call the sisters, Father Provincial, or our Father Bishop for a decision. I am satisfied with everything. A *scientia crucis* [knowledge of the cross] can be gained only when one comes to feel the cross radically. I have been convinced of that from the first moment and have said, from my heart: *Ave, Crux, Spes unica*! [Hail, cross, our only hope!]

Your Reverence's grateful child,

Benedicta

Poetry

"Sign of the Cross"[17] (November 16, 1937)

To stand beside the cross with you!
You wrote these words in a booklet
To one who carries the sign of the cross,
When the shadow of the cross in its immensity
Already rested upon you.
Thereafter, it fell on your shoulder
Hard and heavy.

The one who became human for the sake of humankind,
Gave the fullness of his human life
To the souls he chose for himself.
The one who formed every single human heart
And will someday reveal the secret meaning of its essence
    in a new name,
Which only the one who owns it will understand;
He has united himself with each of the chosen

In a unique, deeply mysterious way.
From the fullness of his human life he gives us
The cross.

What is the cross?
The sign of deepest disgrace.
Whoever touches it is banished from the ranks of human
    beings.
Those who once acclaimed him,
Timidly turn away and know him no longer.
He is defenselessly abandoned to the enemies.
Nothing more remains for him on earth
Than pain, agony, and death.

What is the cross?
The sign which points to heaven.
It towers high over earth's dust and haze and so
Upward into pure light.
Whatever humans are able to lay hold of, let it go,
Open your hands and press close to the cross;
Then take it up yourself
Into the eternal light.

Look up at the cross:
It spreads its beams,
Like one opens his arms,
As though he would embrace the whole world:
Come, all you who labor and are heavily burdened,
Also you who cried out to me: to the cross with him.
It is the image of God who died on the cross.
It rises from the ground of earth to heaven
Like him who ascended to heaven,
And it would like to carry everyone along there.
Just embrace the cross, then you possess him,
Who is the truth, the way, and the life.
If you carry your cross, then it will carry you
And will become blessedness for you.

"THE HOLY FACE"[18]

2nd Sunday of Advent—December 5, 1937

You who loved your own,
As never a person loved on this earth,
Toward the end of your earthly life
You gave us the comforting promise,
That you would be with us until the end of time.

Now you live hidden among us.
Through all times and in all places
From your tabernacle stream out
Comfort, light, and strength down into souls
Who take refuge near you.
They lovingly look up to the small host,
To the silent image of purity and peace.

Yet never silent in the hearts of those who love you,
Is the longing to see you bodily,
The most beautiful of all the children of humanity,
In your human form.
The artist's mind in tireless struggle
Forms image after image:
The child of God in his mother's arms,
The boy in the circle of the scribes,
The master who teaches in the midst of his disciples,
The man of suffering on the cross in the agony of death.
Yet the work of no human gives us
You yourself.

The times came when the power of darkness
Tore faith out of hearts,
Made pale the star of hope,
And cold the embers of love.
Ever smaller becomes the flock of the faithful,
And your dwellings become deserted.
And now in these recent times,

EDITH STEIN

When faith, hope, and love disappeared,
You revealed your holy face,
The face of him who suffered on the cross
And who closed his eyes in the sleep of death.

As behind a veil we look at the suffering
In these holy, sublime features.
So great, so beyond all human measure is this suffering,
That we are not able to grasp and penetrate it.
Yet you suffered silently
And a power was in you
Which overcame the excessive amount of suffering.
You were its Lord, as you yielded yourself to it.
An unfathomable, deep peace
Radiates from these features
And speaks:
It is finished.

You throw the mysterious veil over
Whomever you join to yourself forever:
He suffers with your suffering
And suffers like you
Hidden, silent, and deeply in peace.

THOUGHTS ON BELIEF AND VARIOUS COUNSELS

INTRODUCTION

Edith's stance of respect for the religious beliefs of others could be characterized today as being interreligious and ecumenical. Throughout her life, Edith's circle of friends, acquaintances, and colleagues consisted of both practicing and nonpracticing Jews and Christians, and possibly some nonbelievers as well. Edith's close friend and fellow phenomenologist Hedwig Conrad-Martius, a member of a Protestant free church, was Edith's godmother at her baptism. Edith received a special dispensation for this from the archbishop of Speyer.[1] Beyond her own family, Edith also maintained contacts with Jewish friends after her baptism, although some withdrew their support. She tells us that Trude (Kuznitzky) Koebner was very close to her and shared very deeply in her conversion experience even while Trude herself remained a Jewess. And when Edith's sister Rosa was considering baptism, Edith was most concerned that Rosa and their sister Frieda would forge a strong bond between themselves despite their religious differences.[2]

It is clear that Edith understood that God's love, wisdom, and mercy infinitely exceeds and is far more encompassing than that of humans, and she held convictions that would later be supported by Vatican II. She had no doubt that her mother was united with God at death. About her mother she writes,

> The faith and firm confidence that she had in her God from her earliest childhood until her 87th year remained steadfast, and were the last thing that stayed alive in her

during the final difficult agony. Therefore, I have the firm
belief that she found a very merciful judge and is now my
most faithful helper on my way, so that I, too, may reach
my goal.[3]

She likewise expressed such confident trust in God regarding
her beloved "Master," Edmund Husserl, who was a Lutheran. Near
the time of his death she wrote to a Benedictine sister who had contact with him, "I am not at all worried about my dear Master. It has
always been far from me to think that God's mercy allows itself to be
circumscribed by the visible church's boundaries. God is truth. All
who seek truth seek God, whether this is clear to them or not."[4]

The first five selections are taken from letters written to Roman
Ingarden, a fellow phenomenologist and friend of Edith from their
university years at Göttingen. There are 162 letters that Edith wrote
to him from 1917 until 1938, many of which deal with their philosophical interests and mutual friends. One also gets a glimpse into
their sometimes rocky relationship, and after Edith's baptism, we find
sporadic attempts by Edith to try to explain some of her new religious convictions to him. By the tone of the letters, we get the impression that Ingarden responded with varying degrees of receptivity
toward her religious interests. On her part, we see Edith the intellectual more than ready to challenge her peer honestly and straightforwardly while always remaining respectful and mindful of their
friendship. Edith's frankness also provides some glimpses into her
own faith journey and some of her convictions. For example, she
maintains that there are as many paths on the journey as there are
minds and hearts; that one needs to come to a decision for or against
God without a guarantee of proof; and that it is possible to speak of
religious experience that does not entail a visual perception of God.

Throughout her life, a variety of people sought Edith's advice.
Whether it pertained to practical, academic, professional, or spiritual
matters, her responses come across as objectively weighed and balanced, even if occasionally marked by tough love. At times, they
include a brief counsel of wisdom, such as, "Have patience with yourself; God also has it."[5] The remaining selections are taken from letters
in which Edith offers various types of counsels to the recipients. In

the first of these, Edith expresses her own gradual awareness that the deeper one is drawn into God, the more one must go out to the world to carry the divine life into it. Here and in the remaining selections, we find Edith to be forthright, caring, insightful, and practical.

THE TEXTS

To Roman Ingarden, June 19, 1924[6]

Dear Mr. Ingarden,

...So now I come to a very serious undertaking in my attempt to answer your letter. When I read over the last few lines, I asked myself how it is possible for a person with academic training, who makes a claim for strict objectivity, and without a thorough investigation would never make a judgment on the smallest philosophical question, to dismiss one of the most important problems with a phrase that reminds me of something that might appear in a hick newspaper. I refer to your comment about "the control of the masses with a body of made-up dogma." Do not take that as a personal reproach. Such a view is entirely typical of intellectuals insofar as they have not been brought up in the church, and up until a few years ago, it would have been no different for me.

However, based on our long friendship, allow me to restate the general problem to you as an intellectual matter of conscience. Since religious education at school, how much time have you devoted to the study of Catholic dogma, to its theological foundation, to its historical development? Have you ever once considered how to explain the fact that men like Augustine, Anselm of Canterbury, Bonaventure, Thomas—not to mention the thousands whose names are unknown to those who have no connection to them but who without doubt were no less intelligent than us enlightened folk—that these men have seen in the despised dogma the highest that is available to the human mind and the one thing that deserves the sacrifice of life? With what justification are you able to designate the great teachers and the great holy ones of the church as either idiots or clever defrauders? Certainly one may pronounce such an outrageous suspicion, as each of these words suggests, only after the most thorough examination of all of the facts that come into consideration. Do you not want once and for all objectively to answer these questions, if not for yourself, then for me? Just answer them! You do not have to answer them for me if you do not want to.

I was just interrupted while writing by a young girl from the boarding school who brought me ice cream and cake from the fair being held today in the convent garden. This is just a little image so that you will not paint a picture of such a dark prison life for me. Actually, no one would be less reasonable than I when it comes to dealing with pity. There is no one in the world with whom I would like to change places. And I have learned to love life since I know what I am living for.

Sincere greetings to you and also to your wife and three boys.

Your *Edith Stein*

To Roman Ingarden, December 13, 1925[7]

Dear Mr. Ingarden,

Of course, I did not want to create any grief for you, but I thought I had to run the risk of being completely open in order to reestablish the relationship on a healthy basis, and if I understand you correctly, you give me the right to do so. I believe that writing now will cause me fewer difficulties.

By the way, it is not so much the variety of the "views" that disturbed me as a certain animosity that each letter seemed to express. Catholicism is hardly a "religion of feeling." It concerns itself with the question of the truth, also with matters of life and the heart. And if Christ is the focal point of my life and the church of Christ my home, how could it not be difficult for me to write letters that contain nothing from my heart, nothing that might awaken hostile feelings regarding what is dear and holy to me? ...I can write most freely to someone, with no fear that differences of viewpoint will hinder the exchange, when I feel it is self-evident that we are on equal footing.

As to the other question: of course, in no way do I want to deny that—overlooking everything—we have a genuine friendship and that I view it as something valuable....

Now, I wish you all a really nice Christmas.

Your *Edith Stein*

To Roman Ingarden, November 8, 1927[8]

Dear Mr. Ingarden,

...I hope it is perfectly clear that it is *not* my intention to describe my way as *the* way. I am fundamentally convinced that there are as many ways to Rome as there are human minds and hearts. Perhaps the intellectual way comes off badly with the representation of my way. In the years of preparation for my conversion it had a strong influence on me. However, realistically considered, not "feelings" but real events, along with the concrete image of Christianity in the words of witnesses (Augustine, Francis, Teresa), were decisive for me. However, how shall I describe for you in a few words an image of each "real event"? An infinite world opens up something entirely new when you once begin to live the interior instead of the exterior life. All prior realities become transparent; the genuine sustaining and motivating strengths become perceptible. Previous conflicts become trivial! The individual comes to understand a life filled with passion and blessedness that those living a worldly life do not know and cannot grasp, something that from the outside appears as the most uneventful day in a totally inconspicuous human existence. And how strange it appears when you live among those who see only the superficial and never notice anything else in the world around them.

Are you now scratching your head because of all of these mysterious things? Then do not be angry with me. If you wish, I want to return gladly to the realm of reason where you feel more at home. I have not forgotten how to use it, and I value it even, in its limits, very much more than earlier....

Kind regards, your

Edith Stein

༺༄༅༆༇༈༉༊་༌།༎༏༐༑༒༓༔༕༖༗༘༙༚༛༜༝༞༟༠

To Roman Ingarden, November 20, 1927[9]

Dear Mr. Ingarden,

...I believe we can and must speak of *religious experience.* However, it is not a matter of a "direct intuition" of God. That is possible only in totally exceptional cases (in ecstasy and the like) for which, however, a strict proof is never possible, as with *genuine* revelation. The usual way is via effects that you notice in yourself, in others, and in events in nature and in the lives of people, for which there is no complete proof—taken in itself— that clearly points to God's authorship; events for which no other explanation would be thinkable and that in themselves contain such a proof, many in isolation already so strong that you cannot attribute them to coincidence; events that you can still methodically doubt but cannot really doubt.

...It is not necessary that we come to a correct proof of reli- gious experience before the end of our lives. However, it is nec- essary that we come to a decision for or against God. That is demanded of us: to decide without a guarantee. That is the great wager of faith. The way leads from faith to understanding, not the other way around. Whoever is too proud to go through this narrow gate does not enter. Whoever does enter acquires in this life a brighter clarity and experiences the legitimacy of *"credo ut intelligam"* [I believe in order to understand. (Anselm of Canterbury)]. I also believe that it gains us little to begin with construed or fantasized experiences. Where the actual experience is missing, we have to get it from the testimonies of the religious—and there is no lack of them. According to my experience the most impressive come from the Spanish mystics, Teresa and John of the Cross.

For today, I will just add, kind regards,

Edith Stein

༄

To Roman Ingarden, January 1, 1928[10]

Dear Mr. Ingarden,

...Today I carefully read your long letter from Marburg. When it arrived, I had time only for a quick look. The first letter I received after our conversation here makes me ask myself whether it makes any sense to get involved in such discussions. And now my misgivings have become even stronger. I am not angry with you in the least. The thought that you want to shake me in my beliefs would never occur to me; I do not think you capable of such an absurd undertaking. Also, I do not fear encountering your objections. However, it would be necessary to refute every individual sentence to move on past all of the misunderstandings and presuppositions hidden in the letter. I would not regret the time and trouble if only I could be sure it would help you in some way. However, at the moment, I simply do not believe that is possible. Each of my letters would require a new commentary that would probably not lead to greater understanding than that on which I was commenting. I remember very well how it was with me before the blinders were lifted from my eyes. At the time, I would have only been able to say quite similar things and no theoretical discussion would have swayed me. However, if you experience the change, then you will probably be able to say much better for yourself everything that I could now say. If you are really serious with the search for God, not for the proof of religious experience, then without a doubt you will find a way. I can only advise you with what I wrote earlier, that you should consider the writings of the great saints and mystics because they are the best source material: the autobiography of St. Teresa (I would not recommend that you begin with *Seelenburg* [*The Interior Castle*], although this is the main mystical work) and the writings of St. John of the Cross.

...Now do not be angry with *me* because of this journey. At the present time, it appears to me to be the most correct way.

All the best wishes to you and to yours, your
Edith Stein

To Sr. Callista Kopf, OP, February 12, 1928[11]

Dear Sister Callista,

...Of course, religion is not something to be relegated to a quiet corner or for a few festive hours, but rather, as you yourself perceive, it must be the root and basis of all life: and that, not merely for a few chosen ones, but for every true Christian (though of these there is still but a "little flock"). That it is possible to worship God by doing scholarly research is something I learned, actually, only when I was busy with [the translation of] St. Thomas [Aquinas's *Quaestiones de Veritate* from Latin to German]. (In the little booklet that the sisters here use for the Thomas Sundays, there is a beautiful meditation about that.) Only thereafter could I decide to resume serious scholarly research.

Immediately before, and for a good while after my conversion, I was of the opinion that to lead a religious life meant one had to give up all that was secular and to live totally immersed in thoughts of the Divine. But gradually I realized that something else is asked of us in this world and that, even in the contemplative life, one may not sever the connection with the world. I even believe that the deeper one is drawn into God, the more one must "go out of oneself"; that is, one must go to the world to carry the divine life into it.

The only essential is that one finds, first of all, a quiet corner in which one can communicate with God as though there were nothing else, and that must be done daily. It seems to me the best time is in the early morning hours before we begin our daily work; furthermore, [it is also essential] that one accepts one's particular mission there, preferably for each day, and does not make one's own choice. Finally, one is to consider oneself totally as an instrument, especially with regard to the abilities one uses to perform one's special tasks, in our case, e.g., intellectual ones. We are to see them as something used, not by us, but by God in us.

This, then, is my recipe.... My life begins anew each morning, and ends every evening; I have neither plans nor prospects beyond it; i.e., to plan ahead could obviously be part of one's daily duties—teaching school, for example, could be impossible without that—but it must never turn into a "worry" about the coming day.

After all that, you will understand why I cannot agree when you say I have "become" someone. It does appear as though the orbit of my daily duties is to expand. But that, in my opinion, does not change anything about me. It has been demanded of me, and I have undertaken it, although I am still in the dark about what it will comprise, and what the routine will consist of. I shall be thinking of you on the 15th....

Most cordially, your
Edith Stein

∽∞∾

To Sr. Adelgundis Jaegerschmid, OSB, February 16, 1930[12]

Pax!
Dear Sister Adelgundis,

...There is a real difference between being a chosen instrument and being in the state of grace. It is not up to us to pass judgment, and we may confidently leave all to God's unfathomable mercy. But we may not becloud the importance of these last things. After every encounter in which I am made aware how powerless we are to exercise direct influence, I have a deeper sense of the urgency of my own *holocaustum*. And this awareness culminates increasingly in a: *Hic Rhodus, hic salta* [Here is Rhodes, jump here].[13]

However much our present mode of living may appear inadequate to us—what do we really know about it? But there can be no doubt that we are in the here-and-now to work out our salvation and that of those who have been entrusted to our souls. Let us help one another to learn more and more how to make every day and every hour part of the structure for eternity— shall we, by our mutual prayers during this holy season?

In caritate Christi, your
Edith Stein

To Erna Hermann, December 19, 1930[14]

Pax!
Dear Erna,

Of course, I cannot compete with your beautiful handiwork, but I would also like to send you a small decoration for your room as a Christmas greeting. Of course, were it in my power, I would much rather give you something else, something far more beautiful: the true childlike spirit that opens the door to the approaching Savior, that can say from the heart—not theoretically but practically in each and every case—"Lord, not mine, but thy will be done." I am telling you this because I would like to help you attain the one thing necessary. In the past months I have often been concerned because, repeatedly, I had the impression that there is still something lacking on this most important point, that an obstinate self-will is present, a tenacious clinging to desires once conceived. And if I have seemed to you, perhaps, hard and relentless because I would not give in to your wishes, then believe me, that was not due to coldness or a lack of love, but because of a firm conviction that I should harm you by acting otherwise. I am only a tool of the Lord. I would like to lead to him anyone who comes to me. And when I notice that this is not the case, but that the interest is invested in my person, then I cannot serve as a tool and must beg the Lord to help in other ways. After all, he is never dependent on only one individual.

Won't you make use of these last days of Advent for an honest self-examination, so that you will be granted a truly grace-filled Christmas?....

Now my first wish for you is that you recuperate thoroughly at home, and that you will then be able to return here, strengthened, and with a heart filled with Christmas peace.

I will remember you at Beuron. Most sincerely, your
Edith Stein

☙

To Rose Magold, June 16, 1931[15]

Pax!
Dear Rose,

I know you are aware that you may write me anything you wish. That I will not reply when I cannot find time to do so, I have shown you by this long delay.

...The problem of keeping company with the young teachers is not such a simple one. It is very natural for young people to enjoy the company of other young people. And it is also very natural to find particular enjoyment in being together with people of the opposite sex. I believe both of these experiences were true in your case, and simply admitting it to yourself was all you had to do—after all, there's nothing whatever wrong with it—nor should you have felt it was permissible for you only because of the others. If one is intent on having all of one's life consist exclusively of sacrifices, the danger of pharisaism is around the corner. Of course, when one becomes aware that there is a personal risk in matters that are innocent in themselves, then one must be on guard against them. When one has a clear call to the religious life and is determined to follow it, it is surely advisable not to establish too close a relationship with any man, nor should one encourage a mutual attraction since it cannot attain its natural fulfillment. In most cases that would jeopardize the religious vocation. And it has often concerned me that you have burdened yours in ways that did not serve it well....

Best regards to you and to all acquaintances whom you run into, from your

Edith Stein

To Anneliese Lichtenberger, August 17, 1931[16]

Pax!
Dear Anneliese,

God leads each of us on an individual way; one reaches the goal more easily and more quickly than another. We can do very little ourselves, compared to what is done to us. But that little bit we must do. Primarily, this consists before all else of persevering in prayer to find the right way, and of following without resistance the attraction of grace when we feel it. Whoever acts in this way and perseveres patiently will not be able to say that his efforts were in vain. But one may not set a deadline for the Lord.

Is there an Old Testament or at least a translation of the Psalms available either in your home, or somewhere in the vicinity?... Psalm 118[17] is recited every Sunday in the Little Hours (Prime to None). It is the longest one, but very rich and beautiful.

Obviously it is no small matter for you to return to Speyer. But that's what has been decided for you, and you have no responsibility for it. Do as much as you can, and give your parents a regular account of your standing so there will be no surprise if things go badly at Easter.[18] Then we will see about the future. Among the books you got as a child, do you have Andersen's *Fairy Tales*? If so, read the story of the ugly duckling. I believe in your swan-destiny. Just don't hold it against others if they haven't discovered this yet, and don't let yourself become bitter. You are not the only one to make mistakes day after day—we all do it. But the Lord is patient and full of mercy. In his household of grace he can use our faults, too, if we lay them on the altar for him. "A contrite and humbled heart, O God, you will not scorn" (Ps 50). That, too, is one of my favorite verses.

With best regards and remembering you faithfully, your
Edith Stein

⁂

To Rose Magold, August 20, 1931[19]

Pax!
Dear Rose,

...Surely, Sigrid Undset [Norwegian author] will ruthlessly remove all kinds of scales from your eyes. That won't harm you; rather, it will be useful in many respects. But as for what God wants of you, that you will have to seek to learn from him, eye to eye....

Regards to all you see, from me. Faithfully remembering you, your
Edith Stein

⁂

To Elisabeth Nicola, August 6, 1933[20]

Pax!
Dear Fräulein Nicola,

Thank you so much for your kind letter. I may surely tell you that I have observed with great joy the transformation that has taken place in you during this past year. For there is nothing more beautiful on earth than the work of grace in a soul. If I am supposed to have cooperated therein as a *causa secunda* [secondary cause], it was totally without my knowledge and wholly unintentional on my part. But even if without one's own action one is able to be an instrument [of grace], it creates a very strong bond. And so I believe our common path has not come to an end, even though a lively correspondence and frequent meetings will not be possible....

With best regards, your
Edith Stein

14

FAITH IN ACTION

INTRODUCTION

Referring to the commandment to love one's neighbor as oneself, Edith writes, "The 'neighbor' is not the one whom I 'like,' but any and every human being with whom I come into contact, without exception."[1] Kindness, thoughtfulness, and generosity were characteristic of Edith. These qualities were nurtured in her family home and practiced throughout her life. During World War I, she sent letters and packages to friends who were soldiers, and she herself served in the Red Cross.[2] A teacher in Speyer relates how Edith would put together and secretly deliver packages for the poor at Christmas.[3] In 1926, she offered to pay for Roman Ingarden's trip to Germany. In this regard she writes,

> I have (in addition to free room and board) an income that exceeds my needs, and I always have something left over for other purposes. I never view what I give to others as a gift for I firmly believe that whatever comes into my hands is not my own but is something I hold in trust. On the other hand, I also want to say that I hope such a suggestion is not hurtful to you. Surely it is self-evident that I would not want to hurt anyone.[4]

These are just a few scenarios that present an image of Edith as having a natural tendency to live as those she describes as being poor in spirit in her essay "Blessed Are the Poor in Spirit," included in chapter 9—holding possessions loosely in one's hands with the readiness to give them away. It seems that putting her faith into action by loving her neighbor through acts of kindness came somewhat naturally for her; but that does not imply that it was always easy. She felt the pangs of hurt or rejection as much as anyone else. So, for example, it must have been a challenge for her to reach out to her old friend Fritz Kaufmann when his mother died despite his disapproval of her baptism and no communication with her for five years. Likewise, it had to be difficult at times for her to maintain a long-distance correspondence with Roman Ingarden in what often seems to have been a more one-sided friendship that others would have long abandoned.

When writing about her university years, Edith describes herself as having "an extraordinarily strong social conscience" with a "feeling for the solidarity" of all humankind as well as smaller social groups. Moreover, she states that her love for history was closely tied to "a passionate participation" in current events.[5] Those who might perceive her years in Speyer as reclusive would be mistaken. While combining a contemplative lifestyle with a very active apostolic life of teaching, lecturing, and writing, she stayed aware of current events. Her plan to travel to Rome in 1933 for a private audience with Pope Pius XI to request that he write an encyclical denouncing the actions of the Nazis shows her awareness of the political situation as well as a bold demonstration of putting faith into action by speaking up for the sake of justice. When she learned that a private audience would not be possible, she wrote the pope a letter that was accompanied by a cover letter from her spiritual director, Archabbot Walzer. This letter is found in the first selection. In her request, Edith displays courage, a frank assessment of events, a warning of a coming suppression of Catholics, and humble respect.

The question remains whether her perceptive letter had any influence on Pius XI. Edith documents that she received a blessing from the pope for herself and her relatives, but "Nothing else happened. Later on I often wondered whether this letter might have come to his mind once in a while. For in the years that followed, that which I had predicted for the future of the Catholics in Germany came true step by step."[6] In 1938, Pius XI stated that "anti-Semitism is inadmissible. Spiritually, we are Semites." That same year, a document condemning racism was drafted but never promulgated.[7]

Once she entered Carmel, Edith's way of putting her faith into action was carried out mainly through the apostolate of prayer, her service within her community, and her writing. However, two examples show how her concern for justice also surfaced within the convent walls. In 1938, when some religious were being forced from their convents by the Nazis, the nuns of her Cologne Carmel discussed what they should do regarding the upcoming political election. Knowing that it would be a fixed election, most felt that it would not matter how they voted. But Edith begged the sisters not to vote for Hitler no matter what the personal or community consequences would be.[8] The second example deals with the regulations for the lay or extern sisters in the Carmelite community. Edith found that her community had nothing in writing about the duties of lay sisters, which could result in some unfortunate consequences in practice. She wanted to write something in this regard and asked a Dominican and an Ursuline sister to send information about the guidelines for auxiliary sisters in their respective orders.[9] Here again, Edith anticipated some reforms in religious life that were put into effect after Vatican II.

The remaining selections of excerpts from letters find Edith embracing her life as a Carmelite and explaining the apostolic aspect of the Carmelite lifestyle to others. In addition to duties and interactions within the convent community, she continued her scholarly writing and kept up a considerable amount of correspondence, even though her daily schedule provided little time for this. In her letters, she frequently mentions mail awaiting her responses.[10] Edith also met with quite a number of people who visited her in Carmel and was glad when the visitors could take away some of the peace of Carmel with them. Rather than separating the Carmelites from the people and their concerns outside their walls, she asserts that the walls of Carmel actually serve to bring them even closer. It was Edith's conviction that "God calls no one for one's own sake alone [and]... that he is prodigal in demonstrating his love when he accepts a soul."[11]

In the final selection taken from a letter to Ingarden written nearly four years after she entered Carmel, Edith first points out the fallacy of his assumptions about the Carmelite lifestyle. She then gives a brief explanation of their way of life. Highlighting God's love for the world, she stresses that their lifestyle has nothing to do with any sort of abhorrence of the world; rather, their call is to love and serve.

THE TEXTS

Letter to Pope Pius XI, 1933[12]

Holy Father!

As a child of the Jewish people who, by the grace of God, for the past eleven years has also been a child of the Catholic Church, I dare to speak to the Father of Christianity about that which oppresses millions of Germans.

For weeks we have seen deeds perpetrated in Germany which mock any sense of justice and humanity, not to mention love of neighbor. For years the leaders of National Socialism have been preaching hatred of the Jews. Now that they have seized the power of government and armed their followers, among them proven criminal elements, this seed of hatred has germinated. The government has only recently admitted that excesses have occurred. To what extent, we cannot tell, because public opinion is being gagged. However, judging by what I have learned from personal relations, it is in no way a matter of singular exceptional cases. Under pressure from reactions abroad, the government has turned to "milder" methods. It has issued the watchword "no Jew shall have even one hair on his head harmed." But through boycott measures—by robbing people of their livelihood, civic honor and fatherland—it drives many to desperation; within the last week, through private reports I was informed of five cases of suicide as a consequence of these hostilities. I am convinced that this is a general condition which will claim many more victims. One may regret that these unhappy people do not have greater inner strength to bear their misfortune. But the responsibility must fall, after all, on those who brought them to this point and it also falls on those who keep silent in the face of such happenings.

Everything that happened and continues to happen on a daily basis originates with a government that calls itself "Christian." For weeks, not only Jews but also thousands of faithful Catholics in Germany, and, I believe, all over the world, have been waiting and hoping for the Church of Christ to raise its voice to put a stop to this abuse of Christ's name. Is not this idolization of race and governmental power which is being pounded into the public consciousness by the radio open heresy? Isn't the effort to destroy Jewish blood an abuse of the holiest humanity of our Savior, of the Most Blessed Virgin and the apostles? Is not all this diametrically opposed to the conduct of our Lord and Savior, who, even on the cross, still prayed for his persecutors? And isn't this a black mark on the record of this Holy Year which was intended to be a year of peace and reconciliation?

We all, who are faithful children of the Church and who see the conditions in Germany with open eyes, fear the worst for the prestige of the Church, if the silence continues any longer. We are convinced that this silence will not be able in the long run to purchase peace with the present German government. For the time being, the fight against Catholicism will be conducted quietly and less brutally than against Jewry, but no less systematically. It won't take long before no Catholic will be able to hold office in Germany unless he dedicates himself unconditionally to the new course of action.

At the feet of your Holiness, requesting your apostolic blessing,

Dr. Edith Stein
Instructor at the German Institute for Scientific Pedagogy
Münster in Westphalia, Collegium Marianum

To Sr. Adelgundis Jaegerschmid, August 27, 1933[13]

Dear Sister Adelgundis,

Thank you so much for sharing my joy. Sr. Placida [Laubhardt] can give you an account of what I told her about my first Carmelite joys. We too are *in via* [on the way], for Carmel is a high mountain that one must climb from its very base. But it is a tremendous grace to go this way. And, believe me, in the hours of prayer I always remember especially those who would like to be in my position. Please help me that I may become worthy to live in the inner sanctum of the church and to represent those who must labor outside.

In caritate Christi, your
Edith

꒰꒱

To Sr. Adelgundis Jaegerschmid, January 11, 1934[14]

Pax Christi!
Dear Sister Adelgundis,

...Actual acts of kindness must now be carried out in a different, quiet way. I believe, also, that I will be able to help you more by them than with words. Of course, it is hardly possible to think individually of every intention that is commended to me from so many sides. All one can do is try to live the life one has chosen with ever greater fidelity and purity in order to offer it up as an acceptable sacrifice for all one is connected with. The confidence placed in us, the almost frightening importance placed on our life by so many outside, is a constant stimulus [to do better]....

...All kinds of people have been in our speakroom since I've been here.... Most of the sisters consider it a penance to be called to the speakroom. It is, after all, like a transition into a strange world, and we are happy to flee once more into the silence of the choir and, before the tabernacle, to ponder over those matters that have been entrusted to us. But I still regard this peace, daily, as an immense gift of grace that has not been given for one's exclusive benefit. And when someone comes to us worn out and crushed and then takes away a bit of rest and comfort, that makes me very happy....

In caritate Christi, your
Edith

To Fritz Kaufmann, May 14, 1934[15]

Pax Christi!
Dear Herr Kaufmann,

I am sorry that I could not thank you sooner for your dear letter. I have been writing thank-you letters for four weeks and am far from finished.

You were mistaken in thinking that you had to take leave of me. Naturally, our enclosure is strict: no one may leave or enter, and there is a double grate in the speakroom. But all my visitors who have been close to me have assured me that after a few minutes they are no longer aware of the grates because the spirit moves through them without hindrance. When you are in Cologne some time, you will also make the experiment, won't you? Whoever enters Carmel is not lost to his own, but is theirs fully for the first time; it is our vocation to stand before God for all.

Always with sincerest good wishes for you and yours,
your sister
Teresa Benedicta a Cruce, OCD

EDITH STEIN

To Gisela Naegeli, Autumn 1934[16]

Pax Christi!
Dear Fräulein Naegeli,

...Intentions such as yours are not out of the ordinary for us. Similar ones are brought daily to our door or come in the mail. After all, it is our profession to pray, and many people rely on that. We all pray in common, daily, for the intentions commended to us, and each one adds to that her own contribution for those who are especially under her care. To these, you and your protégés will now belong.

It is often a real source of embarrassment for us when people credit us with special effectiveness in prayer, or with holiness. We can detect nothing extraordinary about ourselves. Despite that it does seem that the Lord gladly helps those who turn to us. It is probably the reward of their confidence, perhaps also the return for our having given ourselves to him. But if the prayer is to be effective for you, then you have to do your part also; in other words, you have to be sensible and do whatever is necessary for your health. God is very pleased when one follows the directions of the doctor and the nurse as though they were his own, and when one uses the time for rest to rest completely, leaving all cares to him....

With best wishes and regards in the love of Christ, your Sister
Teresa Benedicta a Cruce, OCD

To Roman Ingarden, Summer 1937[17]

The Peace of Christ!
Dear Mr. Ingarden,

...If I wanted to get involved in a dispute, I would say that the assumptions you express about our attitude to life fail to take into account the fact that we believe that life does not come to an end. It will be better if I explain something quite simple about our life. We believe it pleases God to choose a small flock of people who will take a special part in his own life, and we believe we belong to this fortunate group. We do not know the basis of the selection. In any case, it is not based on rank or merit, and therefore the blessing of the call does not make us proud, rather small and thankful. Our task is to love and to serve. God never abandons the world he created and above all loves humans very much. Therefore, it is impossible for us to despise the world and humanity. We have not left them because we hold them worthless, but to be free for God. And if it pleases God, we have to maintain connections with many who are on the other side of our grille. All people are the same for us whether they peel potatoes, wash windows, or write books. In general, however, we do what we are best suited to do, and therefore I have peeled potatoes less often than I have written....

With kind regards and greetings for you and your loved ones, your Sister
T. Benedicta of the Cross, OCD

RETREAT REFLECTIONS

INTRODUCTION

Edith made a private retreat from April 10 to 21, 1938, in preparation for her final vows, which she professed on April 21, 1938. The retreat began on Palm Sunday. The following selections include her personal retreat reflections from Holy Thursday until Easter Tuesday, with a poem comprising her reflection for Good Friday. In them, Edith places much focus on Mary, the patroness of the Carmelites. Addressing Mary with ease, she reflects on Mary's presence and reactions during events recounted in Scripture. Edith calls Jesus' fleeting Easter appearances a passing over, and notes that similarly, union with Jesus in Holy Communion is also a passing over.

Her final meditation focuses on the interplay between truth and mercy: "Truth is merciful, and mercy, true." Within the meditation, she brings up an area within herself that she seems to have had to work on her entire life. Edith had a quick and sharp sense of observation, especially of human behavior. As noted in the introduction, she straightforwardly admits that during her university years, she became aware of her use of ridicule or sarcasm to highlight the weaknesses and faults of others. At that time, she learned to let go of the need always to "be right" and began using her awareness of others' vulnerabilities as a means to protect them. Experience also taught her that trying to correct others was useless unless they themselves wanted to improve and were open to another's critique.[1] At this point in her life, we see her further transformation in this area. Edith now sees that revealing another's shortcomings must be driven only by pure love, with consideration for what the other is able to bear, awareness of one's own blindness, and in reliance on God's guidance.

THE TEXTS[2]

(April 14) Holy Thursday—Mary at the Last Supper

Scripture does not say, but it need not really be doubted, that the Mother of God was present. Certainly, she went along to Jerusalem for the Passover feast as always and celebrated the Passover meal with all of Jesus' followers. She who kept all of Jesus' words in her heart—how she will have taken in his farewell discourse. "I have ardently desired to celebrate this Passover meal with you" [Luke 22:15]. At that, did she not think of the wedding at Cana? Now his hour had come. Now he could give what he could only symbolically allude to at that time. The footwashing: he was among them as one who serves. So had she seen him throughout his entire life. So had she herself lived and would continue to live. She understood the mystical meaning of the footwashing: whoever joins in the sacred meal must be entirely pure. But only his grace can give this purity. My Mother, your Holy Communion! Was it not like a return to that incomprehensible unity as when you nourished him with your flesh and blood? But now he nourishes you. In this hour, don't you see before you the entire Mystical Body that is to arise through this sacred meal? Don't you already accept it as a mother, as it is to be entrusted to you beneath the cross tomorrow? Don't you also see all the offenses which will befall the Lord under these forms and make amends for it? O Mother, teach us to receive the body of the Lord as you received it.

(April 15) Good Friday

To Stand beside the Cross with You

Today I stood with you beneath the cross
and felt so clearly, as never before,
that beneath the cross you became our Mother.

How even an earthly mother faithfully ensures
fulfilling her son's last will.
But you were the handmaid of the Lord,

and for the being and life of God's becoming flesh
completely gave your being and life.

So you have taken into your heart those who belong
    to him,
and by the life blood of your bitter pains
you have purchased new life for every soul.
You know us all: our wounds, our weaknesses,
you also know the heavenly radiance which your son's
    love
would like to pour out on us in eternal brightness.
So you carefully direct our steps,
no price is too high for you to lead us to the goal.
But those chosen by you as companions
will someday surround you at the eternal throne,
they must stand with you here at the cross
and with the life blood of bitter pains
purchase the heavenly radiance for the precious souls,
whom God's Son entrusts to them as an inheritance.

(April 16) Holy Saturday: To Wait in Silence for the Salvation of God

Your Holy Saturday: How are we to imagine it otherwise than in complete silence? After the closing of the tomb, St. John surely led you to the house in Jerusalem where he enjoyed hospitality. It will have happened in silence. Reverence before your sorrow had to seal all lips. You will have only intimated that you wanted to be alone. It was just impossible to go to the temple as usual for the Sabbath and the feast, among the people who had crucified him and now would point their fingers at you. Being alone was the only relief. At one point the tears certainly had to flow. If the Lord wept over the death of Lazarus, should you not weep after everything that had taken place? His entire life, which was your life, will have once again come before your soul—all the allusions to the suffering, all the prophetic passages. With this, also the announcement of the resurrection. You told yourself what the Savior made clear to the disciples on the way to Emmaus: Did not the Christ have to suffer all of that in order to enter into his glory? So your sorrow changed to thanks for the "It is finished" and to silent, faith-filled anticipation of Easter morning—on the third day he will arise. I can't imagine it otherwise than that you yourself were present. Didn't the angel of announcement silently lead you from the house of the guests and guide you to the tomb before daybreak? Didn't the Alleluia from the angel's mouth at the tomb sound like the Gloria in the fields of Bethlehem? In the rosy early morning surrounded in brightness, didn't he step out of the tomb into the garden which blossomed like a paradise? No one has reported this reunion to us. No human eye saw it, no ear heard it, and nor has it occurred to any human heart what the Lord prepared for his mother who loved him above all human understanding.

If the time between the resurrection and ascension was dedicated, above all, to the preparation of the developing church, then we may assume that the Lord initiated his mother before all others into all the mysteries of the Mystical Body. She would have died of sorrow at the cross and of joy at the resurrection if a special strengthening of grace had not preserved her for the church. She did not first need the descent of the Holy Spirit like the disciples to understand the mysteries of the kingdom. She will have received information about the mystery of the church, the sacraments, and the priesthood in order to then help form the church in the years after the ascension.

(April 17) Easter Sunday: I Have Risen and I Am with You!

The Risen One is always with you [Mary]! Actually, I believe that he never left you. Yes, the resurrected body was no longer bound to the conditions of the earthly body. He could be in more than one place (as also in the sacramental presence). And if he appeared to the disciples, passing now here, now there, then he could certainly be with you continuously. In earthly life, you helped to carry the cross, even the cross of separation and loneliness. Now you share the blessedness of the Risen One which is free of suffering and receive thanks for your motherly joy in love unceasingly given and in godlike fullness of life. He placed his hand upon you and took your life entirely into his own. So also has he placed his hand upon me, and you have placed your hand upon me, that I will carry the cross with both of you and through the cross, attain the blessed life of resurrection. Our house is yours, Queen of Peace. When I vow myself here to you and your Son forever, then at the same time, I thereby vow myself to this, your family. I must carry its cross and commit myself so that true Easter peace comes to every soul.

Oh my beloved Mother, the Lord has entrusted the mysteries of his kingdom to you and has committed his Mystical Body to you. Your glance overlooks all times; you know every member and his task, and seek to guide him in it. You have accepted our order as your own and guide its destiny. You called our house into being. Each of us is called by you and obliged to your service. I thank you for having called me before I yet knew that the call comes from you. I don't know what you have in mind for me. But I considered it a great, undeserved grace that you have chosen me as your instrument. I would like to place myself entirely into your hands as a pliable instrument. I trust in you, most wise, benevolent, and powerful Virgin, that you will make this dull instrument useful. Here I am—receive me!

Now I may still celebrate Easter with you entirely silent and hidden. You were surely with the Lord not far from the tomb when the women came. He showed himself to Magdalene while the others already returned to the city. Peter and John arrive at the news of the women. After having seen for themselves that the tomb is empty, Peter wants to tell the other disciples and meets the Lord on the way. According to Luke's report of the Emmaus disciples, it must have only been later, after both apostles had already reported to the others about the empty tomb. John surely parted from him in order to find you and bring you the news. Perhaps you had returned to his lodgings. And now you surely went with him to the circle of disciples and were present when he appeared to them through the closed door. For that was an event that concerned the young church. And now you are always present with them because you are the heart of the church.

(April 18) Easter Monday: Emmaus

In the appearances of Eastertime, why does the Lord show himself in a form in which the disciples don't immediately recognize him? His appearance, as they had known him in life, was certainly still indelibly imprinted upon them. St. Gregory defends the eternal truth against the suspicion of a lie. He calls the Savior a graphic artist who so shapes his appearance as it corresponds to the disciples' state of mind. As they speak of him, he is near them; as they doubt, they don't see his true form. But doesn't a manifestation of the new, resurrected nature lie precisely in this changeable and, compared to his familiar appearance, altered form? The Risen One has an entirely different power and freedom in relation to the body than under earthly conditions. He is much more the "Creator." It's shown—as also by entering through the closed door—that the Savior did not return as he was, but rather in a transfigured body. (Thus also, no doubt could arise as to whether he really died.)

They recognize the Lord in the breaking of the bread. The sacramental presence allows them to recognize him inwardly and opens their eyes. But then he disappears. All Easter appearances are only a Passover, a passing over. The union in Holy Communion is also only a passing over. If only we would know to appreciate these moments properly and our heart would remain burning because of them. The effect surely ought to be a lasting one. His blood is truly drink and his body truly food. Thus, we become one body with him and in our mortal body is placed the seed of the immortal glorious body. Now we ought to be wholly members of his body and moved only by his Spirit. Insofar as we don't open our souls to his Spirit and don't allow him to lead us, we are dead members and disfigure the Mystical Body.

Priests are the dispensers of the mysteries of God. The Mystical Body is formed through their service. Seeing the Lord in the hands of unworthy priests must be as painful to Mary as seeing him in the hands of the executioners. Indeed, they inspired our holy Mother [Teresa of Avila] to so urgently inculcate in her order the need for prayer and sacrifice for priests.

My Mother, today was already like a leave-taking day. Both of the next two days I will already be busy with external preparations and may no longer be so entirely silent near you and with you near the Lord. For that reason, I have prayed to you once again wholly from my heart to make me ready for the hour of the marriage. Above all, for an ardent remorse to burn out everything in me which was in the way of union with the Lord. Make it that I be like you, as though I am not, that I no longer have any life than the life of Jesus, that I forget myself and only know him more.

I know that what I have said and written about truth very strictly obliges me. Always remind me of that when I slip from true being into something illusory.

(April 19) Easter Tuesday: Mercy and Truth Have Met

Truth and mercy have met in the work of salvation. They are one in God. The dreadfulness of sin and the power of darkness became apparent in the suffering and death of Jesus. It is mercy that we don't perish, but rather are healed by his wounds, are led to the Father by his abandonment, and gain life through his death. Thus, truth is merciful and mercy, true. Even in your heart, Most Blessed Virgin, truth and mercy are one. You did not close your eyes before the terrible sight of suffering and yet you had mercy on us and with the Lord said: Father, forgive them. If we are truthful, we don't close our eyes before our own sins and failings, but rather we see and openly confess them. And if we truthfully believe in mercy, then it meets us and sets us free. And we are also merciful with respect to others when we are true—when we see and reveal their shortcomings to help set them free. But we are only truly true when we are true in mercy—when only pure love drives us, when we show consideration for what the other is able to bear, when we ourselves are clear about our own blindness, and for that reason, invoke Divine Mercy and not trust our own light, but rather place ourselves under the guidance of divine light.

Truth and mercy are one in the Most Blessed Sacrament. It is truth that we need physical nearness and palpable presence. It is incomprehensible mercy that you took your abode in this form in our midst. It is truth that your sacrifice on the cross would be a vague fact of antiquity if it were not daily present on our altars. Your entire life which was lived for us would be "past" if your mercy were not present to us again and again in the cycle of the church year. The Divine Office is truly sacred and sanctifying service which reveals and makes effective in the present the merciful truth of salvation history—a service which wholly approximates the priestly service. It is incomprehensible truth and mercy that the Almighty God stoops to raise up a wretched creature to himself in bridal union. You say it and I believe that this union is the highest that can happen to a creature on earth, only to be surpassed by [the life of] glory. If we take the sacred vows very earnestly, free ourselves for you through them, and truly believe in the transforming power of your grace and mercy, then this eternal covenant is also not surpassed by mystical marriage. How does one make oneself worthy for that? I'm not able to do it. But I trust in your grace and in the mighty help of your Mother.

NOTES

Brackets in the notes for Stein's selected texts indicate material added by the editor or the translator.

Foreword

1. Edith Stein, from the appendix to Teresa of Avila's *Interior Castle*, in *Endliches und ewiges Sein, Edith Stein Gesamtausgabe* 11/12 (Freiburg: Herder Verlag, 2006), 501.

Introduction

1. Edith Stein, "The Prayer of the Church," in *The Hidden Life*, trans. Waltraut Stein, CWES 4 (Washington, DC: ICS Publications, 1992), 13–16.

2. Pope John Paul II, "Apostolic Letter Issued *Motu Proprio* Proclaiming Saint Bridget of Sweden, Saint Catherine of Siena, and Saint Teresa Benedicta of the Cross Co-Patronesses of Europe," October 1, 1999, no. 3, http://w2. vatican.va/content/john-paul-ii/en/motu_proprio/documents/hf_jp-ii_ motu-proprio_01101999_co-patronesses-europe.html; accessed July 15, 2015.

3. Ibid., no. 9.

4. Raphael Walzer, "Letter to Sr. Maria Aloisia, OCD," December 2, 1946, originally written in English. A copy of the letter was given to me in June 2002 by Sr. Amata Neyer, OCD, at that time archivist of the Edith Stein Archives at the Cologne Carmel. Walzer's English is a bit stilted. Part of this letter is found in Teresia Renata Posselt, *Edith Stein: The Life of a Philosopher and Carmelite*, ed. Susanne Batzdorff, Josephine Koeppel, and John Sullivan (Washington, DC: ICS Publications, 2005), 149–54. However, since there are some variations from the original, it seems to be a retranslation into English from the German translation of the original.

5. Ibid.

EDITH STEIN

6. Edith Stein, *Self-Portrait in Letters 1916-1942*, trans. Josephine Koeppel, CWES 5 (Washington, DC: ICS Publications, 1993), 77, letter 75; hereafter, *Letters*.

7. Edith Stein, "The Mystery of Christmas," in *Writings of Edith Stein* (Westminster, MD: Newman, 1956), 27-28.

8. Edith Stein, *Life in a Jewish Family 1891-1916: An Autobiography*, trans. Josephine Koeppel, CWES 1, ed. Lucy Gelber and Romaeus Leuven (Washington, DC: ICS Publications, 1986), 72; hereafter, *Life*.

9. Erna Biberstein, "Reminiscences," in editor's foreword to Stein, *Life*, 17.

10. Stein, *Life*, 99, 104, 110, 114, 232-36, 273-74, 332-33.

11. Ibid., 138, 152, 217, 219.

12. Stein, *Letters*, 35-36, 44, letters 31, 36.

13. Edith Stein, *Letters to Roman Ingarden*, trans. Hugh Candler Hunt, CWES 12 (Washington, DC: ICS Publications, 2014), 170, letter 68.

14. Ibid., 310-11, letter 151.

15. Stein, *Life*, 424.

16. Edith Stein, "How I Came to the Cologne Carmel," in *Edith Stein: Selected Writings*, trans. Susanne M. Batzdorff (Springfield, IL: Templegate Publishers, 1990), 18.

17. Stein, *Letters*, 143, letter 142a.

18. Ibid., 347-48, letter 337.

19. Lucy Gelber, "Chronology," in *Life*, 429-32.

20. Stein, *Life*, 73-75.

21. Ibid., 216.

22. Stein, *Letters*, 272, letter 259.

23. Stein, *Life*, 195-96.

24. Ibid., 234.

25. Ibid., 276-78, 281-84.

26. Stein, *Letters*, 38-40, letter 32a.

27. Stein, *Life*, 293, 324-64.

28. Stein, *Letters to Roman Ingarden*, 59, letter 14.

29. Stein, *Letters*, 41, letter 34.

30. Ibid., 46, letter 38a.

31. Ibid., 92, letter 93.

32. Edith Stein, *Selbstbildnis in Briefen II (1933-1942)*, ESGA 3 (Freiburg: Herder, 2006), letter 781.

33. Stein, *Letters to Ingarden*, 230, letter 96.

34. Ibid., 326, letter 159.

Notes

35. Stein, *Life*, 160 and 71–72, respectively.
36. Ibid., 138, 148, 213.
37. Ibid., 189–90, 211, 213, 260.
38. Ibid., 316.
39. Ibid., 261.
40. Ibid., 401.
41. Stein, *Letters to Roman Ingarden*, 49–50, letter 9.
42. Posselt, *Edith Stein: Life of a Philosopher and Carmelite*, 59–60, 246n12.
43. Sarah Borden, *Edith Stein* (NY: Continuum, 2003), 6.
44. Edith Stein, *Selbstbildnis in Briefen 1 (1916–1933)*, ESGA 2 (Freiburg: Herder, 2010), letter 11, cited and translated in Josephine Koeppel, *Edith Stein: Philosopher and Mystic* (Scranton, PA: Scranton University Press, 2007), 63.
45. Stein, *Letters to Roman Ingarden*, 136–37, letter 51.
46. Ibid., 139–40, letter 53.
47. Erich Przywara, "Edith Stein zu ihrem zehntnen Todestag," in *Die Besinnung 7*, (1952): 238–43; Erich Przywara, "Die Frage Edith Stein," in *In und Gegen* (Nuremberg, 1955), 61–67.
48. Stein, *Letters to Roman Ingarden*, 189, letter 76n4; See also Stein, *Letters*, 161, letter 158a.
49. Posselt, *Edith Stein: Life of a Philosopher and Carmelite*, 64–65; Gelber, "Chronology," in *Life*, 421.
50. Stein, *Letters to Roman Ingarden*, 259, letter 115.
51. Stein, *Life*, 238.
52. Stein, *Letters*, 195, 209–10, 212, letters 190, 203, 205.
53. Ibid., 171, 198, 203, 327, letters 168, 193, 198, 316.
54. Ibid., 339, letter 328.
55. Ibid., 281–82, letter 270 and n5.
56. Ibid., 291, letter 281.
57. Stein, *Letters to Roman Ingarden*, 248, letter 106n1.
58. Stein, "How I Came to the Cologne Carmel," 16; Stein, *Letters*, 63, 235, letters 55n2, 225.
59. Walzer, "Letter to Sr. Maria Aloisia."
60. Stein, *Letters*, 57, letter 49.
61. Ibid., 110, letter 112.
62. Ibid., 182, letter 178.
63. Ibid., 327, letter 316.
64. Walzer, "Letter to Sr. Maria Aloisia."

65. Harvey Egan, *An Anthology of Christian Mysticism*, 2nd ed. (Collegeville, MN: Liturgical Press, 1996), xx–xxi.

66. Stein, *Letters to Ingarden*, 259–60, letter 115.

67. Roman Ingarden, "Zur Philosophie Edith Steins," in *Edith Stein: eine grosse Glaubenszeugin*, ed. Waltraud Herbstrith (Anweiler, Germany: Verlag Thomas Plöger, 1986), 211, 213–14.

68. Posselt, *Edith Stein: Life of a Philosopher and Carmelite*, 154.

69. Stein, *Letters*, 187, letter 182.

70. Stein, "How I Came to the Cologne Carmel," 16–17.

71. Ibid., 18.

72. Ibid., 19.

73. Posselt, *Edith Stein: Life of a Philosopher and Carmelite*, 167–68; Stein, *Letters to Roman Ingarden*, 332, letter 161; Stein, *Letters*, 251, 275, letters 239, 262; Gelber, "Chronology," in *Life*, 427.

74. Stein, *Letters*, 274–75, letter 262.

75. Edith Stein, "Selig sind die Armen im Geiste," in *Geistliche Texte II*, ESGA 20 (Freiburg: Herder, 2007), 102–9, translation mine.

76. Edith Stein, "Eucharistische Erziehung," in *Bildung und Entfaltung der Individualität*, ESGA 16 (Freiburg: Herder, 2001), 63–66, translation mine.

77. Edith Stein, "Exaltation of the Cross—*Ave Crux, Spes Unica!*" in *The Hidden Life*, trans. Waltraut Stein, CWES 4 (Washington, DC: ICS Publications, 1992), 94–96.

78. Edith Stein, *Finite and Eternal Being: An Attempt at an Ascent to the Meaning of Being*, trans. Kurt Reinhardt, CWES 9 (Washington, DC: ICS Publications, 2002); hereafter, *FEB*.

79. Edith Stein, "Grundlagen der Frauenbildung," and Ergänzung zum Vortrag, in *Die Frau*, ESGA 13 (Freiburg: Herder, 2000), 30–45, translation mine. Cf. "Fundamental Principles of Women's Education," in *Essays on Woman*, trans. Freda Mary Oben, CWES 2, 2nd ed. rev. (Washington, DC: ICS Publications, 1996), 129–45.

80. Edith Stein, "Das heilige Antlitz," in *Geistliche Texte II*, 49–51., translation mine.

81. Edith Stein, "Ich bleibe bei Euch…," in *Geistliche Texte II*, 179–82., translation mine.

82. Edith Stein, "Letter to Pope Pius XI," trans. Susanne Batzdorff, Josephine Koeppel, and John Sullivan, available at http://www.baltimorecarmel.org/saints/Stein/letter%20to%20pope.htm; accessed July 3, 2015.

83. Stein, *Letters to Roman Ingarden*.

84. Roman Ingarden, "Edith Stein on Her Activity as an Assistant of Edmund Husserl, *Philosophy and Phenomenological Research* 23, no. 2 (December 1962): 155.

85. Edith Stein, "Christliches Frauenleben," in *Die Frau*, 79–114, translation mine. Cf. Edith Stein, "Spirituality of the Christian Woman," in *Essays on Woman*, 87–128.

86. Edith Stein, "Zur Idee der Bildung," in *Bildung und Entfaltung der Individualität*, 35–49, translation mine.

87. Edith Stein, "Die Mitwirkung der klösterlichen Bildungsanstalten an der religiösen Bildung der Jugend," in *Bildung und Entfaltung der Individualität*, 50–62, translation mine.

88. Stein, "The Prayer of the Church," 7–17.

89. Edith Stein, "Probleme der neueren Mädchenbildung," in *Die Frau*, 127–208, translation mine. Cf. Edith Stein, "Problems of Women's Education," in *Essays on Woman*, 147–235.

90. Edith Stein, "Vorbereitungsexerzitien für die ewigen hl. Gelübde," in *Geistliche Texte II*, 57–64, translation mine.

91. Edith Stein, *The Science of the Cross*, trans. Josephine Koeppel, CWES 6 (Washington, DC: ICS Publications, 2002).

92. Edith Stein, "Sentient Causality," in *Philosophy of Psychology and the Humanities*, trans. Mary Catharine Baseheart and Marianne Sawicki, CWES 7 (Washington, DC: ICS Publications, 2000).

93. Stein, *Letters*.

94. Edith Stein, "Signum Crucis," in *Geistliche Texte II*, 47–49, translation mine.

95. Edith Stein, "Die theoretischen Grundlagen der sozialen Bildungsarbeit," in *Bildung und Entfaltung der Individualität*, 15–34, translation mine.

96. Edith Stein, "Wahrheit und Klarhheit im Unterricht und in der Erziehung," in *Bildung und Entfaltung der Individualität*, 1–8, translation mine.

Chapter 1

INTRODUCTION

1. Edith Stein, *Self-Portrait in Letters 1916–1942*, trans. Josephine Koeppel, CWES 5 (Washington, DC: ICS Publications, 1993), 289n2.

EDITH STEIN

2. Edith Stein, *Finite and Eternal Being: An Attempt at an Ascent to the Meaning of Being*, trans. Kurt Reinhardt, CWES 9 (Washington, DC: ICS Publications, 2002), 356–57, 376–77.

3. Ibid., 464, 596n1, 604n88.

4. Edith Stein, *Der Aufbau der menschlichen Person: Vorlesungen zur philosophischen Anthropologie*, ESGA 14 (Freiburg: Herder, 2004), 98, 105–6.

THE TEXTS

5. Edith Stein, "Ich bleibe bei Euch…," in *Geistliche Texte II*, ESGA 20 (Freiburg: Herder, 2007), 180.

6. Stein, *Self-Portrait in Letters*, 288–89, letter 278.

7. Stein, *FEB*, 58–60.

8. Martin Heidegger, *Being and Time*, trans. John Macquarrie and Edward Robinson (NY: Harper & Row, 1962), 310–11.

9. Cf. the third way of St. Thomas in *Summa Theologiae* 1, q.2, a 3.

10. Ibid., 1, q.3, a 4.

11. Ibid., 1, q.11, a 3.

12. Hedwig Conrad-Martius has formulated a demonstration of the existence of God in this way: "*If* temporal existence…*then* also of necessity eternal existence," but she never personally "followed up the implications of this rational conclusion." [See "Die Zeit," *Philosophischer Anzeiger II*, 2 and 4 (1927/28): 371ff.]

13. Augustine, *De consensus Evangelistarum* IV, 10, 20; cf. Erich Przywara, *Analogis entis* (Munich: Kösel-Pustet, 1932), 207ff.

14. Augustine, *In Psalmos* 99, 5ff.; cf. Przywara, *Analogis entis*, 201.

15. Ibid., 134, 6; cf. Przywara, *Analogis entis*, 203ff.

16. Stein, *FEB*, 342–45.

17. The Hebrew words, *Ah'jäh, aschér äh' jäh*, have been translated and interpreted in a number of ways: "I am who I am"; "I shall be who I shall be"; "I shall be who I am." We follow the above-mentioned Augustinian version, according to which God enunciates in the "I am" his own name in the strictest and truest sense. (Cf. *FEB*, 59–60.)

18. It seems to me that Leibniz's "monad" shows some of this peculiar characteristic.

19. Cf. Stein, *FEB*, chap. II, §6 and 7.

20. Ibid., 349–51.

21. Ibid., 418–20.

22. Cf. ibid., chap. III, §2 and 12; chap.VI. §4.6.

23. *Catechismus Catholicus*, 11th ed. (Rome, 1933), chap. III, q. 86, p. 112.
24. Ibid., chap. III, q. 119, p.123.
25. Cf. Stein, *FEB*, chap. VI. §5.
26. Cf. Duns Scotus, *Quaestiones disputatae de rerum principio*, q. 4, §6.
27. Cf. Augustine, *On the Trinity* XV, 17ff.
28. We speak here of an "image" and not, like St. Thomas, of a mere "vestige," because we find in creaturely autonomy of being and in creaturely fullness of meaning and life a genuine likeness of divine autonomy and plenitude of meaning and life, not a mere sign or trace of the authorship of the Triune God. (cf. *FEB*, chap. VII, n.1).
29. Stein, *FEB*, 423.
30. Ibid., 424–27.
31. Ibid., 462–64.

Chapter 2

Introduction

1. Edith Stein, *Finite and Eternal Being: An Attempt at an Ascent to the Meaning of Being*, trans. Kurt Reinhardt, CWES 9 (Washington, DC: ICS Publications, 2002), 57–58.
2. Edith Stein, *Self-Portrait in Letters 1916–1942*, trans. Josephine Koeppel, CWES 5 (Washington, DC: ICS Publications, 1993), 261, 270, letters 248, 257.
3. Ibid., 314, letter 306.
4. Edith Stein, "Sentient Causality," in *Philosophy of Psychology and the Humanities*, trans. Mary Catharine Baseheart and Marianne Sawicki, CWES 7 (Washington, DC: ICS Publications, 2000), 84n115.

The Texts

5. Ibid., 84–85.
6. Stein, *Letters*, 51, letter 42a.
7. Ibid., 86–87, letter 89.
8. [An orator's distinctive, familiar phrase, habitually used to close every talk.]
9. Stein, *Letters*, 184–86, letter 181.
10. Ibid., 308–9, letter 300.

11. Edith Stein, "Wahrheit und Klarhheit im Unterricht und in der Erziehung," in *Bildung und Entfaltung der Individualität*, ESGA 16 (Freiburg: Herder, 2001), 7.

12. Edith Stein, "Zur Idee der Bildung," in *Bildung und Entfaltung der Individualität*, 49.

Chapter 3

INTRODUCTION

1. Edith Stein, *Finite and Eternal Being: An Attempt at an Ascent to the Meaning of Being*, trans. Kurt Reinhardt, CWES 9 (Washington, DC: ICS Publications, 2002), 526.

THE TEXTS

2. Edith Stein, *Endliches und Ewiges Sein: Versuch eines Aufstiegs zum Sinn des Seins*, ESGA 11/12 (Freiburg: Herder, 2006), 100–2, 105–7, translation mine; hereafter, *EeS*. I translate from the German in cases where my translation differs from the extant English translation. Cf. *FEB*, 106–8, 111–14.

3. [Cf. J.W. von Goethe, *Faust I*, trans. David Luke (Oxford University Press, 2008), 1178ff.]

4. Cf. Thomas Aquinas, *Disputed Questions on Truth*, q. 4, a 1, ad 5/6.

5. According to the maxims of St. Anselm, "Faith seeking understanding" and "I believe so that I may understand." Cf. Alexandre Koyré's introduction to his Latin-French work on Anselm's *Proslogion*, which appeared under the title *Fides quaerens intellectum* (Paris, 1930).

6. "All"—"all things" means all that is created.

7. Thus, I [Stein] am trying to translate *synestēken* = "*constant*" [Latin].

8. Cf. the Athanasian Creed.

9. The same interpretation is found in Josef Dillersberger, *Das Wort vom Logos* [*The Word of the Logos*] (Salzburg: Anton Pustet, 1935), 35, with references from Augustine and Origen.

10. The divine essence is not a "*universale*" [universal], but rather a "*commune*" [one in common].

11. This decision was pronounced on the occasion of the condemnation of the *Ontologism* of A. Günther. See Denziger-Bannwart, *Enchiridion Symbolorum*, 11th ed. (Freiburg im Breisgau, 1910), 1659–65.

12. Thomas states that the essential differences among things are unknown to us; we could only characterize them with the aid of the "accidental" differences that derive from the essential ones. (*De ente et essentia*, chap. V). Cf. what is stated about essence and the knowledge of essence in *FEB* III. §11.

13. Aquinas, *Disputed Questions on Truth*, q. 2 a 5 corp.

14. Stein, *EeS*, 210–11, translation mine; cf. *FEB*, 241–42.

15. Cf. *FEB*, III. §12.

Chapter 4

INTRODUCTION

1. Edith Stein, *Life in a Jewish Family 1891–1916: An Autobiography*, trans. Josephine Koeppel, CWES 1, ed. Lucy Gelber and Romaeus Leuven (Washington, DC: ICS Publications, 1986), 397.

2. Edith Stein, *The Science of the Cross*, trans. Josephine Koeppel, CWES 6 (Washington, DC: ICS Publications, 2002), 5.

3. Edith Stein, *Finite and Eternal Being: An Attempt at an Ascent to the Meaning of Being*, trans. Kurt Reinhardt, CWES 9 (Washington, DC: ICS Publications, 2002), 52, 374–76.

4. See Marian Maskulak, *Edith Stein and the Body-Soul-Spirit at the Center of Holistic Formation* (NY: Peter Lang, 2007), 12, 65–66.

5. Ibid., 202.

6. Stein, *FEB*, 549–50n29.

7. Ibid., 460.

8. Edith Stein, *Endliches und Ewiges Sein: Versuch eines Aufstiegs zum Sinn des Seins*, ESGA 11/12 (Freiburg: Herder, 2006), 236, translation mine; cf. *FEB*, 272.

9. Stein, *FEB*, 217.

10. Edith Stein, *Der Aufbau der menschlichen Person: Vorlesungen zur philosophischen Anthropologie*, ESGA 14 (Freiburg: Herder, 2004), 101–2.

11. Stein, *Science of the Cross*, 112.

12. Ibid., 114.

13. Stein, *Aufbau der menschlichen Person*, 115, translation mine.

14. Edith Stein, "Probleme der neueren Mädchenbildung," in *Die Frau*, ESGA 13 (Freiburg: Herder, 2000), 193; cf. Edith Stein, "Problems of Women's Education," in *Essays on Woman*, trans. Freda Mary Oben, CWES 2, 2nd ed. rev. (Washington, DC: ICS Publications, 1996), 217.

15. Stein, *Aufbau der menschlichen Person*, 115, translation mine.

THE TEXTS

16. Stein, *Science of the Cross*, 153–66.

17. Here one must recall that in these distinctions we are using a spatial image for something that is not spatial. Actually, the soul "has no parts, and there is no difference as to inward and outward." Cf. John of the Cross, *Living Flame of Love*, 1.10 [in *The Collected Works of St. John of the Cross*, trans. Kieran Kavanaugh and Otilio Rodriguez, rev. ed. (Washington, DC: ICS Publications, 1991)].

18. What can here merely be indicated in a few words about spiritual being is explained in detail in *Finite and Eternal Being*.

19. *Living Flame of Love* 1.12. [The expression "point of rest" was copied literally by Edith from the translation by Aloysius, p. 13. In a long footnote, the German translator pointed out that St. John of the Cross wrote at a time when science had not yet arrived at the designation "center of gravity." The concept St. John used did not come from physics, but rather from the philosophy of his day that held that whatever was material was attracted by what was "more" material—a stone fell to the earth because it was the smaller of the two and it would have kept "falling" until it reached the very center of the earth, where the earth's material weight was greatest. Hereafter, "point of rest" will usually be translated as "deepest center," but it should be noted that it describes not merely a place but also an activity. The soul has not only arrived at a point, but it is "actively" resting there.]

20. John of the Cross, *Ascent of Mount Carmel*, 2.26.14 [in *The Collected Works of St. John of the Cross*].

21. Cf. Thomas Aquinas, *Disputed Questions on Truth*, q.8 a 11 c [as found in Edith's German translation].

22. Ibid., q.8 a 8 ad 7.

23. Cf. *Living Flame of Love*, 2.32–33.

24. Our Mother St. Teresa of Jesus likens the soul to a castle with many dwelling places. In her principle mystical work, *The Interior Castle*, she tells of seven dwelling places. Teresa of Avila, *The Interior Castle*, 1.1 [in *The Collected Works of St. Teresa of Avila*, trans. Kieran Kavanaugh and Otilio Rodriguez, vol. 2 (Washington, DC: ICS Publications, 1980, 2012)].

25. Our holy Mother [Teresa of Avila] calls the body the outer wall of the castle.

26. Aquinas, *Disputed Questions on Truth*, q.9 a 4.

27. Cf. John of the Cross, *Living Flame of Love*, 4.14–16.

28. Teresa of Avila, *Interior Castle*, VII.1.3.

29. John of the Cross, *Living Flame of Love*, 1.9
30. Ibid., 3.78ff.

Chapter 5

INTRODUCTION

1. Edith Stein, *The Science of the Cross*, trans. Josephine Koeppel, CWES 6 (Washington, DC: ICS Publications, 2002), xxi.

THE TEXTS

2. Edith Stein, *Endliches und Ewiges Sein: Versuch eines Aufstiegs zum Sinn des Seins*, ESGA 11/12 (Freiburg: Herder, 2006), 376, translation mine; cf. Edith Stein, *Finite and Eternal Being: An Attempt at an Ascent to the Meaning of Being*, trans. Kurt Reinhardt, CWES 9 (Washington, DC: ICS Publications, 2002), 446–47.

3. Regarding the commandment to love one's enemy, St. Jerome says: Many measure the commandments of God according to their weakness, not according to the strengths of the saints, and therefore think that what is commanded is impossible…. So one must know that Christ does not demand the impossible, but that which is perfect. *Commentary on Matthew* 5–6, book 1; Roman Breviary, Ferial VI after Ash Wednesday.

4. Stein, *EeS*, 385, translation mine; cf. *FEB*, 457.

5. *EeS*, 385–86, translation mine; cf. *FEB*, 457–58.

6. Edith Stein, *Self-Portrait in Letters 1916–1942*, trans. Josephine Koeppel, CWES 5 (Washington, DC: ICS Publications, 1993), 137, letter 137.

7. Ibid., 149–50, letter 147.

8. Ibid., 154–55, letter 153.

9. Ibid., 318–20, letter 311.

10. [Ps 18 in the Greek Septuagint and Latin Vulgate numbering corresponds to Ps 19 in the Hebrew numbering.]

Chapter 6

INTRODUCTION

1. Edith Stein, "Sendung der katholischen Akademikerin," in *Die Frau* ESGA 13 (Freiburg: Herder, 2000), 224, translation mine; cf. Edith Stein,

EDITH STEIN

"Mission of the Catholic Academic Woman," in *Essays on Woman*, trans. Freda Mary Oben, CWES 2, 2nd ed. rev. (Washington, DC: ICS Publications, 1996), 267.

2. Edith Stein, *Finite and Eternal Being: An Attempt at an Ascent to the Meaning of Being*, trans. Kurt Reinhardt, CWES 9 (Washington, DC: ICS Publications, 2002), 243.

The Texts

3. Edith Stein, *Endliches und Ewiges Sein: Versuch eines Aufstiegs zum Sinn des Seins*, ESGA 11/12 (Freiburg: Herder, 2006), 422–23, translation mine; cf. *FEB*, 504–6.

4. Like everything created, the soul could be annihilated by God, but this would not be a "natural end."

5. Edith Stein, *Self-Portrait in Letters 1916–1942*, trans. Josephine Koeppel, CWES 5 (Washington, DC: ICS Publications, 1993), 103–4, letter 104.

6. Ibid., 286–87, letter 277.

7. Edith Stein, "Probleme der neueren Mädchenbildung," in *Die Frau*, ESGA 13 (Freiburg: Herder, 2000), 179–80. Cf. Edith Stein, "Problems of Women's Education," in *Essays on Woman*, 201–2.

Chapter 7

Introduction

1. Edith Stein, *Der Aufbau der menschlichen Person: Vorlesungen zur philosophischen Anthropologie*, ESGA 14 (Freiburg: Herder, 2004), 134, translation mine.

The Texts

2. Edith Stein, "Grundlagen der Frauenbildung," in *Die Frau*, ESGA 13 (Freiburg: Herder, 2000), 32; cf. "Fundamental Principles of Women's Education," in *Essays on Woman*, trans. Freda Mary Oben, CWES 2, 2nd ed. rev. (Washington, DC: ICS Publications, 1996), 130.

3. Edith Stein, *Finite and Eternal Being: An Attempt at an Ascent to the Meaning of Being*, trans. Kurt Reinhardt, CWES 9 (Washington, DC: ICS Publications, 2002), 507–10.

4. The appendix in *EeS* on *The Interior Castle* will make this clear.

5. It was laid down by dogmatic definition that angels do not proceed from one another (Denziger 533) [H. Denzinger and C. Bannwart, *Enchiridion symbolorum, definitionum et declarationum de rebus fidei et morum* (Freiburg: Herder, 1928), 533.] In everything else, dogmatic theology leaves a great deal of freedom regarding the different views on angels. The church teaches in its dogmatic declarations merely that angels are pure spirits created by God (Denzinger 428, 1783).

6. Thus, the one-sidedness of nationalism, internationalism, etc.

7. Edith Stein, "Die theoretischen Grundlagen der sozialen Bildungsarbeit," in *Bildung und Entfaltung der Individualität*, ESGA 16 (Freiburg: Herder, 2001), 16–34.

Chapter 8

INTRODUCTION

1. Edith Stein, "Probleme der neueren Mädchenbildung," in *Die Frau*, ESGA 13 (Freiburg: Herder, 2000), 168; cf. "Problems of Women's Education" in *Essays on Woman*, trans. Freda Mary Oben, CWES 2, 2nd ed. rev. (Washington, DC: ICS Publications, 1996), 189.

2. See Maximilian Mary Dean, "Dumb Ox or Dunce—Part II E," *The Absolute Primacy of Christ* (blog), http://absoluteprimacyofchrist.org/dumb-ox-or-dunce-part-ii-e/, accessed June 27, 2015.

3. Edith Stein, *Finite and Eternal Being: An Attempt at an Ascent to the Meaning of Being*, trans. Kurt Reinhardt, CWES 9 (Washington, DC: ICS Publications, 2002), 513–14.

4. John Hardon, "The Church as the Mystical Body of Christ," *Catholic Faith* 3, no. 4 (July–August 1997): 5–10, The Real Presence Eucharistic Education and Adoration Association, http://www.therealpresence.org/archives/Mystical_Body/Mystical_Body_004.htm, accessed June 28, 2015.

5. "Dogmatic Constitution on the Church," in *Vatican Council II: The Conciliar and Post-Conciliar Documents*, ed. Austin Flannery, rev. ed. (Collegeville, MN: Liturgical Press, 2014), 15, 16, 69.

6. Edith Stein, *Self-Portrait in Letters 1916–1942*, trans. Josephine Koeppel, CWES 5 (Washington, DC: ICS Publications, 1993), 272, letter 259.

THE TEXTS

7. Stein, *FEB*, 523–27.

8. Aquinas, *Summa Theologiae* III, q. 8, a 4, corp.

Chapter 9

Introduction

1. Edith Stein, *Self-Portrait in Letters 1916-1942*, trans. Josephine Koeppel, CWES 5 (Washington, DC: ICS Publications, 1993), 277-78, letter 265.

2. Ibid., 236, letter 225n1.

3. Ibid., 235, letter 225.

4. Ibid., 211, letter 204.

5. Ibid., 218-19, letter 212.

6. Pope Francis, *The Joy of the Gospel* (Frederick, MD: The Word Among Us Press, 2013), no. 259.

7. Stein, *Letters*, 66, letter 58.

8. Ibid., 88, letter 91.

9. Edith Stein, *Life in a Jewish Family 1891-1916: An Autobiography*, trans. Josephine Koeppel, CWES 1, ed. Lucy Gelber and Romaeus Leuven (Washington, DC: ICS Publications, 1986), 70-71.

10. For example, see *Catechism of the Catholic Church*, no. 1096.

11. Edith Stein, "Aufgabe der Frau als Führerin der Jugend zur Kirche," in *Die Frau*, ESGA 13 (Freiburg: Herder, 2001), 216; cf. "Church, Women, and Youth," in *Essays on Woman*, trans. Freda Mary Oben, CWES 2, 2nd ed. rev. (Washington, DC: ICS Publications, 1996), 245.

The Texts

12. Edith Stein, "Selig sind die Armen im Geiste," in *Geistliche Texte II*, ESGA 20 (Freiburg: Herder, 2007), 102-9.

13. [Augustine, *True Religion*, in *On Christian Belief*, trans. Edmund Hill, The Works of Saint Augustine: A Translation for the 21st Century, part 1, vol. 8 (Hyde Park, NY: New City Press, 2005), 39, 72.]

14. Edith Stein, "The Prayer of the Church," in *The Hidden Life*, trans. Waltraut Stein, CWES 4 (Washington, DC: ICS Publications, 1992), 7-17.

15. Judaism had and has its richly formed liturgy for public as well as for family worship, for feast days, and for ordinary days.

16. "Praise to you, our Eternal God, King of the Universe, who brings forth bread from the earth…who creates the fruit of the vine."

17. For example, before awakening Lazarus (John 11:41–42).

18. Cf. N. Glatzer and L. Strauss, *Sendung und Schicksal: Aus dem Schriftum des nachbiblischen Judentums* [Mission and fate: from the writings of post-biblical Judaism] (Berlin: Schocken-Verlag, 1931), 2ff.

19. Erik Peterson, in *Buch von dem Engeln* [Book of the angels] (Leipzig: Verlag Hegner, 1935), has shown in an unsurpassed way the union of the heavenly and earthly Jerusalem in the celebration of the liturgy.

20. Naturally, it is a prerequisite that one is not burdened with serious sins; otherwise, one could not receive Holy Communion "in the proper spirit."

21. Because the limits of this essay do not permit me to cite Jesus' entire high priestly prayer, I must ask readers to take up St. John's Gospel at this point and re-read chapter 17.

22. Teresa of Avila, *The Way of Perfection*, in *Schriften der heiligen Teresa von Jesus*, vol. 2, ch. 1 (Regensberg, 1907). [English translation in *The Collected Works of St. Teresa of Avila*, trans. Kieran Kavanaugh and Otilio Rodriguez, vol. 2 (Washington, DC: ICS Publications, 1980), chap. 1, sec. 1 and 5, pp. 41 and 42].

23. Ibid., ch. 3. Both of these passages are regularly read in our order on Ember Days [in Edith Stein's time].

24. Teresa of Avila, *Interior Castle*, seventh dwelling place, ch. 2, sec. 1.

25. Marie de la Trinité, *Lettres de "Consummata" à une Carmélite* (Carmel d'Avignon, 1930), letter of September 27, 1917. Published in German as *Briefe in den Karmel* (Regensberg: Pustet, 1934), 263ff.

26. "There is one interior adoration…adoration in Spirit, which abides in the depths of human nature, in its understanding and in its will; it is authentic, superior adoration, without which outer adoration remains without life." From *"O mein Gott, Dreifaltiger, den ich anbete": Gebet der Schwester Elisabeth von der Heligisten Dreifaltigkeit* ["O my God, Trinity whom I adore": Prayer of Sister Elizabeth of the Trinity], interpreted by Dom Eugene Vandeur, OSB (Regensburg, 1931), 23. [English translation: *Trinity Whom I Adore*, trans. Dominican Nuns of Corpus Christi Monastery (NY: Pustet, 1953)].

27. [There are oblique references in this sentence to the Carmelite *Rule* and to St. Thérèse, who said she wished to be love in the heart of the church.]

28. St. Augustine, "Tract. 27 in Joannem," from the Roman Breviary [of Edith Stein's day], readings 8 and 9 of the third day in the octave of Corpus Christi.

29. St. John Chrysostom, "Homily 61 to the People of Antioch," fourth reading, from the Roman Breviary [of Edith Stein's day].

30. Roman Missal [of Edith Stein's day], post-Communion for the first Sunday after Pentecost.

31. Edith Stein, "Eucharistische Erziehung," in *Bildung und Entfaltung der Individualität*, ESGA 16 (Freiburg: Herder, 2001) 63–66.

32. Stein, *Letters* 141, letter 140–41.

Chapter 10

INTRODUCTION

1. Edith Stein, *Self-Portrait in Letters 1916–1942*, trans. Josephine Koeppel, CWES 5 (Washington, DC: ICS Publications, 1993), 182, letter 178.

2. Josephine Koeppel, *Edith Stein: Philosopher and Mystic* (Scranton, PA: University of Scranton Press, 2007), 83, 120.

THE TEXTS

3. Edith Stein, *Endliches und Ewiges Sein: Versuch eines Aufstiegs zum Sinn des Seins*, ESGA 11/12 (Freiburg: Herder, 2006), 373–74, translation mine. Cf. Edith Stein, *Finite and Eternal Being: An Attempt at an Ascent to the Meaning of Being*, trans. Kurt Reinhardt, CWES 9 (Washington, DC: ICS Publications, 2002), 443–44.

4. Augustine, *Homilies on the Gospel of John 1–40*, 15, 25 [trans. Edmund Hill (New Hyde Park, NY: New City Press, 2009)].

5. Augustine, *Soliloquies*, 2, 6, 9 [trans. Kim Paffenroth (New Hyde Park, NY: New City Press, 2000)].

6. But such a renunciation of the world and the self will only be meaningful and fruitful under the direction of grace and in the boundaries which it prescribes.

7. John of the Cross, *The Collected Works of St. John of the Cross* [trans. Kieran Kavanaugh and Otilio Rodriguez, rev. ed. (Washington, DC: ICS Publications, 1991)].

8. Edith Stein, *The Science of the Cross*, trans. Josephine Koeppel, CWES 6 (Washington, DC: ICS Publications, 2002), 111–22.

9. John of the Cross, *Living Flame of Love*, 1.10. Explanation of the third line of the first stanza.

10. Augustine, *The Trinity*, XII, 4 and 7 [trans. Edmund Hill (Brooklyn, NY: New City Press), 1991].

Notes

11. In actuality, Thomas connects the memory with sensuality because it recognizes the past *as* past, therefore distinguishing it from the present: this, he says, is a function of sensuality. Because the intellect recognizes not only the present, but also *that* it recognizes, so to say, that it possessed this knowledge before, the memory may be counted as belonging to the spiritual part of the soul. (*Quaestiones disputatae de veritate* q.10 a 2 corp; [Investigations of truth, 1, 266ff]). [This is the work of Aquinas that Edith translated from Latin into German.]

12. In explaining the manifold concepts covered by the word *faith*, I am following here the distinctions that St. Thomas makes in the *Quaestiones disputatae de veritate*, q 14 a 7 ad 7.

13. [See John of the Cross, *Ascent of Mount Carmel*, 2.29ff.]

14. Cf. John of the Cross, *Ascent of Mount Carmel*, 2.14.2 ff.: "The Short Treatise on the Dark Affirming and Negating Knowledge of God."

15. See ibid., 2.3 and 2.5.4.

16. Ibid., 2.7.11ff.

17. Pseudo-Dionysius the Areopagite, *Mystica Theologia*, I, 1.

18. Stein, *Science of the Cross*, 169–79.

19. John of the Cross, *The Ascent of Mount Carmel*, 2.5ff. Here, only this life is taken into consideration; the union in glory, which is again different, is not included.

20. John of the Cross, *Spiritual Canticle*, 11.3 [in *The Collected Works of St. John of the Cross*].

21. Teresa of Avila, *The Interior Castle*, V.1.10.

22. Aquinas, *Disputed Questions on Truth*, q. 14, a 2, corp.

23. Teresa of Avila, *Interior Castle*, V.3.

24. Ibid., V.1.12; V.2.9, 12.

25. Ibid., V.1.6.

26. [This and the preceding quotations are from *Interior Castle*, V.1.9–11.]

27. [Ibid., VI.4.1]

28. John of the Cross, *Living Flame of Love*, 3.25.

29. We shall see later that also in the *Spiritual Canticle* the explanation is not completely uniform.

30. John of the Cross, *Ascent to Mount Carmel*, 2.32.2.

31. Cf. Jean Baruzi, *Saint Jean de la Croix et le problème de l'expérience mystique*, vol. 1: "Les Textes" (Paris: Editions Salvator, 1999), as well as the introduction in the most recent critical edition by Silverio de Santa Teresa, *Obras completas de San Juan de la Cruz* (Burgos: El Monte Carmelo, 1929).

32. Teresa of Avila, letter to M. Ana de Jésus, October 1578.

33. John of the Cross, *Spiritual Canticle*, 13.7.

34. When in one and the same created being the indwelling modifies itself, it is in fact a modification [a change in mode] and not a combination of one mode with another. When a soul receives sanctifying grace, God does not then dwell in her in two differing modes; rather, the indwelling of presence and that of grace are a single unit.

35. John 2:23–24; cf. Augustine, *Tract. in Joan.* 11–12, Migne, P.L., XXXV, 1474ff.

36. Teresa of Avila, *Interior Castle*, V.1.9; John of the Cross, *Dark Night of the Soul*, 2.20.3 [in *The Collected Works of St. John of the Cross*], and *Spiritual Canticle*, 13.2.

37. Teresa of Avila, *Interior Castle*, VI.6.9; John of the Cross, *Spiritual Canticle*, 14–15.2.

38. Teresa of Avila, *Interior Castle*, VII.1.5; John of the Cross, *Spiritual Canticle*, 22.2.

39. It is impossible here and now to examine how far this can be validly applied to human interpersonal relations.

40. John of the Cross, *Living Flame of Love*, 3.78.

41. In the discussion of the *Living Flame*, we will arrive at it at once. St. Teresa describes the Blessed Trinity's descending to the mystical marriage in *The Interior Castle*, VII.1.

Chapter 11

INTRODUCTION

1. Edith Stein, *Finite and Eternal Being: An Attempt at an Ascent to the Meaning of Being*, trans. Kurt Reinhardt, CWES 9 (Washington, DC: ICS Publications, 2002), 247–48.

2. Ibid., 274.

3. Edith Stein, "Probleme der neueren Mädchenbildung," in *Die Frau*, ESGA 13 (Freiburg: Herder, 2000), 185–86; cf. Edith Stein, "Problems of Women's Education," in *Essays on Woman*, trans. Freda Mary Oben, CWES 2, 2nd ed. rev. (Washington, DC: ICS Publications, 1996), 208.

4. Edith Stein, *Self-Portrait in Letters 1916-1942*, trans. Josephine Koeppel, CWES 5 (Washington, DC: ICS Publications, 1993), 54–55, letter 45.

5. Edith Stein, "Aufgabe der Frau als Führerin der Jugend zur Kirche," in *Die Frau*, 216; cf. "Church, Women, and Youth," in *Essays on Woman*, 245.

THE TEXTS

6. Edith Stein, "Die Mitwirkung der klösterlichen Bildungsanstalten an der religiösen Bildung der Jugend," in *Bildung und Entfaltung der Individualität*, ESGA 16 (Freiburg: Herder, 2001), 50–62.

7. [This seems to be a reference to Goethe's *Torquato Tasso* 2, 969: "Thus one feels the intention and is upset."]

8. [*Singmesse*—Beginning in the eighteenth century, name given to Mass arrangements and accompanying songs that were sung by the faithful in German.]

9. Stein, "Grundlagen der Frauenbildung," in *Die Frau*, 39; cf. "Fundamental Principles of Women's Education," in *Essays on Woman*, 138–39.

10. Stein, Ergänzung zum Vortrag, "Grundlagen der Frauenbildung," 43–45; cf. "Fundamental Principles of Women's Education," 143–45.

11. [Excerpt from Latin hymn *Nunc Sancti Nobis Spiritus* ascribed to St. Ambrose. John Henry Newman translated the lines as: "Let love light up our mortal frame, till others catch the living flame."]

12. Stein, "Christliches Frauenleben," in *Die Frau*, 95, 96, 113; cf. "Spirituality of the Christian Woman," in *Essays on Woman*, 106, 107, 127–28.

Chapter 12

INTRODUCTION

1. Edith Stein, *The Science of the Cross*, trans. Josephine Koeppel, CWES 6 (Washington, DC: ICS Publications, 2002), 9–10.

2. Edith Stein, *Self-Portrait in Letters 1916–1942*, trans. Josephine Koeppel, CWES 5 (Washington, DC: ICS Publications, 1993), 151, letter 148.

3. Ibid., 295, letter 287.

4. Ibid., 305, letter 296.

5. Ibid., 327, letter 316.

6. Ibid., 341, letter 330n3.

7. Ibid., 253–55, 256–57, 262–63, letters 241, 242, 244, 249.

8. Ibid., 267–68, letter 254.

The Texts

9. Edith Stein, "Exaltation of the Cross—*Ave Crux, Spes Unica!*" in *The Hidden Life*, trans. Waltraut Stein, CWES 4 (Washington, DC: ICS Publications, 1992), 94–96. [For this title, Waltraut Stein translated Kreuzerhöhung as "elevation of the cross," rather than "exaltation of the cross."]

10. Stein, *Letters*, 52–53, letter 44.

11. [Stein's translation of J. H. Newman, *Briefe und Tagebücher bis zum Übertritt zur Kirche* (John Henry Newman's letters and diaries to his conversion), (Munich, 1928).]

12. Stein, *Letters*, 128, letter 129.

13. Ibid., 196–97, letter 192.

14. Ibid., 341, letter 330.

15. [Father Johannes Hirschmann, SJ, member of the Jesuit community at Valkenburg (Limburg, Netherlands)].

16. [Edith refers to her *stabilitas loci*, that is, her incorporation in the [chapter of the] monastery of the nuns in Echt. Unlike Benedictines, Carmelites do not take a vow of stability as such, but they are assigned conventuality to a particular monastery. Since efforts were already being made to have Edith go to another monastery outside the Netherlands, the involved canonical procedure of incorporation at Echt would have to be superseded by a subsequent one. If it were delayed at this point, the transfer could be effected directly from Cologne to the new Carmel.]

17. Edith Stein, "Signum Crucis," in *Geistliche Texte II*, ESGA 20 (Freiburg: Herder, 2007), 47–49.

18. Stein, "Das heilige Antlitz," in *Geistliche Texte II*, 49–51.

Chapter 13

Introduction

1. Edith Stein, *Letters to Roman Ingarden*, trans. Hugh Candler Hunt, CWES 12 (Washington, DC: ICS Publications, 2014), 199, letter 81n1.

2. Edith Stein, *Self-Portrait in Letters 1916–1942*, trans. Josephine Koeppel, CWES 5 (Washington, DC: ICS Publications, 1993), 236–37, letter 226.

3. Ibid., 238, letter 227.

4. Ibid., 272, letter 259.

5. Ibid., 110, letter 112.

THE TEXTS

6. Stein, *Letters to Roman Ingarden*, 207–9, letter 85.
7. Ibid., 229–31, letter 96.
8. Ibid., 258–60, letter 115.
9. Ibid., 262–63, letter 117.
10. Ibid., 265–67, letter 120.
11. Stein, *Letters*, 54–55, letter 45.
12. Ibid., 59–60, letter 52.
13. [See ibid., 63, letter 55, where Edith refers to this as her motto.]
14. Ibid., 77, letter 76.
15. Ibid., 92–93, letter 94.
16. Ibid., 100–101, letter 102.
17. [Psalm 118 in the Greek Septuagint and Latin Vulgate numbering corresponds to Psalm 119 in the Hebrew numbering.]
18. [In many German schools, Easter was the time for final reports and promotions.]
19. Stein, *Letters*, 102, letter 103.
20. Ibid., 153, letter 150.

Chapter 14

INTRODUCTION

1. Edith Stein, *Finite and Eternal Being: An Attempt at an Ascent to the Meaning of Being*, trans. Kurt Reinhardt, CWES 9 (Washington, DC: ICS Publications, 2002), 446.

2. Edith Stein, *Life in a Jewish Family 1891-1916: An Autobiography*, trans. Josephine Koeppel, CWES 1, ed. Lucy Gelber and Romaeus Leuven (Washington, DC: ICS Publications, 1986), 309–10, 318–65.

3. Teresia Renata Posselt, *Edith Stein: The Life of a Philosopher and Carmelite*, ed. Susanne Batzdorff, Josephine Koeppel, and John Sullivan (Washington, DC: ICS Publications 2005), 73.

4. Edith Stein, *Letters to Roman Ingarden*, trans. Hugh Candler Hunt, CWES 12 (Washington, DC: ICS Publications, 2014), 236–38, letter 101.

5. Stein, *Life*, 190.

6. Edith Stein, "How I Came to the Cologne Carmel," in *Edith Stein: Selected Writings*, trans. Susanne M. Batzdorff (Springfield, IL: Templegate Publishers, 1990), 17.

7. See Georges Passelecq and Bernard Suchecky, *The Hidden Encyclical of Pius XI*, trans. Steven Rendall (New York: Harcourt Brace & Company, 1997); *La Documentation Catholique* 39 (1938):1459–60, cited in Emma Fattorini, *Hitler, Mussolini, and the Vatican: Pope Pius XI and the Speech That Was Never Made* (Malden, MA: Polity Press, 2011), 161.

8. Posselt, *Edith Stein: Life of a Philosopher and Carmelite*, 182; Josephine Koeppel, *Edith Stein: Philosopher and Mystic* (Scranton, PA: Scranton University Press, 2007), 86.

9. Edith Stein, *Self-Portrait in Letters 1916–1942*, trans. Josephine Koeppel, CWES 5 (Washington, DC: ICS Publications, 1993), 319, 322, letters 311, 312.

10. For example, see Stein, *Letters*, 262, 274, letters 249, 262.

11. Ibid., 275, letter 262.

THE TEXT

12. Edith Stein, "Letter to Pope Pius XI," trans. Susanne Batzdorff, Josephine Koeppel, and John Sullivan, available at http://www.baltimorecarmel.org/saints/Stein/letter%20to%20pope.htm; accessed July 3, 2015.

13. Stein, *Letters*, 154, letter 152.

14. Ibid., 166–67, letter 164.

15. Ibid., 177–78, letter 174.

16. Ibid., 187–88, letter 183.

17. Stein, *Letters to Roman Ingarden*, 330–32, letter 161.

Chapter 15

INTRODUCTION

1. Edith Stein, *Life in a Jewish Family 1891–1916: An Autobiography*, trans. Josephine Koeppel, CWES 1, ed. Lucy Gelber and Romaeus Leuven (Washington, DC: ICS Publications, 1986), 234.

THE TEXTS

2. Edith Stein, "Vorbereitungsexerzitien für die ewigen hl. Gelübde," in *Geistliche Texte II*, ESGA 20 (Freiburg: Herder, 2007) 57–64.

BIBLIOGRAPHY

CRITICAL EDITIONS

Thematic listing as arranged in the Edith Stein Gesamtausgabe (ESGA):

Stein, Edith. *Aus dem Leben einer jüdischen Familie und weitere autobiographische Beiträge*. Edited by Maria Amata Neyer and Hanna-Barbara Gerl-Falkovitz. ESGA 1. Freiburg: Herder, 2010.

———. *Selbstbildnis in Briefen I (1916–1933)*. Edited by Hanna-Barbara Gerl-Falkovitz and Maria Amata Neyer. ESGA 2. Freiburg: Herder, 2010.

———. *Selbstbildnis in Briefen II (1933–1942)*. Edited by Hanna-Barbara Gerl-Falkovitz. ESGA 3. Freiburg: Herder, 2006.

———. *Selbstbildnis in Briefen III: Briefe an Roman Ingarden*. Edited by Maria Amata Neyer and Eberhard Avé-Lallemant. ESGA 4. Freiburg: Herder, 2005.

———. *Zum Problem der Einfühlung*. ESGA 5. Freiburg: Herder, 2010.

———. *Beiträge zur philosophischen Begründung der Psychologie und der Geisteswissenschaften*. Edited by Beate Beckmann-Zöller. ESGA 6. Freiburg: Herder, 2010.

———. *Eine Untersuchung über den Staat*. Edited by Ilona Riedel-Spangenberger. ESGA 7. Freiburg: Herder, 2006.

———. *Einführung in die Philosophie*. Edited by Claudia Mariéle Wulf and Hanna-Barbara Gerl-Falkovitz. ESGA 8. Freiburg: Herder, 2010.

———. *"Freiheit und Gnade" und weitere Beiträge zur Phänomenologie und Ontologie (1917–1937)*. Edited by Beate Beckmann-Zöller and Hans Rainer Sepp. ESGA 9. Freiburg: Herder, 2014.

———. *Potenz und Akt: Studien zu einer Philosophie des Seins*. Edited by Hans Rainer Sepp. ESGA 10. Freiburg: Herder, 2005.

———. *Endliches und ewiges Sein: Versuch eines Aufstiegs zum Sinn des Seins*. Edited by Andreas Uwe Müller. ESGA 11/12. Freiburg: Herder, 2013.

EDITH STEIN

————. *Die Frau: Fragestellungen und Reflexionen.* Edited by Maria Amata Neyer. ESGA 13. Freiburg: Herder, 2000.

————. *Der Aufbau der menschlichen Person: Vorlesungen zur philosophischen Anthropologie.* Edited by Beate Beckmann-Zöller. ESGA 14. Freiburg: Herder, 2004.

————. *Was ist der Mensch? Theologische Anthropoligie.* Edited by Beate Beckmann-Zöller. ESGA 15. Freiburg: Herder, 2005.

————. *Bildung und Entfaltung der Individualität: Beiträge zum christlichen Erziehungsauftrag.* Edited by Beate Beckmann-Zöller and Maria Amata Neyer. ESGA 16. Freiburg: Herder, 2001.

————. *Wege der Gotteserkenntnis: Studie zu Dionysius Areopagita und Übersetzung seiner Werke.* Edited by Beate Beckmann-Zöller and Viki Ranff. ESGA 17. Freiburg: Herder, 2013.

————. *Kreuzeswissenschaft: Studie über Johannes vom Kreuz.* Edited by Ulrich Dobhan. ESGA 18. Freiburg: Herder, 2013.

————. *Geistliche Texte I.* Edited by Ulrich Dobhan. ESGA 19. Freiburg: Herder, 2009, 2014.

————. *Geistliche Texte II.* Edited by Sophie Binggeli. ESGA 20. Freiburg: Herder, 2007.

————, trans. *Übersetzung I: John Henry Newman: Die Idee der Universität.* Edited by Hanna-Barbara Gerl-Falkovitz. ESGA 21. Freiburg: Herder, 2010.

————, trans. *Übersetzung II: John Henry Newman: Briefe und Texte zur ersten Lebenshälfte (1801–1846).* Edited by Hanna-Barbara Gerl-Falkovitz. ESGA 22. Freiburg: Herder, 2009.

————, trans. *Übersetzung III: Des Hl. Thomas von Aquino: Untersuchungen über die Wahrheit—Quaestiones disputatae de veritate 1.* Edited by Andreas Speer and Francesco Valerio Tommasi. ESGA 23. Freiburg: Herder, 2008.

————, trans. *Übersetzung IV: Des Hl. Thomas von Aquino: Untersuchungen über die Wahrheit—Quaestiones disputatae de veritate 2.* Edited by Andreas Speer and Francesco Valerio Tommasi. ESGA 24. Freiburg: Herder, 2008.

Conrad-Martius, Hedwig, and Edith Stein. *Übersetzung V: Alexandre Koyré, Descartes und die Scholastik.* Edited by Hanna-Barbara Gerl-Falkovitz. ESGA 25. Freiburg: Herder, 2005.

Stein, Edith, trans. *Übersetzung VI: Thomas von Aquin: Über das Seiende und das Wesen—De ente et essentia.* Edited by Andreas Speer and Francesco Valerio Tommasi. ESGA 26. Freiburg: Herder, 2010.

———. *Miscellanea thomistica: Übersetzungen—Abbreviationen—Exzerpte aus Werken des Thomas von Aquin und der Forschungsliteratur.* Edited by Andreas Speer and Francesco Valerio Tommasi. ESGA 27. Freiburg: Herder, 2013.

ENGLISH TRANSLATIONS

Stein, Edith. *Edith Stein: Selected Writings.* Translated by Susanne M. Batzdorff. Springfield, IL: Templegate Publishers, 1990.

———. *Essays on Woman.* Translated by Freda Mary Oben. 2nd ed., revised. CWES 2. Washington, DC: ICS Publications, 1996.

———. *Finite and Eternal Being: An Attempt at an Ascent to the Meaning of Being.* Translated by Kurt F. Reinhardt. CWES 9. Washington, DC: ICS Publications, 2002.

———. *The Hidden Life: Hagiographic Essays, Meditations, Spiritual Texts.* Translated by Waltraut Stein. CWES 4. Washington, DC: ICS Publications, 1992.

———. *An Investigation Concerning the State.* Translated by Marianne Sawicki. CWES 10. Washington, DC, 2006.

———. *Knowledge and Faith.* Translated by Walter Redmond. CWES 8. Washington, DC: ICS Publications, 2000.

———. *Letters to Roman Ingarden.* Translated by Hugh Candler Hunt. Washington, DC: ICS Publications, 2014.

———. *Life in a Jewish Family 1891–1916: An Autobiography.* Translated by Josephine Koeppel. CWES 1. Washington, DC: ICS Publications, 1986.

———. "Martin Heidegger's Existential Philosophy." Translated by Mette Lebech. *Maynooth Philosophical Papers* 4:55–98.

———. *On the Problem of Empathy.* Translated by Waltraut Stein. CWES 3. 3rd ed., revised. Washington, DC: ICS Publications, 1989.

———. *Philosophy of Psychology and the Humanities.* Translated by Mary Catharine Baseheart and Marianne Sawicki. CWES 7. Washington, DC: ICS Publications, 2000.

———. *Potency and Act: Studies toward a Philosophy of Being.* Translated by Walter Redmond. CWES 11. Washington, DC: ICS Publications, 2009.

———. *The Science of the Cross.* Translated by Josephine Koeppel. CWES 6. Washington, DC: ICS Publications, 2002.

————. *Self-Portrait in Letters 1916–1942.* Translated by Josephine Koeppel. CWES 5. Washington, DC: ICS Publications, 1993.

————. *Writings of Edith Stein.* Translated by Hilda Graef. Westminster, MD: The Newman Press, 1956.

SECONDARY SOURCES

Alles Bello, Angela. "Edmund Husserl and Edith Stein: The Question of the Human Subject." Translated by Antonio Calcagno. *American Catholic Philosophical Quarterly* 82, no. 1 (Winter 2008): 143–60.

————. "The Study of the Soul between Psychology and Phenomenology in Edith Stein." In *The Philosophy of Edith Stein: The Eighteenth Annual Symposium of the Simon Silverman Phenomenology Center,* 3–17. Pittsburgh, PA: Silverman Institute for Phenomenology at Duquesne University, 2001.

Baseheart, Mary Catharine. "Edith Stein's Philosophy of Woman and of Women's Education." *Hypatia* 4, no. 1 (Spring 1989): 120–31.

————. *Person in the World: Introduction to the Philosophy of Edith Stein.* Dordrecht, Netherlands: Kluwer, 1997.

Batzdorff, Susanne M. *Aunt Edith: The Jewish Heritage of a Catholic Saint.* Springfield, IL: Templegate Publishers, 1998.

Beckmann, Beate, and Hanna Barbara Gerl-Falkovitz, eds. *Edith Stein: Themen—Bezüge—Dokumente.* Würzburg: Königshausen and Neumann, 2003.

Beckmann-Zöller, Beate. "Edith Stein's Theory of the Person in Her Münster Years (1932–1933)." *American Catholic Philosophical Quarterly* 82, no. 1 (Winter 2008): 47–70.

Berkman, Joyce, ed. *Contemplating Edith Stein.* Notre Dame, IN: University of Notre Dame Press, 2006.

Borden, Sarah. *Edith Stein.* Outstanding Christian Thinkers. Edited by Brian Davies. New York: Continuum, 2003.

————. "Edith Stein's Understanding of Woman." *International Philosophical Quarterly* 46, no. 2 (June 2006): 171–90.

Borden Sharkey, Sarah. "Edith Stein and John Paul II on Women." In *Karol Wojtyla's Philosophical Legacy,* edited by Nancy Mardas Billias, Agnes Curry, and George McLean, 265–76. Washington, DC: The Council for Research in Values in Philosophy, 2008.

————. "Edith Stein and Thomas Aquinas on Being and Essence." *American Catholic Philosophical Quarterly* 82, no.1 (Winter 2008): 87–103.

Bibliography

————. *Thine Own Self: Individuality in Edith Stein's Later Writings.* Washington, DC: Catholic University of America Press, 2010.

Brenner, Rachel Feldhay. *Writing as Resistance: Four Women Confronting the Holocaust.* University Park, PA: The Pennsylvania State University Press, 1997.

Calcagno, Antonio. "Die Fülle oder das Nichts? Edith Stein and Martin Heidegger on the Question of Being." *American Catholic Philosophical Quarterly* 74, no. 2 (2000): 269–85.

————. "Edith Stein: Is the State Responsible for the Immortal Soul of the Person?" *LOGOS: A Journal of Catholic Thought and Culture* 5, no.1 (Winter 2002): 62–75.

————, ed. *Edith Stein: Women, Social-Political Philosophy, Theology, Metaphysics and Public History: New Approaches and Applications.* Heidelberg, Germany: Springer Verlag, 2015.

————. *The Philosophy of Edith Stein.* Pittsburgh, PA: Duquesne University Press, 2006.

Conrad-Martius, Hedwig. "Edith Stein: Kreuzweg der Liebe." *Der christliche Sonntag* (1958): 293–94.

Courtine-Denamy, Sylvie. *Three Women in Dark Times: Edith Stein, Hannah Arendt, Simone Weil.* Ithaca, NY: Cornell University Press, 2000.

Devaux, André A. "L'Idée de Vocation dans la Vie et Dans la Pensée d'Edith Stein." *Les Études Philosophiques* 3 (July–September 1956): 423–46.

Dobhan, Ulrich. "Teresa von Avila und Edith Stein." *Internationale Katholische Zeitschrift Communio* 6 (1998): 494–514.

Fitzgerald, Constance. "Passion in the Carmelite Tradition: Edith Stein." *Spiritus: A Journal of Christian Spirituality* 2, no. 2 (2002): 217–35.

Garcia, Laura. "The Primacy of Persons: Edith Stein and Pope John Paul II. *LOGOS: A Journal of Catholic Thought and Culture* 1, no. 2 (1997): 90–99.

Gerl, Hanna-Barbara. *Unerbittliches Licht: Edith Stein—Philosophie, Mystic, Leben.* Mainz, Germany: Matthias-Grünewald Verlag, 1991.

Gerl-Falkovitz, Hanna-Barbara. "*Endliches und ewiges Sein*: Der Mensch als Abbild der Dreifaltigkeit nach Edith Stein." *Internationale Katholische Zeitschrift Communio* 6 (1998): 548–62.

Graef, Hilda C. *The Scholar and the Cross: The Life and Works of Edith Stein.* London: Longmans, Green and Co., 1955.

Herbstrith, Waltraud. *Edith Stein: A Biography.* Translated by Bernard Bonowitz. San Francisco, CA: Ignatius Press, 1985.

————, ed. *Edith Stein: Ein Lebensbild in Zeugnissen und Selbstzeugnissen.* Mainz, Germany: Matthias-Grünewald Verlag, 2001.

EDITH STEIN

——, ed. *Edith Stein: Eine grosse Glaubenszeugin.* Annweiler, Germany: Verlag Thomas Plöger, 1986.

——, ed. *Never Forget: Christian and Jewish Perspectives on Edith Stein.* Translated by Susanne Batzdorff. Carmelite Studies 7. Washington, DC: ICS Publications, 1998.

Ingarden, Roman. "Edith Stein on Her Activity as an Assistant of Edmund Husserl." *Philosophy and Phenomenological Research* 23, no. 2 (December 1962): 155–75.

——. "Über die philosophischen Forschungen Edith Steins." In *Edith Stein: Eine grosse Glaubenszeugin,* edited by Waltraud Herbstrith, 203–29. Annweiler, Germany: Verlag Thomas Plöger, 1986.

Kavunguvalappil, Antony. *Theology of Suffering and Cross in the Life and Works of Blessed Edith Stein.* Frankfurt am Main, Germany: Peter Lang, 1998.

Koeppel, Josephine. *Edith Stein: Philosopher and Mystic.* Scranton, PA: University of Scranton Press, 2007.

Lebech, Mette. "Edith Stein's Philosophy of Education in *The Structure of the Human Person.*" *Religion, Education, and the Arts* 5, no. 5 (2005): 55–70.

——. "Edith Stein's Thomism." *Maynooth Philosophical Papers* 7 (2013): 20–32.

——. *On the Problem of Human Dignity: A Hermeneutical and Phenomenological Investigation.* Würzburg, Germany: Verlag Königshausen and Neumann, 2009.

——. "Stein's Phenomenology of the Body. The Constitution of the Human Being between Description of Experience and Social Construction." *Maynooth Philosophical Papers* 5 (2008): 16–20.

——. "What Can We Learn from Edith Stein's Philosophy of Woman?" *Yearbook of the Irish Philosophical Society* (2009): 215–24.

——. "Why Do We Need the Philosophy of Edith Stein?" *Communio* 38 (2011): 682–727.

Madden, Nicholas. "Edith Stein on the Symbolic Theology of Dionysius the Areopagite." *Irish Theological Quarterly* 71 (2006): 29–45.

Maskulak, Marian. "Edith Stein and Simone Weil: Reflections for a Theology and Spirituality of the Cross." *Theology Today* 64, no. 4 (January 2008): 445–57.

——. *Edith Stein and the Body-Soul-Spirit at the Center of Holistic Formation.* NY: Peter Lang Publishers, 2007.

Bibliography

———. "Edith Stein: A Proponent of Human Community and a Voice for Social Change." *LOGOS: A Journal of Catholic Thought and Culture* 15, no. 2 (Spring 2 012): 64–83.

McIntyre, Alisdair. *Edith Stein: A Philosophical Prologue, 1913–1922.* Lanham, MD: Rowman and Littlefield, 2006.

Müller, Andreas Uwe, and Maria Amata Neyer. *Edith Stein: Das Leben einer ungewöhnlichen Frau.* Zürich: Benziger Verlag, 1998.

Neyer, Maria Amata. *Edith Stein: Her Life in Photos and Documents.* Translated by Waltraut Stein. Washington, DC: ICS Publications, 1999.

Oben, Freda Mary. "Edith Stein as Educator." *Thought* 65, no. 257 (June 1990): 113–26.

———. *Edith Stein: Scholar, Feminist, Saint.* New York: Alba House, 1988.

———. *The Life and Thought of St. Edith Stein.* New York: Alba House, 2001.

Payne, Steven. "Edith Stein and John of the Cross." *Teresianum* 50, nos.1–2 (1999): 239–56.

Posselt, Teresia Renata. *Edith Stein: The Life of a Philosopher and Carmelite*, edited by Susanne Batzdorff, Josephine Koeppel, and John Sullivan. Washington, DC: ICS Publications, 2005.

Sawicki, Marianne. *Body, Text, and Science: The Literacy of Investigative Practices and the Phenomenology of Edith Stein.* Phaenomenologica 144. Edited by R. Bernet et al. Dordrecht, Netherlands: Kluwer, 1997.

———. "Empathy before and after Husserl." *Philosophy Today* 22 (1997): 123–27.

———. "Personal Connections: The Phenomenology of Edith Stein." In *Yearbook of the Irish Philosophical Society: Voices of Irish Philosophy 2004*, 148–69. Maynooth, Ireland, 2004.

Schudt, Karl C. "Edith Stein's Proof for the Existence of God from Consciousness." *American Catholic Philosophical Quarterly* 82, no. 1 (Winter 2008): 105–26.

Schulz, Peter. *Edith Steins Theorie der Person: Von der Bewußtseinsphilosophie zur Geistmetaphysik.* Freiburg: Verlag Karl Alber, 1994.

———. "Faith and Reason in the Philosophy of Edith Stein." *Faith and Reason* 27, nos. 2–4 (Summer–Winter, 2002): 295–326.

———. "Toward the Subjectivity of the Human Person: Edith Stein's Contribution to the Theory of Identity." *American Catholic Philosophical Quarterly* 82, no. 1 (Winter 2008): 161–76.

Stallmach, Josef. "The Work of Edith Stein: The Tension between Knowledge and Faith." Translated by Stephen Wentworth Arndt. *Communio* 15 (Fall 1988): 376–83.

Sullivan, John, ed. *Edith Stein Symposium/Teresian Culture*. Carmelite Studies IV. Washington, DC: ICS Publications, 1987.

———, ed. *Holiness Befits Your House: Canonization of Edith Stein—A Documentation*. Washington, DC: ICS Publications, 2000.

Van den Berg, Regina. *Community with Christ according to Saint Teresa Benedicta of the Cross*. San Francisco: Ignatius Press, 2015.

Wright, Terrence. "Artistic Truth and the True Self in Edith Stein." *American Catholic Philosophical Quarterly* 82, no.1 (Winter 2008): 127–42.

———. "Edith Stein: Prayer and Interiority." In *The Phenomenology of Prayer*, edited by Bruce Benson and Norman Wirzba, 134–41. Bronx, NY: Fordham University Press, 2005.

INDEX